*Funu**

The Unfinished Saga
of East Timor

Jose Ramos-Horta

Preface
by
Noam Chomsky

The Red Sea Press, Inc.
Publishers & Distributors of Third World Books
556 Bellevue Avenue
Trenton, New Jersey 08618

The Red Sea Press, Inc.
556 Bellevue Avenue
Trenton, NJ 08618

First Printing, January 1987

Typeset by TypeHouse of Pennington

Covery design by Joaquim de Britto

Library of Congress Catalog Card Number: 86-60188

ISBN: 0-932415-14-8 Cloth
       0-932415-15-6 Paper

* *Funu* is the Tetun word for war.

Funu, guerra. - A guerra
há-de terminar
a sorrir amor.

Semente a partir-se
tem seu fim na flor.

June 17, 1986
Fernando Sylvan*

(Funu, war.-The war/ will end/ smiling love/ Seed
that ruptures/ blossoms into a flower.)

*Born in East Timor, Fernando Sylvan was raised and educated in Portugal
where he is chairman of the Portuguese Language Society. He has
published an extensive list of poetry and other writings.

Acknowledgement

For my tormented country,
in memory of those whose lives
were taken away; my friends
murdered and "disappeared";
also in memory of Nuno, Guy and
Mariazinha, whose souls are now
wandering in Mt. Matebian;*
in honor of the heroic
combatants, men and women, of
Loro Monu and Loro Sah'e, Taci
Fetu and Taci Man.**

I am indebted to Sue Roff for her encouragement to write an "autobiography" even when I protested that it would be too presumptious on my part to pretend to have lived enough to warrant a biography; Cora Weiss, of Rubin Foundation; Art Van Der Heide; Prof. Robert Betchov; the Swedish Social Democratic party; and an anonymous friend who sent me a check when I was broke.

Last but not least, I thank Kassahun Checole, my publisher, for his patience, understanding and constant support.

* Mount Matebian, rugged and inaccessible mountain region. Matebian in the Tétun language means soul.
** Loro Monu—where the sun sets, or East; Loro Sah'e—where the sun rises, or West; Taci fetu—"Female sea" or the South Sea. The Timorese attribute the female name to the rough seas, and Taci Mane, or Male sea, to the North coast, which is much calmer.

Contents

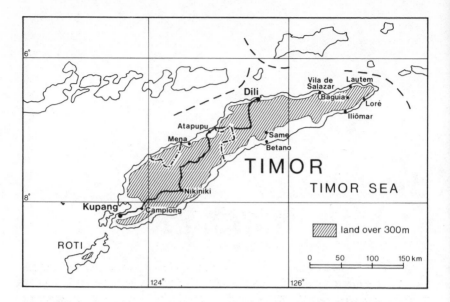

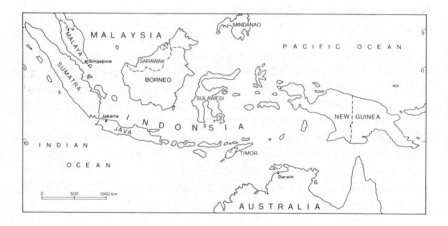

Jorgen Ulrich/IWGIA

Preface

Noam Chomsky

The *New York Times* of June 5, 1939, features a front-page story under the headline: "Roosevelt Appeals to World to Join in Moral Rearming." It reports a message sent by the President, joined by "distinguished persons from many parts of this country and the world," to the National Meeting for Moral Rearmament held in Constitution Hall in Washington. The President's message, read by Senator Harry Truman, advocated a worldwide program of "moral rearmament" because "the underlying strength of the world must consist in the moral fiber of her citizens." In an adjacent column, the headline reads: "Refugee Ship Idles off Florida Coast." It reports another day in the saga of the liner St. Louis, carrying 900 Jewish refugees from Germany to whom the Roosevelt Administration denied asylum, finally sending them back to Europe where many ended their lives in Hitler's extermination camps.

In the issue of September 1, 1983, the *Times* reports a bitter denunciation of the United Nations by US delegate Charles Lichenstein, who accuses the organization of "utter futility as an effective instrument of international peace and security" and of "fundamental irrelevance to the realities of international gangsterism"—referring to its failure to adopt the American position on intervention in Chad by Libya, which was at that time one of several foreign states engaged in the civil wars there. The adjacent column is headed: "Indonesians Pressing Drive in East Timor." It begins: "Indonesia's armed forces have mounted an offensive against guerrillas fighting for the independence of East Timor" and quoted General Benny Murdani, the chief of the Indonesian armed forces as saying that there would be "no mercy" for rebels who do not surrender under Indonesian terms. 20,000 troops are reported to be engaged in this new Indonesian offensive. The column does not remind the reader—nor has the *Times* ever done so—that the United Nations has failed entirely to constrain the Indonesian aggression, now entering its second decade, because the US delegation has ensured that the United Nations will "prove utterly ineffective in whatever measures it undertook," in the words of the US official who organized these successful efforts at ensuring the "utter futility" of the United Nations as an "effective instrument of international peace and security," and guaranteeing "fundamental irrelevance to the realities of international gangsterism"; in this case, gangsterism by the United States and its client vastly exceeding anything chargeable to Libya; and a case of outright and murderous aggression in which the perpetrators, Indonesia and the United States, have no case whatsoever except for the case provided by their overwhelming power to destroy and to silence.

These two pages of the world's leading newspaper, almost half a century apart, illustrate one of the most striking features of the modern age. Moral principles are intoned with much solemnity, accompanied by great anguish and heartfelt concern for the victims of the other fellow's crimes. This impressive display of moral fervor, which evokes much self-congratulation, coexists easily with the most callous inhumanity.

The front page of the June 5, 1939, edition of the *New York Times* also carries a report of a speech by Adolf Hitler expressing defiance in the face of Britain's "encirclement policy," and his commitment to strengthen "German defense measures" against this threat. Illustrated here is another major theme of modern history: the true nature of what political leaders and their acolytes invariably call "defense." For the Indonesian invasion of East Timor on December 7, 1975, the aggressors relied almost entirely on US arms granted to Indonesia on the explicit condition that they were to be used only for self-defense; and the invasion continued, through 1983 and until today, thanks to an increasing arms flow from the United States designed to facilitate the aggression and subsequent slaughter. It must be, then, that the Indonesian invasion was another act of "self-defense," like Hitler's invasion of Poland and the Low Countries. And indeed, the official US position, as expressed by the State Department to Congress, was that "we made it clear to [the Indonesians] that we understood the situation they were in; we understood the pressures they felt and their concern about the fighting that was going on and the potential for instability that would be caused by developments as they saw them." In fact, no fighting was going on prior to the Indonesian invasion, apart from Indonesian border attacks against East Timor that were conveniently ignored or falsified in the US press. And the threatened "instability" was of the usual kind: fear that social and economic progress in this extremely poor and undeveloped corner of the former Portuguese empire, however meager, might "infect" Indonesia, causing "the rot to spread" (as American planners like to put it) and encouraging people suffering under the Western-backed system of exploitation and misery in Indonesia to attempt to improve their own lot, thus harming the interests of their oppressors, the United States included.

The transition from the front page of the *New York Times* on June 5, 1939, to the story of Timor, Indonesia and the West during the past ten years is all too easy, though the parallels are not exact: Roosevelt did not supply Hitler with the means to exterminate the Jews.

The Western-backed invasion and subsequent massacre in East Timor, still in progress, reveals with much clarity the hypocrisy of Western posturing about human rights; the utter fraudulence of the show of anguish over a certain well-defined class of terrible atrocities (namely, those that are ideologically serviceable, since the perpetrators are official enemies); the casual acceptance of acts that would be described as genocidal were we not responsible for them; and the device of cloaking aggression in the guise of defense, almost too common to bear mention. The story is so revealing that it cannot be known, and indeed is not known, and indeed is not known except in tiny circles. Furthermore, the truth of the matter cannot be permitted to survive, and one can predict with some confidence that these events will find their way into Orwell's useful memory hole, and will be as well-known in the United States and elsewhere in the West as the US massacre of hundreds of thousands of Filipinos at the turn of the century, the genocidal destruction of Native Americans, and other matters not suitable to be enshrined in official history.

The background to the tragedy of East Timor lies in US global planning in the post-World War II period. The political problems of Southeast Asia were to be solved in such a way as to enable the region "to fulfill its major function as a source of raw materials and a market for Japan and Western Europe," the State Department explained in 1949. Indonesia, with its wealth of raw materials, was to play a central role in the emerging global system, with Japanese and Western European capitalism reconstructed within a broader framework managed by the United States and ultimately subordinated to US interests. The Portuguese colony of East Timor, to which Indonesia laid no claim prior to its 1975 invasion, was also mentioned by the planners of the postwar world. Sumner Welles held that it should receive the right of self-determination, though with a slight delay: "it would certainly take a thousand years," he explained, expressing the familiar racist contempt for the "lesser breeds." For Indonesia, self-determination—of a sort—would be permitted at once.

The United States supported the termination of Dutch colonialism, which, like other regional systems that the US did not control, would be an impediment to plans for organizing the global system to fit US requirements. But dissatisfied with the outcome of Indonesian independence, the US attempted to overthrow President Sukarno in 1958 through a "rebellion" of Indonesian dissidents and mercenaries trained by the CIA in the Philippines. Even when a US pilot (for an airline that was a CIA front) was shot down, the US press was not sufficiently interested to inquire into charges that were dismissed by Bernard Kalb of the *New York Times* as "Communist propaganda." This attempt to overthrow the Indonesian government failed, but the efforts continued along a different path, one that the US has pursued with some regularity in overthrowing governments, including democratic governments, that it finds offensive to its taste: Chile under Allende is a well-known case. The US maintained close contact with the Indonesian military and provided military aid while relations with the government became increasingly hostile. In 1965, six generals were murdered in what official doctrine (including much of scholarship) describes as a "Communist coup," which miraculously spared the pro-US General Suharto, while targeting elements of the military considered anti-American. Suharto then carried out an actual military coup, which led to the slaughter of a half a million people in a few months, mostly landless peasants, and crushed the popular-based Communist Party; at the same time, incidentally, turning Indonesia into a "paradise for investors."

The West observed all of this with much pleasure, even delight. Secretary of Defense Robert McNamara was asked in congressional hearings whether the military aid to Indonesia during a period of frost US-Indonesian relations had "paid dividends," and he agreed that it had. Congress agreed as well, as did the press, which welcomed the "gleam of light in Asia," "the West's best news for years in Asia," "hope . . . where once there was none," and so on. Western liberals hailed the "dramatic changes" that had taken place in Indonesia as justification for the US attack against South Vietnam (called here "the defense of South Vietnam"). The US attack provided a "shield" behind which the Indonesian generals were encouraged to carry out their necessary work of purging the society and freeing it for Western exploitation. By now, respected journalists are able to write that the Communist Party "subjected the country to a bloodbath" (George McArthur); and that "thousands were slaughtered" in 1965 "when the nation's military foiled a bloody attempt by President Sukarno and the Chinese-backed Communist Party of Indonesia to replace the parliamentary government with a dictatorship" (Robert Toth). The victims have become the perpetrators of the massacre, and its level is reduced by a factor of 100 with the US role suppressed—all of which is the norm in regard to atrocities committed by the "good guys" on our side, paying the dividends for our assistance.

A CIA study of the 1965 Indonesian operation remains secret. Former CIA agent Ralph McGhee, who was custodian of that study but is not permitted to discuss it, states that on the basis of the study, "I know the specific steps the agency took to create the conditions that led to the massacre of at least half a million Indonesians."

With the political opposition demolished in one of the great massacres of the modern era, and 750,000 arrested, many to remain in jails and concentration camps for 15 years, Indonesia was welcomed into the Free World. It continues to serve today as a loyal outpost of liberty and democracy in the approved style, including: impoverishment of much of the population of a potentially rich society; terror and torture; a political system that does not even merit the term "fraudulent"; but, crucially, few barriers to foreign exploitation apart from the rapacity of the Indonesian generals and their local associates.

In 1974, with the overthrow of Portuguese fascism, steps toward independence were undertaken in the Portuguese colony of East Timor. Indonesian-supported elements attempted a coup in August, 1975, but the attempt was beaten back in a brief but bloody civil war in which two to three thousand people were killed. By early September, the country was in the hands of Fretilin, described by knowledgeable observers on the scene as "populist Catholic" in general orientation. International relief officials, journalists and other observers praised the moderate and constructive efforts to move toward development and independence. But Indonesia had other ideas in mind, and the United States and its allies were happy to oblige, as long as the profits kept flowing.

Indonesian aggression began at once in the border areas, and there was little doubt that Indonesia would soon invade outright. Secret US cables, leaked in Australia, reveal that the US Embassy in Jakarta was under instructions from Henry Kissinger not to involve itself in the matter and "to cut down its reporting on Timor" (Australian Ambassador Woolcott). The personal view of US Ambassador David Newsom, as reported by the Australian Ambassador, was that if Indonesia were to intervene they should do so "effectively, quickly, and not use our equipment." The latter hope was mere deceit: its meaning was that Indonesia should not use our equipment too flamboyantly. Ninety percent of Indonesian military supplies were from the United States, granted on the condition that they be used only for self-defense; but as the remarks by Hitler and the State Department cited earlier illustrate, the concept of "defense" can be construed quite broadly, when necessary.

On December 7, 1975, Indonesia invaded outright, initiating a mass slaughter that may have cost the lives of some 200,000 people by 1979, while reducing the survivors to the level of Biafra or the Thai-Cambodian border. The United States, contrary to official lies, participated with enthusiasm. The US government claimed to have initiated a secret six-month arms moratorium; as later exposed the moratorium was so secret that Indonesia did not know about it, and during this period arms continued to flow and the US even made new offers of equipment particularly useful for counterinsurgency operations. By 1977, Indonesia had actually begun to exhaust its military supplies in this war against a country of 700,000 people, so the Carter Administration took time out from its pieties and self-acclaim about its devotion to human rights ("the Soul of our Foreign Policy") to arrange a large-scale increase in the flow of arms to Indonesia, in the certain knowledge that they would be used to consummate a massacre that was approaching genocidal proportions.

As for the American media, they required no instructions from the State

Department "to cut down reporting from Timor." Understanding their role, they virtually eliminated the topic from view. In the *New York Times*, for example, coverage of Timorese issues had been substantial in 1975, but declined as Indonesia invaded and reached zero as the atrocities reached their peak with the new equipment provided by Carter's "Human Rights" administration in 1978. The occasional news reports carefully avoided interviewing the many Timorese refugees in Portugal and Australia, choosing to rely instead on Indonesian generals, who assured readers that the Timorese who had been "forced" to the mountains by Fretilin were now fleeing from its "control" to Indonesian protection. These "facts" were presented as facts by the "free press," when it deigned to consider the slaughter at all. Later, the nature and scale of the atrocities were partially conceded, behind a curtain of deception and with the role of the US government and the complicity of the press carefully excised.

While the US was the major foreign participant in the slaughter, others tried to profit as they could and kept their silence. In Canada, the major Western investor in Indonesia, the government and the press were silent. The Canadian government now claims that "Groups opposed to the Fretilin politcal faction requested the assistance of Indonesia and the Indonesian military intervened. Subsequently representatives of the anti-Fretilin factions submitted a formal request to the Indonesian government for the integration of East Timor and Timor is now an integral part of the Republic of Indonesia." That is all; Goebbels would have been impressed. *Le Monde* reported in September, 1978, that the French government would sell arms to Indonesia while abstaining from any UN discussion of the invasion, and in general doing nothing to "place Indonesia in an embarrassing position." The Paris intellectuals, much impressed at the time with their own courage in denouncing Communist crimes in Indochina (which presumably washed clean a century of French atrocities there, in Africa and elsewhere), had no time to object to France's complicity in the ongoing massacre; and they now haughtily inform us that Timor was too "geographically and historically marginal" to have merited concern (Gerard Chaliand). British journalists who were denouncing Cambodian autogenocide and even Vietnamese "genocide" in Cambodia present us with a "more structurally serious explanation" for the failure to cover what was happening in Timor: "there were not many refugees; there was no 'border' for journalists to visit"; and "there has been a comparative lack of sources" (William Shawcross). We are thus being informed, with a straight face, that Lisbon, two hours by air from London, is harder to reach than the Thai-Cambodia border; and that the voluminous record provided by church sources, smuggled letters, refugee studies by highly competent authorities, *etc.*, does not exist. Some 40,000 Timorese died during World War II assisting Australian commandos fighting the Japanese; Australia registered its thanks by at first tacitly, and now openly, supporting the Indonesian aggression. The story is the same throughout the civilized world, with very rare exceptions, providing a certain insight into the nature of "civilization."

US participation in the massacre extended beyond the level of material support and complicity on the part of the ideological institutions. The US government also lent diplomatic support to the Indonesian invasion. It was particularly concerned with blocking action at the United Nations to deter the aggression in the early days, when such action might have been effective. UN Ambassador Daniel Patrick Moynihan was assigned this task, and describes his success in performing it with much pride. In a secret cable of January 23, 1976, to Secretary of State Kissinger, he cited his success in blocking UN action on Timor as part of the "considerable progress' he had achieved by arm-twisting tactics at the United Nations. In his memoirs, he explains why the UN was unable to act in a meaningful way:

> The United States wished things to turn out as they did and worked to bring this about. The Department of State desired that the United Nations prove utterly ineffective in whatever measures it undertook. This task was given to me, and I carried it forward with no inconsiderable success.

Moynihan also made it clear that he understood the nature of his accomplishment very well. He cites a February 1976 estimate by an Indonesian client in Timor "that some sixty thousand persons had been killed since the outbreak of the civil war" in August (recall that some two to three thousand had been killed during the civil war, the remainder since the Indonesian invasion in December) and remarks that this is "10 percent of the population, almost the proportion of casualties experienced by the Soviet Union during the Second World War." Thus Moynihan is taking credit for an achievement that he proudly compares to Hitler's in Eastern Europe.

Moynihan is highly admired for ridiculing Idi Amin, and similar acts of heroism during his tenure at the United Nations; and he received much acclaim for his denunciation of the United Nations as "the scene of acts we regard as abominations," which the US will "never forget." These oratorical flourishes were issued exactly at the time he was working to ensure that the United Nations would place no impediment in the path of the US-backed Indonesian aggression. Moynihan is also much praised as a spokesman for the Rule of Law and for his criticism of the "the totalitarian left," with its "Orwellian" distortions that have "blunted . . . perceptions within the democracies." In December 1980, Moynihan was the main speaker at a conference of the Committee for United Nations Integrity, which denounced the UN as "no longer the guardian of social justice, human rights and equality among nations" because it is "perverted by irrelevant political machinations" and is "in danger of becoming a force against peace itself." The Committee was not referring to the success of its honored speaker in implementing a huge massacre in Timor by perverting the United Nations, but rather with the fact that the UN has supported Palestinian rights, a major crime in US eyes.

More recently, Moynihan explained that the Senate Select Committee on Intelligence, of which he was then vice-chairman, had approved Administration requests for funding to support the *contra* attack on Nicaragua—"on the grounds that international law not only authorized the United States" to support paramilitary operations in Central America "but even obligated it to do so, it being the case that the Government of Nicaragua was supporting efforts to subvert its neighbor, El Salvador." Moynihan has a subtle and discriminating sense of what constitutes "aggression." A trickle of aid to those being massacred by US clients constitutes "aggression" obligating a foreign invasion by a proxy army (so that, *a fortiori*, the USSR has the right, even the obligation, to attack Pakistan, China and the United States because of their support for efforts to "subvert" the legally recognized government of Afghanistan); but direct and outright aggression by a US client with full and crucial US support, leading to one of the major massacres of the modern period, does not constitute "aggression"—and it is our right, even our obligation, to undermine international efforts to impede it, with applause from liberal Western opinion.

On December 12, 1975, when Moynihan was carrying out his assigned task with much relish, he received the highest award from the International League for the Rights of Man (now the International League for Human Rights), honoring his role as "one of the most forthright advocates of human rights on the national and international scene." On December 10, 1982, the League announced that it would bestow the same award to former President Jimmy Carter "in recognition of outstanding achievement in the field of human rights," one notable example being his dedication to ensuring that Indonesia would have the military means and diplomatic support to bring its noble work in Timor to fruition. The League, incidentally, is well aware of the facts and the US role, and indeed is one of the few groups with a respectable record of protest on the matter.

In 1977, when the death toll in Timor had perhaps reached one hundred thousand, and Jimmy Carter authorized increased military aid to Indonesia to drive it still higher, the West was consumed with agony and outrage over atrocities in Cambodia. From mass circulation journals such as the *Readers Digest* and *TV Guide* to intellectual journals such as *The New York Review of Books*, the Khmer Rouge were condemned as the equals of Hitler and Stalin, perhaps worse, with their "boast" that they had "eliminated" one-fourth of the population, some two million people. (The source, Jean Lacouture, conceded a few weeks later that the story was a fabrication and that the actual toll may have been in the thousands, but explained that a factor of 1000 was of no significance; the two million figure remained orthodoxy in the West despite this acknowledgement.) Two years earlier, when the Khmer Rouge had killed perhaps thousands of people, it was accused of "genocide" by the *New York Times*. By mid-1977, according to US intelligence, the death toll had reached "tens if not hundreds of thousands," mostly from disease, malnutrition and overwork, the result primarily of "brutal, rapid change," not "mass genocide"; this assessment, ignored at the time since it did not satisfy current propaganda requirements, is now generally confirmed by subsequent scholarship. This was in a country with ten times the population of East Timor, a country that had been ravaged by a US attack that was responsible for the death of hundreds of thousands in the first half of the decade, and where people were dying from this attack at the rate of one hundred thousand a year in the city of Phnom Penh alone. No one knew, or cared to explore, what was happening in the countryside, subjected to one of the fiercest bombardments in history prior to the Khmer Rouge takeover. The outrage over the Khmer Rouge was not only extensive in scale, but also unprecedented in character, with some of the most astonishing fabrication and deceit on record. The actual atrocities of the Khmer Rouge, gruesome enough as recognized with no question (apart from the qualifications of US intelligence, the only people who knew anything about what was happening) were not deemed sufficient for the crucial purpose at the time: to shift the moral onus for the Indochina wars to the victims. The merits and nature of this outrage are revealed with much clarity by the reaction in the same circles to the simultaneous and quite comparable atrocities in Timor.

One must, however, take note of several crucial differences between these two cases, the most important being that in the case of Cambodia, the outrage, while ideologically serviceable and hence intense, was quite impotent; no one suggested any way to bring the atrocities to an end, though later there was discussion about the legitimacy of intervention to protect the victims. In the case of Timor, the silence was crucial; it was of critical importance to ensure that the public was unaware of what was happening so that there would be no impediment to the ongoing slaughter. To bring the atrocities to an end required no intervention; it would have sufficed to call off the hounds. The example provides much insight into the nature of the Western conscience and its moral concerns, as does the fact that the Indonesian atrocities continue today, arousing no interest in the West, which prefers farcical debates about what should have been done in Cambodia.

When the truth about Timor finally became partially known for a brief period in 1980 (before being restored to its proper oblivion) the comparison to Cambodia was raised in establishment circles, as it had been before in the obscurity of protest. The *Wall Street Journal* was troubled by the comparison, which it quickly put to rest with reasoning that need not detain us here. But the *Journal* and others need no longer be troubled by the "inconsistency" between our opposition to Khmer Rouge massacres and our support for comparable Indonesian massacres. The "inconsistency" has now been overcome, since the US now supports both Pol Pot and the Indonesian murderers. The US openly backs the Democratic Kampuchea coalition, based largely on the Khmer Rouge, who are supported directly by the US allies China and Thailand. The reasons were explained by John Holdridge of the State Department in congressional hearings in September 1982. Asked whether "the opposition in Cambodia (the Khmer Rouge-based Democratic Kampuchea coalition) is more representative of the Cambodian people than the Fretilin is of the Timorese people," Holdridge replied: "Unquestionably, because there has been this continuity since the very beginning."—namely, the continuity with the Pol Pot regime.

Those who prefer a more orderly world may now rest easy, "inconsistencies" having been resolved.

The torture of the people of Timor will continue as long as we are willing to look the other way. The Timorese will survive at best "under arrest," in the words of a recent West German parliamentary delegation, describing what they saw in a country where "people do not laugh." Meanwhile, Western journalists on guided tours will applaud the efforts being undertaken by the Indonesians to bring the benefits of civilization to the benighted Timorese, who will soon suffer the fate of the people of West Papua, cynically consigned to Indonesia by the West years earlier, now facing obliteration as their territory becomes the site of "the largest colonization program in history," Survival International informs us. But profits flow, and all is well, while Western moralists weep about the crimes of the Evil Empire and its clients, mimicking the commissars who are their models, who impress an honest person no less with their agonies over Western crimes.

There is one bright spot in this sordid tale. Thanks to the efforts of a handful of young people, some knowledge of the facts at last reached parts of the population, members of Congress, and even—briefly—the press. One result of these efforts was that the International Red Cross was permitted intermittent access to Timor and some relief flowed, perhaps saving tens of thousands of lives. This too teaches a lesson: there is a great deal that can be done to mitigate and overcome state terror and atrocities, if we are willing to escape the grip of the commissars and look honestly at what is happening in the world. It remains possible, though the likelihood diminishes with each passing year, that the Indonesian aggression can be terminated by public pressure on the US government that provides it with the critically needed support; and that the people of East Timor, those who have survived the onslaught, may yet enjoy the right of self-determination that the US professes to uphold, perhaps even sooner than 1000 years hence.

Noam Chomsky
November 20, 1985

Introduction

On December 7, 1975, 10,000 Indonesian troops, supported by a large naval task force of Russian-built destroyers, American-supplied landing crafts, amphibious tanks, fighter planes and helicopters, invaded the Portuguese colony of East Timor. For almost 500 years, East Timor had been a Portuguese possession inhabited by 700,000 people of Melanesian and Malay background. A small half-island less than 400 miles north of Australia, roughly the size of El Salvador, East Timor did not weigh heavily in the geopolitical equation. Hours before the invasion, President Ford and his Secretary of State, Henry Kissinger, had been in Jakarta conferring with President Suharto of Indonesia on security matters in the region. East Timor was high on the agenda. Suharto was concerned about a possible adverse American reaction. The United States Congress's decision to cut off aid to Turkey after its invasion of Cyprus in 1974 caused Suharto to worry that a similar sanction might be applied against Indonesia if he were to invade East Timor. Suharto knew perfectly well that his army was almost entirely dependent upon American aid. [1]

If Suharto was worried about the American reaction, he was soon reassured by Ford and Kissinger that the United States "understood" Indonesia's interests in East Timor and the actions he would be "forced" to take. Ford's trip to Indonesia was the last leg of an extended Asian tour designed to reassure American allies in the region that, in spite of the Indochinese debacle, the United States could still be relied upon. After the fall of the three Indochinese dominoes, Suharto did not have much difficulty persuading his American guests that East Timor, if left to become an independent state, would soon fall under communist control. Another domino could not be tolerated; this explains Ford's and particularly Kissinger's "understanding" of Indonesia's actions on December 7, 1975.

More than ten years after the brutal invasion of the tiny island by its giant neighbor, the East Timorese are still fighting the invaders at an enormous cost. Out of a population of 700,000 in 1974, by 1981 Indonesia's own official statistics indicated a population of a little over 500,000. A frightening conclusion: some 200,000 East Timorese died between 1975 and 1980! It is beyond doubt that tens of thousands of men, women, children, the elderly, combatants and non-combatants, have died from mass executions, indiscriminate shooting, and aerial strafing of populated areas and fragmentation bombs. A number of witnesses have told of the use of napalm and other chemical weapons, particularly during the 1977 summer offensive against FRETILIN strongholds in the Matebian mountains. Hundreds of FRETILIN supporters, mainly women and children, died in the three-week siege of Matebian. However, on the basis of independent accounts, I believe that the death toll was largely the result of a deliberate strategy of starvation through destruction of food crops and continuous military operations that left the population unable to cultivate the land. No relief organization was allowed into East Timor between 1975 and 1979, and thousands simply died of hunger. By 1982, when Pulitzer Prize winner Rod Nordland of the *Philadelphia Inquirer* visited East Timor, he summed up the tragedy with this headline: "Under Indonesian control, Timor remains a land of hunger, oppression and misery."[2]

The former papal representative in predominantly Catholic East Timor, Monsignor Martinho da Costa Lopes, witnessed the invasion from his window:

> The sun was rising. It was about five in the morning. I opened the window, looked at the sky and saw Indonesian military aircraft flying low and dropping paratroopers.
>
> The warships and airplanes continued to fire on Dili with rockets and cluster bombs. They burned everything and everybody.
>
> The Indonesians broke into the houses. They ransacked the shops, looted the houses. They raped women . . . sometimes even in front of their husbands. It was very bad. That day remained forever engraved in my memory. I will never forget.

Msgr. Lopes, aged 60, was until 1983 the head of the Catholic Church of East Timor. Having witnessed the cruelty of the invading troops, and after several years of discreet approaches to the Indonesian military authorities, without much success, Msgr. Lopes began to speak out publicly. He gained the love and respect of the East Timorese, and because of his actions, the Church saw its membership leap from 200,000 in 1974 to over 400,000 in 1983. However, he did not ingratiate himself with the Indonesian authorities or the Vatican. In May 1983, the outspoken Timorese churchman was invited by the Vatican to resign. He complied with the Pope's and Indonesia's wishes.

Later, sitting with me in a hotel room in Lisbon, the Monsignor told me of the anguish he had experienced since 1975, after seeing with his own eyes the monstrosities perpetrated by the invaders: the pain, the rape, the executions of our people. He asked me plaintively: "What is the United Nations doing? Why don't they help us? What are the Americans doing? They are the ones who give the weapons to the Indonesians, so they have the power to stop the war. You have been in the United Nations. Tell me, why isn't the United Nations doing anything?"

The Monsignor, a deeply moral man, sees the world through the prism of his Christian beliefs and could not comprehend the immorality of international politics. He protested when I tried to explain to him that East Timor was an expendable pawn in the international power game. With no big patrons, we were left to the mercy of the Indonesian Army.

The conversation reminded me of the day in 1975 that I and two other FRETILIN leaders left Dili in a hurry, a few days before the invasion. That was the last time I saw my mother and eldest sister, Romana. Numerous other brothers and sisters were scattered. One brother, Arsenio, had been taken prisoner by FRETILIN during the brief civil war between FRETILIN and UDT. He was in jail on the outskirts of the city. Chico, an elder brother, was a UDT prisoner and had been taken to West (Indonesian) Timor by the fleeing UDT forces. Unlike myself, Arsenio and Chico were only bystanders in East Timor's confusing political landscape; they became prisoners because they happened to be in the wrong place at the wrong time when the civil war broke out in August 1975. My sister Rosa was the wife of the UDT *putschist*, Joao Carrascalao, my political adversary but personal friend; he lost the civil war and fled to Indonesia with his wife and children. Romana, along with her husband and children, escaped the confusion and was not detained by either side during the civil war. She was at the airport with a letter which she asked me to bring to our aunt Noemia in Lisbon. Fear was in Romana's eyes; she knew the Indonesians were coming any day. In the letter to our aunt, she expressed her hope that "Jose will get the United Nations to help us. He is going to talk to big powers. This is our only hope."

My sister's hope was the hope of everybody else. Her fears were the fears of an entire nation that felt abandoned by Portugal, a country with which East Timor shared almost half a millenium of common history. The Portuguese had left with neither honor nor dignity, abandoning a whole country to the mercy of a ruthless neighbor. I had my own hopes and illusions about the United Nations. Ten years after the invasion, and as many General Assembly and Security Council resolutions later, Indonesian forces are still entrenched in East Timor. The killing, torture and rape continue. And my illusions are gone.

What is the United Nations doing? What is the rest of the world doing? I have been asked these questions again and again by Timorese refugees in Australia and Portugal, and by other concerned people who cannot understand the inability of the United Nations to bring about a just solution to the tragic Timor situation. To answer these questions and many others, I decided to write this book. I will focus on three main themes: a) the Timorese people's right to self-determination and independence; b) Indonesia's invasion of East Timor and subsequent atrocities; c) the United Nations' role. I shall analyze the attitudes of the major powers; the socialist bloc, including China, Vietnam, Cambodia and Laos; the African and the Latin American groups; the Arab bloc, etc. Much attention will be devoted to the role of the Portuguese, their colonial relationship with the Timorese, and the 1974 coup and its implications for East Timor. The role of non-governmental organizations (NGOs), humanitarian organizations, such as the International Committee of the Red Cross (ICRC), UNICEF, the Indonesian Red Cross, will be reviewed in light of their response (or lack of it) to the tragedy in East Timor.

A word of caution: Having been involved in the Timor struggle from the very first day, I do not pretend to be an impartial scholar. It is clear where I stand, and that is on the side of my people in our struggle for national independence. The book is an attempt to offer readers an understanding of the Timor problem from the perspective—be it subjective—of a Timorese who has represented his country at the United Nations and around the world for the past ten years. This is a personal account, not an official one, and I alone am responsible for its contents.

NOTES

1. Montealegre, Flora E. *The Invasion of East Timor and United States Military Assistance, Background Information on Indonesia*, Institute for Policy Studies, Washington, D.C.: May 1982.
2. Nordland, Rod. *The Philadelphia Inquirer*, May 28, 1982, pp 1, 2, 21-A.

1

Childhood Memories

I was born after World War II and was therefore spared the brutal Japanese occupation of East Timor. Mother lived through the ordeal and lost almost all her immediate and distant family members, except for one sister. She hardly ever talked about it, but putting together the bits and pieces I overheard over the years, I could reconstruct her tragedy. The Japanese came to the village one day and gathered everybody for interrogation. They wanted to know the whereabouts of the Australian soldiers. There was silence. The Japanese commanding officer then ordered everybody into half a dozen houses made of bamboo, palm and grass. They set fire to the huts, then trained their machine-guns on the doors and shot those trying to escape. Mother's sister Noemia managed to leave for Portugal, while mother stayed on in East Timor after the war. They never saw each other again, to this day.

Mother still lives today in the same palm tree house with a tin roof that we built on the outskirts of Dili in the late 1960s. I have not seen her since I left in 1975. I cannot but admire her courage and endurance in the midst of the tragedy that has engulfed the country and almost every family in East Timor. She raised ten children. Some of us were brats that could drive any mother insane. Yet she survived us as she did the Japanese occupation— and several years of hardship in the mountains as well, roaming the countryside with the FRETILIN cadres and the thousands of displaced people fleeing the Indonesian troops and aerial incursions.

Mother saw my sister Mariazinha, then 17 years old, a blossoming young woman, torn apart by rockets fired upon a civilian concentration by two "Bronco" aircraft. The village was burnt to the ground and 20 other children were killed. That same year she lost my younger brother, Guy, then 15 years old, to an Indonesian helicopter-borne assault on the village. In 1978, a third brother, Nuno, then 23, mother's favorite, was captured by the Indonesian forces and executed. Nuno was the *bete noire* of the family. Dumb in school, a rebel at home, he managed to generate a rare consensus among his brothers and sisters against him. When he was drafted into the Portuguese Army in the early 1970s, he spent more time in prison for breach of discipline than in the army itself. Then he joined FRETILIN in 1974, and by 1976 was a unit commander. His military exploits became known to the Indonesians, and we all knew that if he were ever captured, he would be shot on the spot.

In European homes, mothers tell the kids that babies are flown from Paris by a big bird. In our backward but peaceful village of Laklubar, mother told us a different story. When the fifth of us was to be delivered, I remember asking mother how *it* was going to come. She wanted us as far as possible from the house, so she told us to pack some food and go on a picnic at the river, because *it* would come down the river. In the early morning, Romana, Chiquito, Arsenio and I all rushed to the river and trained our eyes on the currents. We waited all day and got excited whenever some object appeared in the distance. There it comes! There it comes! We would shout excitedly, pointing our dirty little fingers and jumping up and down. But it was just another piece of tree that was floating on the current. When the sun began to turn yellow and dark, we headed back home, puzzled that our new brother or sister had not come. When we got close to home, we heard a baby's cries. Nuno, the fifth in the family, had arrived, and he was going to be a real pain in the ass in the years to come. He's gone now, murdered by Indonesian troops. Mother suffered immensely. We all forgave Nuno for our childhood quarrels and miss him terribly.

When I was 18, in 1970, I left Dili for exile in Mozambique. I had spent an evening carousing with an American from New Jersey and a group of Australian hippies. Under the influence of alcohol I had uttered some "subversive" statements, ridiculing the Portuguese "civilizing mission." Perhaps more serious, for a fascist regime, was my suggestion that "if Portugal is too poor to develop Timor, better give it to the Americans." For this, I was called into the Portuguese security police headquarters for interrogation, which lasted six full hours. That was my first encounter with the dreaded PIDE*, and I was so shaken that when a detailed report of that evening's incidents was read to me, I admitted to every charge and could only say: "I'm so sorry. I didn't mean to say all these things." The senior police officer who interrogated me, *Senhor* Biscaia, a man with a bulldog face, said: "You are done. You are burnt for the rest of your life. The only thing I envy is your age."

PIDE was omnipresent and powerful, feared and hated by everyone. In

---

Polícia Internacional de Defasa do Estado, the Portuguese Security police. Following the death of Salazar, the new fascist Prime Minister Marcello Caetano changed the name to *Direcção Geral de Segurança* (DGS). Its power to arrest and torture remained undiminished.

Portugal, Angola and Mozambique, it used both brutal and refined methods of torture to extract "confessions" from its victims. Like the German GESTAPO, the Russian KGB or the American CIA, it had its own network of informers and its own army that operated autonomously in the jungles of Angola and Mozambique, fighting the indigenous nationalist movements there. In East Timor, I never heard of any systematic use of force against suspects. Its presence in East Timor was mainly to monitor Indonesia's moves and to neutralize any pro-Indonesia movement in the territory.

After my interrogation, the colonial governor, Valente Pires, decided I should be fired from my job and leave the country for a while to allow things to cool down. The evening of my departure for Mozambique, almost the entire town came to the harbor to see the *Timor*, an old cargo and passenger boat, departing with the Portuguese troops who had completed their two years of tedious duty in the "province." The yearly visit of the *Timor* was a major event in Dili. During the week that the ship was anchored in the harbor, thousands of Timorese, Portuguese and Chinese would flock aboard for a few drinks in the bar, or just to stare out at the horizon, dreaming of voyages across the Indian Ocean, around the Cape, up the West African coast to Lisbon, the old "metropole."

Almost my entire family was there—mother, sisters and brothers. My aged and sick father could not make the trip from Laga, a distant coastal town. I had gone there earlier for a visit before my departure. Father hardly ever talked to any of us. He was a quiet, withdrawn man whose most faithful companion was a short-wave radio with tall bamboo antennas that enabled him to monitor Lisbon and the BBC. He followed very anxiously the events in his distant native land, always hoping for the news of a coup overthrowing the Portuguese dictator Salazar, who had sent him into exile in East Timor in the late 1930s.

I learned of my father's exploits, not from him directly, but from his old comrades; he never talked about his political past. Many of his comrades are still alive (I met one in Maputo recently, and several in Lisbon) and relish remembering those "wonderful times," as they put it. It was the time of the Spanish Civil War in 1936. Fascists from Portugal, Italy and Germany went to Spain to fight on Franco's side. Leftist brigades also went from Portugal and many other countries. Father was then a gunner in the Portuguese navy. He and his comrades-in-arms in the frigates *Afonso de Albuquerque* and *Dão* rebelled; then put to sea in the two warships and headed toward Spain to fight on the Republican side. However, dictator Salazar, whose sympathies were with Franco, learned of their plan and intercepted the rebel forces as they sailed out of the Tagus river. There was exchange of fire and the rebel navy was neutralized. Subsequently, father ended up in exile in East Timor while others were deported to Portugal's African colonies.[1]

Father wasn't the first in the family to have been shipped off to East

Timor. Grandfather, whom I never met, was deported first to the Azores in 1925, and from there transferred to the Cape Verde Islands, then to Guinea, and finally to East Timor, where he arrived toward the end of 1927. Arsénio José Filipe, my grandfather, was a notorious *anarcho-sindicalista* in Lisbon, responsible for countless bomb explosions in the 1920s. He actually manufactured the bombs in his small apartment in Rua do Solao, Rato, a narrow alley with decaying buildings where monthly rents are still around US$2.00! My uncle Armando and Noémia still live in the same old apartment, and their monthly rent is less than US $4.00—after a recent 100 percent increase.

In those times, the anarcho-sindicalists were so feared that often judges wouldn't show up for their trials. It happened that a few had been shot soon after they read the verdict. When World II broke out in East Timor with Dutch, Australian and Japanese landings, both grandfather and father joined the allied forces. Grandfather, *the bomb thrower*, became a sophisticated "chef" for one of the Australian units, while father, a former naval gunner, was deployed in the Remexio area as a fighter. Both were evacuated to Australia before the end of the war. In Australia, grandfather was put in an internment camp for attending a May Day parade! (I guess that was Australia's way of showing gratitude to those who helped the allied cause.)

That hot tropical evening in 1970, I was dressed in my first suit ever, custom-made by a local Chinese tailor. I had started life barefoot and had always worn shorts made of cheap material. Now, at 18, I was wearing a suit and traveling overseas—though in disgrace. *Senhor* Biscaia was there also, very conspicuously observing my movements. I was terrified and tried to hide my fears. What if he decided that I should not board the vessel and escorted me instead to a prison? I greeted everybody I could. I noticed that some were avoiding me, lest they also become suspects in the eyes of Sr. Biscaia. I gave my mother a kiss and hugged her. Tears rolled over her face. I was trying to maintain a cool appearance, hiding my emotions. Licinia, my little sister, an adorable creature who was then four years old, succeeded in pulling aside the masks I used to hide my emotions. As I lifted her up for a kiss, she said in that angelic voice of hers: "Don't ever die, *está bem?*" Tears flooded my eyes and began to roll down my face. I rushed to the boat.

Senhor Biscaia was at the gate. "Now he is going to arrest me," I thought. I stopped, and in a studied humble tone, said goodbye to him. To my surprise and relief, he patted me on the back and told me in a (sincere or pretending) fatherly way: "Don't get into troubles there." I boarded the vessel and went straight to my cabin, which I shared with six other people. I found out later that one of them was a PIDE informant.

I grew up in different places on the island—in Soibada, Laklubar, Barike, Atsabe, Venilale, Laga and Dili. As the son of a Portuguese, even a disgraced *deportado*, I was in a privileged position. Mother delivered me in the hospital, instead of in the bush like other babies not "fortunate" enough to have been conceived by a European with a native woman. All this I observed early on without understanding it; or without realizing how unjust it was. In a backwater colony, a European, no matter how dumb or illiterate, was considered a superior species. The son of a Portuguese *deportado*, even though his father was a dissident, had more advantages than the son of a native peasant.

I traveled almost everywhere in the island. By truck in the company of pigs, goats, and chickens; by motorbike or on a pony, I came to know my country like my own backyard. When I was seven my parents sent me to Soibada, a remote village which had a place on the map only because of its old Catholic mission school. Hundreds of children came there from around the country to begin their basic education. Located in a region of heavy rainfall, Soibada was blessed with luxuriant vegetation, but travel in and out was a nightmare. Roads were impassable during the rainy season, even for our tiny but tough ponies. There wasn't one single motor vehicle in the entire region; and whenever a truck or a jeep arrived in Soibada—when the rains subsided—it was a major event. The daily means of transportation there, as in most of East Timor, was the faithful pony, so overworked that usually they displayed awful wounds on their backs.

Soibada was the oldest Catholic mission school in the land. It was run by dedicated Portuguese and Goanese missionaries in a fashion that would delight an arch-conservative. The teachers were all Timorese. They, too, were dedicated, with one exception: the notorious *mestre* Jaime. A big man with a ferocious look on his monstrous face, *mestre* Jaime was the terror of the students. Impatient and temperamental, he would lose control of himself if a student failed to understand a lesson with the first explanation. Julio Alfaro, a classmate of mine, was once the target of his fury. Punches and kicks sent poor, skinny Julio flying to the floor. Then, *mestre* Jaime, excited with the pain he was inflicting on his student, smiled and licked his lips. With a wooden stick, he continued the beating until Julio fell unconscious. He seemed to derive sexual gratification from the punishment he inflicted on the youngsters. Of course, this interpretation of a teacher's sadistic behavior came to me much later in life. I, too, suffered his wrath on numerous occasions. Each time I would cry out loudly in the hope that one of the priests would come to my rescue. *Mestre* Jaime always guessed my intentions and became more infuriated. Those times when I crash-landed on the floor, I missed my home, father, and mother. I ran away a few times, only to be picked up and returned to school.

For seven years, that was the routine in Soibada. We were beaten for minor faults such as speaking Tétun or any of the Timorese languages. Of the hundreds of students who entered Soibada each year, less than one percent could muster a few words of Portuguese. Yet, we were supposed to communicate with each other only in Portuguese! The only way to get around the problem was to keep silent for days on end, or to speak to classmates with maximum discretion.

Every day we were made to recite a heavy dose of prayers—prayers to the Virgin Mary, Jesus, the saints, the Pope, the Bishop, and prayers for the health and wisdom of Salazar, the Portuguese fascist dictator. We started the day at 5 a.m., and by 6 we were at the chapel for the morning mass in Latin!

The food was awful. For seven years we ate corn—old rotten corn, with no vegetables or meat. There was never a glass of milk for any of us. At Christmas we were treated to a plate of boiled rice and a stew of deer meat. What a treat that seemed!

Christmas was a happy season. Relatives came from distant villages bringing tons of goodies. My parents never came for Christmas, because they were too far away in Atsabe near the border with West Timor. I didn't mind, because *Liurai* Tito, a local tribal chief whose eldest daughter had married my eldest brother, Antonio, would visit us. As a tribal chief, he had much more food to offer us than my mother could. We would gorge, desperately trying to stuff as much as we could into our stomachs. The feast would only last one day. The next day the schoolyards, stairs, the shower area and the streets would be spattered with vomit. Some of us could hardly move.

I'll never forget my first encounter with *Mano* António, my half-brother. I was only four or five, and still living at home. Nobody in the house had thought it necessary to explain to me that I had a half-brother, or that he would be arriving that afternoon. I sensed, though, that something unusual was about to happen. There was heavy traffic in the kitchen. Mother was beating eggs into a large pan, mixing them with sugar and flour. When she wasn't looking, I would dig my finger into the pan. Suddenly, I felt a sharp, painful slap on my cheek. "Out! Out! *Fora daqui!*" my mother shouted. With tears rolling down my face, I ran to the front yard. *Mother doesn't like me, my father doesn't like me, nobody likes me!* With these thoughts, I cried louder and louder. I decided to lay on the green grass right in the middle of the road. The village was visited by a truck only once a year, so there was never any danger of being run over. Lying on my skinny back, I stared at the sky. The stars of the evening began to surface. I started to count them, lost count, and started again. I thought of going to the backyard and tormenting Xica, the monkey mother had bought in the market. Poor animal. I thought of her only when some mean idea came into my head.

Then *Mano* António arrived. It was early evening. I do not remember the exact year. He had left high school in Dili and was coming home to stay. There he was, on a black horse, looking very impressive from where I lay on the road, looking up. He and the horse seemed gigantic against the stars.

In the next few years, we grew close. A few years later, Antonio got a job in Bualaka, as remote as any place could be. Laklubar could claim to see a truck once a year; Bualaka could only be reached on foot or by pony. Oil had been found there back in the thirties, but there was never any serious attempt by the Portuguese to exploit it, until the district authority took upon itself the task of squeezing a bit out of the ground to fill its miserable budget. Antonio became the local oil magnate. The crude was lifted from three wells in the same rudimentary manner as tribesmen anywhere in Africa or Asia pull water from the earth. A rope, a bucket, a few semi-enslaved workers did the job. Then the crude was refined, again in a very rudimentary fashion, just as one would extract alcohol from palm wine. Antonio's "corporation" produced half a dozen barrels of diesel and gasoline a month, which was sold to the villagers and the Catholic Mission of Soibada. He made Bualaka his permanent residence. How he adapted to such a primitive environment was amazing to me. In retrospect, what amazes me still was his ability to absorb the way of life, values, habits, and languages of the various tribes of the area.

Sometime in the late 1950s or early 1960s, he married Alzira, the eldest daughter of *Liurai* (local chief) Tito, a powerful and popular local leader. Their wedding was attended by hundreds, mainly representatives of the various tribal communities that were ruled by *Liurai* Tito. Along with my brother Chiquito, I got dispensation from Soibada to attend Antonio's wedding. The people had donated dozens of buffalos for the big day. A group of tribal elders were debating the union of their king's daughter with the *malae oan* (son of the European). They debated on through the night, in a musical oratory that to my ears sounded beautiful, though I did not have the foggiest idea what was going on. They finally gave their blessing. The wedding was held in the local Catholic Church, and Father Carlos came from Soibada for the occasion. According to local usage, the man had to donate a substantial dowry of buffalos, swords, silver, and gold. I do not recall what *Mano* António had to put up for such a royal wedding, but it had to be quite a bit because of the social status of the bride's parents.

What I remember most from the days of the wedding was the abundance of food. What a contrast with Soibada, where my diet was corn, corn and corn! There were dozens of local specialties, as well as some European pastries. My eyes surveyed the immense table, my heartbeat increased, my mouth grew wet, my hands started shaking and I began to eat and eat and eat. I loaded my pockets, just in case there would be no food the next day. But it kept coming. The feast went on for three days and nights. At night, the educated caste danced to "modern" music, played on an ancient record player. Somebody had been assigned to wind it whenever the music slowed. Outside, in the calm night air, under millions of stars, the tribesmen had their own fun. Buffalos were roasted, palm wine was passed around, men jumped the *dahur** and women played the *tebe.***

---

*Timorese dance performed usually by men.
**Timorese drums played by women.

When the war came in 1975 and I left East Timor, I had not seen Antonio for three years, and had not been to Laklubar, Bualaka or Barike for a long time. I left without my dearest brother who had looked after me and everyone else in the family during our years in Soibada. Antonio was forced to leave Bualaka—to leave his oil operations and his small farms that never produced much. Most painful of all, he was forced to leave his people and his way of living, and return to Dili, the town he had left some 20 years before. Now he has a small street shop in Dili, selling matches, cigarettes, etc. I have often inquired about the fate of his people—his in-laws, Alzira, her brothers, Marcos and Carlitos. The entire area, once remote from Portuguese administration, was affected by war when Indonesian troops moved into the region to chase FRETILIN forces that had made Soibada a bastion. Fighting has been going on there for years. Thousands have died from the war itself, and from war-induced famine. I often wonder what has become, or will become, of the once happy and simple people of Soibada, Barike, Laklubar and Bualaka. I cannot face the thought that they are all gone, a whole people physicially extinguished.

Soibada marked me profoundly. There were no roses in my seven years there, but I can only recall Soibada with love and *saudades* (nostalgia). Two Portuguese priests, Fathers Januario and Carlos, both from the Azores Islands, were part of Soibada's history. They were different, both physically and in their characters. Father Januario, the older, was tall and very tolerant; he was most likable. Father Carlos was short and skinny. A religious zealot and disciplinarian, he enjoyed saying mass in Latin (it didn't matter that no one understood it). Worse, he would deliver the sermon three times: in Latin, in Portuguese and finally in his own version of Tetun. When Father Januario was transferred to Dili after 20 years in Soibada, we all cried and missed him terribly. Father Carlos took over and immediately began imposing on us his austere and orthodox habits. One rule was that all the students should wear shorts long enough to cover the knees. As we all had shorts of normal length, we had to add a few inches. The following year, the fashion was baggy shorts covering the knee cap.

In spite of his weird notions of discipline, Father Carlos was regarded as some sort of saint. On one of his well-looked-after horses or on foot, he would visit the remotest villages, bringing along the words of Christ. Much later in life, I learned that the gossips went around saying that not all of his frequent trips to the bush were for spreading the Word.

Father Carlos was a friend of my family, and in Soibada he took good care of my soul. Every evening I had to confess to him my sins of the day. More often than not, I could not recall any sins; in those innocent years, even a solitary masturbation was not in my thoughts or vocabulary. So I could not think of anything bad to confess to Father Carlos. However, he didn't trust me and insisted I confess. To get off the hook, I made up vague "sins," saying "Today I was bad."

"How bad?" he would ask.

"Just bad, very bad."

"What did you do? You must confess everything," the Inquisitor would probe, hoping for a major revelation. After I made up some credible stories, Father Carlos would finally recommend a long list of *Ave Marias* and *Salve Rainhas*. I had visions of Hell and the prospect of being condemned to the eternal flames really frightened me, so I always doubled the prayers he recommended, just to be on the safe side.

I finished my basic education in Soibada with distinction. Father Guterres, a demanding instructor, prepared me thoroughly for the admission tests to enter high school in Dili. I was among the first two or three candidates from Soibada to move on to higher learning. For most Timorese, Soibada was the end of their education. A Portuguese Bishop once said, "The Timorese need only to read and write, and then we should give them a hoe and an axe." His remarks were common knowledge and much resented.

The admission test was demanding, but it was a walk-through for me, and I won entry into the exclusive *Liceu Dr. Francisco Veira Machado*. The moment I found myself in Dili, away from the round-the-clock supervision of religious zealots, I began to distance myself more and more from the traditional Church. The more I learned about the politics of the Church and the sexual escapades of the priests, the more cynical I became. Yet, I still have fond memories of the old Soibada mission, to which I owed so much of my early education and formation.

Liceu Dr. Francisco Veira Machado was theoretically open to all, but in practice restricted to a few privileged individuals. I was among the lucky few. Leaving the austere environment of Soibada for the relatively open atmosphere of Dili, I was confronted for the first time with a dramatic change in my life. My parents remained in a mountain village, so I was entrusted to a family I had never met before, though they were most caring. I missed Soibada, Laklubar, Atsabe, Barike and all the villages where I grew up in peace and happiness. This change immediately affected my studies. Though I was good in history, Portuguese, French and geography, I failed miserably in math and physics. The next year, I passed narrowly, and from then on I had no major problems. I completed senior high school with average marks, except in languages, history and philosophy, in which I excelled.

I cheated quite often. I joined with other schoolmates and formed a gang to steal examination forms. Sometimes, when we failed to get hold of the questions beforehand, we would enter the instructor's office in the middle of the night to replace the original test with one that we had already solved. Two of our schoolmates, Nuta and Gabriela, had suspicions about our activities, and began to demand that we share with them the tests we stole. I argued against this, and remember my words quite vividly: "Let us not allow women involved in this. They will mess up everything. What if they report us to Maria Benfica?" (Maria Benfica was our math teacher. That was not her real name, but we nicknamed her Benfica because she often wore red, the color of Portugal's most popular soccer club.)

We decided with a vote, and all but me voted to share the tests with the two sisters who, sure enough, passed them on to two girlfriends. The rest was predictable. Maria Benfica started questioning the women; soon, we were all caught. I then decided to draft a long, elegant letter addressed to the school's rector, making use of all my incipient gentlemen's instinct, asking that only we, the boys, be punished, and not the girls. We got the expected reactions. We were punished with only one week's suspension from class, but won a commendation for our chivalry! We all laughed a great deal with that and spent a week at the beach enjoying ourselves and catching up on our homework.

It is not the purpose of this book to describe my brief experience in Mozambique. I was never bothered by the authorities, though my dossier followed me from East Timor. After a brief period working as a journalist on a local daily, the editor, a priest, fired me abruptly because I was dating one of his secretaries. I did not know she was the priest's lover. This incident took place on November 15, 1970. I remembered because on the same day I received a telegram announcing my father's death. On the way home in the middle of the night, I was indifferent to the rain that was soaking me. I was oblivious to the world around me.

I was happy to return home when my exile was over. The Portuguese military chief in Lorenzo Marques authorized me to leave on the condition that I travel on a vessel chartered by the army to ferry troops for their tour of duty in East Timor. I found my beloved country much the same as I had left it. East Timor, under the Portuguese, seemed to sit still in history. The clock of development didn't tick there. For centuries the Portuguese neglected the East Timorese. The colony was only maintained as a symbol of empire, for the Portuguese valued myths and symbols.

Nevertheless, even though the Portuguese neglected the economic development of the territory, not to mention the education of its inhabitants, at least they left the indigenous peoples to their daily lives and rituals, secure in their ancestral *knuas*.* Five hundred years of Portugal's "civilizing mission" had little if any impact on Timorese animist religion and culture.

---

*Groups of huts housing families belonging to the same clan, usually built in remote mountainous regions.

NOTE

1. Talon, Vicente. *Portugal, Golpe o Revolucion*, CVS Ediciones (Madrid: 1974). "Movianiento Contra la Dictadura (1927-1974).

2

Colonial Beginnings

East Timor is roughly half of Timor Island, the largest of the islands of the Lesser Sundas. It is situated less than 400 miles off the northwest coast of Australia, with an area of 18,889 square kilometers and a population of about 700,000 in 1975. It is as large or larger in area and/or population than more than 30 independent states around the world. It is larger and potentially richer than most of the South Pacific island states, with the exception of Papua New Guinea, and most of the Caribbean islands, with the exception of Jamaica. The other half of the Timor Island belongs to Indonesia.

The island is of recent geological formation. The eastern sector is very mountainous with several peaks reaching over 5,000 feet in altitude. Tata Mai Lau, the highest peak, reaches 10,000 feet above sea level. The rugged nature of the terrain covered with tropical vegetation makes East Timor a most suitable sanctuary for guerrilla fighters. During World War II, a small group of Australian commandos pinned down 20,000 Japanese with ambushes and hit-and-run tactics. The same terrain is an ideal rear base for the Timorese resistance fighters who have been fighting the Indonesian occupation since 1975.

The population of East Timor "manifests an ethnic heterogeneity which characterizes the entire region . . . "[1] noted Shepard Forman, an American anthropologist with The Ford Foundation. Malays, Makassarese, and Papuans came to Timor and left traces of their presence. However, the proto-Malay type predominates. Two dominant language families—the Malayo-Polynesian, or Austronesian, and the Papuan, or non-Austronesian—break into more than thirty distinct linguistic groups in East Timor. However, Tétun has become a sort of *lingua franca*.

The Portuguese arrived in Timor two years after their conquest of Malacca in 1511. Before the European intrusion, Timor Island was ruled by two powerful kingdoms, Serviao in the west and Belu in the east. The Portuguese arrival did not alter the political dominance and independence of the two kingdoms until much later, after several centuries of cunning political manipulation, trade, religious conversion and outright use of force when this was possible. Only in 1912 were the Portuguese able to establish firm control over most of the Eastern part of the island, when Dom Boaventura, the last of East Timor's powerful indigenous chiefs, was subdued after almost two decades of rebellion.

Long before the arrival of the Portuguese, the island of Timor was known for its riches. The Portuguese were certainly the first Europeans to reach the shores of Timor, but not the first outsiders to "discover" it. Chinese traders had discovered the riches of the island almost a century before the Portuguese. According to C. R. Boxer, a Chinese chronicle of 1436 remarked that "the mountains are covered with sandal trees."[2]

A Portuguese historian wrote:

> Well before the arrival of the Portuguese (between 1511 and 1513), the island of Timor was already renowned for its riches in sandal wood, particularly the white sandal. Arab and Chinese merchants found in Timor their best supply of this wealth and tried to control its commercial monopoly.[3]

Antonio Pigafetta, a historian with the Magellan expedition, also made reference in his diary to the riches of the Timor Island in 1522: "There was a lot of white sandal wood, buffalos, pigs, goats, and also chickens. We also had rice, bananas, sugar cane, beans, and lemons."[4]

It seems clear that even before the European intrusion, the island of Timor was a political entity in itself, largely untouched by the Hindu, Buddhist and Moslem empires that flourished in the region between the 7th and 13th centuries. According to Forman, who lived in the eastern sector of East Timor with his wife, Leona, and their children for over a year in 1973-74, Timor

> ... did not come under the aegis of the early Javanese/Islamic principalities ... Indo-Javanese and Islamic influences barely can be noted, except in so far as Dutch hegemony later effected the spread of some ideas, particularly in the political domain, to western (now Indonesia) Timor. East Timor, under Portuguese rule, was largely exempted from those influences.[5]

Following the conquest of Malacca, a first Portuguese settlement was established on the island of Solor. A Dominican Friar, Antonio Taveira, began a campaign to propagate the Catholic faith; to protect the new converts from Moslem attackers, he built a fortress on the island. Around this enclave a community of *Topasses* developed from the marriage of Portuguese sailors, soldiers and traders with local women. After Solor, other settlements were established on Flores and Timor. The *Topasses* soon became an important political factor in the Lesser Sundas, challenging the Portuguese at times, or siding with them against the Dutch. They were led by two powerful families, the Hornays and the da Costas, who had established such a firm grip on the islands that the Portuguese were forced to recognize their authority to win their allegiance in the struggle with the Dutch.[6]

Throughout the 16th and 17th centuries, the Portuguese crown had little authority on Timor, which was theoretically ruled from Goa by a viceroy. The Topasses were the *de facto* rulers of the islands and challenged the viceroy's representatives when they were not happy with them. It was not until the 18th century that the seat of government was established on the island of Timor itself. The first official governor, Antonio Coelho Guerreiro, was appointed in 1701. He began a strategy of divide and rule that was to characterize the Portuguese colonialism for the next two centuries. Through bribes, military ranks offered to loyal chiefs, and alliances cunningly exploiting tribal rivalries, Guerreiro managed to undermine, one by one, the authority of the indigenous rulers. However, Portuguese authority was still tenuous at best.[7]

The Dutch meanwhile pursued their efforts to achieve hegemony over the entire region. The first major defeat for the Portuguese was the seizure of Malacca by the Dutch, followed by Kupang in West Timor. The Portuguese, a smaller and weaker maritime power, began to see their presence in the Far East being gradually reduced to the eastern half of Timor. A first border agreement between the Dutch and the Portuguese was concluded in 1858, but it was not until 1913 that the present boundary dividing East and West Timor was ratified with the Hague *Sentença Arbitral*. As a result of this border agreement between two European powers, Dutch West Timor became part of the Indonesian Republic in 1945, even though as seen earlier, the whole island of Timor was *never* part of any of the early Hindu or Islamic empires that covered the rest of the archipelago.

Portuguese control of East Timor was tenuous at best through the 19th century. Its presence was limited to a few coastal outposts. The countryside was effectively ruled by powerful chiefs like Dom Boaventura, regarded today as the first nationalist fighter against the Portuguese. An educated and astute leader, Dom Boaventura united the tribes on the island and launched a bloody campaign against the Portuguese that lasted a full 17 years. The rebels overran the capital, ransacked the colonial Governor's palace and established a seat of government in the Manufahi region. However, with Mozambiquan troops drafted into the Portuguese Army and superior European firepower, Dom Boaventura was finally subdued. Thousands died and 3,000 rebel troops were taken prisoner.[8]

Dom Boaventura's war was only one in a series of uprisings against Portuguese domination. Portuguese textbooks attempted to portray the "natives" of East Timor as "docile," unlike those in Angola and Mozambique. The island was conquered "with a cross, not with a sword"—a claim based on the fact that it was a Franciscan missionary who first set foot on Timor's shores. The noted historian Basilio de Sa was less romantic in his appraisal of the Timorese:

> Timor was the last colony to be completely pacified. In 1912, the Portuguese presence on the island was still very much in danger, threatened by the rebellion of the most important native king, Dom Boaventura . . . Until this date, the history of Timor has been a long story of rough campaigns, continuous changes, tight vigilance to establish, consolidate and protect the Portuguese domain on the island . . . Throughout it, epic deeds were registered, fought in desperation for life and death, so that the Portuguese flag would not be pulled down forever in those lands. Lifau, Mena, Cova, Ai-tutun, Laku-Maras, Kailaku, Manatuto, etc. were scenes of the indigenous determination to extinguish, in slaughter and blood, the Portuguese name.[9]

The defeat of Dom Boaventura marked the beginning of Portuguese control of the territory and penetration of the interior mountains. Coffee, which had been introduced in 1815, became the most important export item, accounting for about 80 percent of the total volume of exports. Needless to say, the beneficiaries of this economy were not the Timorese. A full 40 percent of the coffee production was owned by a Portuguese firm whose proprietors almost never set foot in the colony. Another 40 percent was owned by half a dozen Portuguese families, and the rest by a few Timorese tribal chiefs. The coffee monoculture flourished to the detriment of less profitable food crops that were vital to the vast majority of the inhabitants.

The defeat of Dom Boaventura marked the beginning of a period of relative peace in the colony. The outbreak of World War II ended that peace. Although Portugal declared its neutrality in the conflict, Japan invaded and occupied East Timor. The Japanese landed on the beaches of the north coast early in 1942, not long after the December 7, 1941, attack on Pearl Harbor. But the Japanese were not the first foreign troops to violate Portuguese "neutrality." A contingent of Australian and Dutch troops had landed in East Timor around Christmas, 1941, in spite of the protests of the Portuguese authorities. East Timor became a battleground.

The Timorese were forced to take sides. It wasn't their war; it was a war fought between imperialist rivals, and it spilled over to countries that had no stake whatsoever in the outcome. Arrogant Japanese attitudes, and their brutal practices of raping local women, confiscating livestock and crops, and summary execution of entire families, soon turned the Timorese against them. The 400 Australian commandos operating in the territory, with hardly any support from the outside, won the sympathy and allegiance of the vast majority of the Timorese tribal chiefs and their people. Other chiefs remaining loyal to Portugal joined in the fight against the Japanese, since they saw in them a threat to continued Portuguese presence on the island.

No doubt the Australian commandos operating in East Timor performed superbly, and their courage must go down in history as one of the great epics of the war. However, no matter how courageous and ingenious they were, their success and even physical survival was due to the support of the Timorese people. Of the 400 Australian troops fighting in the colony for three years, only 40 died, and most of them from disease and accidents. The Timorese, on the other hand, paid heavily. Thousands were gunned down, burnt inside their huts, or starved to death.[10]

The end of the war saw East Timor a devastated country. Its miserable economy, the work of Portuguese mediocrity and mendacity, was further ruined by the war. Its people were broken physically and psychologically. The Australians and the Portuguese celebrated the Allied victory. The Timorese, who bore the brunt of the Japanese occupation while the Portuguese maintained their "neutrality," were ignored during the victory celebrations. For Europe, there was a Marshall Plan. For Indonesia, where Sukarno and his nationalist followers had collaborated actively with the Japanese, there was the reward of independence. For East Timor, there was the return of the backward colonial power ruled by a fascist dictator whose sympathies during the war were with the Axis powers. Yet the Allied powers, influenced by England, which entertains with Portugal the oldest treaty alliance in history, favored the recolonization of East Timor by the Portuguese.

> The Portuguese government of Timor is a most miserable one. Nobody seems to care the least about the improvement of the country . . . after three hundred years of occupation, there has not been a mile of road made beyond the town, and there is not a solitary European resident anywhere in the interior. All the government officials oppress and rob the natives as much as they can, and yet there is no care taken to render the town defensible should the Timorese attempt to attack it.[11]

So wrote Lord Alfred Wallace in 1869. His description of the Portuguese record in East Timor, written in the 19th century, was equally true in the period after World War II. For many centuries, East Timor had been the bastard colony—the most remote, the most rebellious and the most neglected. Portuguese officials dubbed it the "*ante-camara do inferno*" (gateway to hell) because the island was plagued by malaria and other tropical diseases. Yet, the Portuguese did little to improve the country's conditions in the post-war period.

East Timor was at the bottom of the Portuguese national budget and development plans. No senior cabinet minister ever set foot on the island. It was the dumping ground for political dissidents, failed professionals and incompetent bureaucrats. It was only in the 1960s that the capital city, Dili, was provided with electricity; the rest of the country continued to rely on firewood and candles. By 1974, only a few main streets in Dili had been paved. Education had improved by the late 1960s; senior high school and a technical secondary institution were turning out a number of Timorese with education beyond simple writing and reading ability. Still, only a handful of Timorese managed to obtain scholarships to pursue university studies in Portugal.

In the early 1970s, with the appointment of a new governor, Colonel Fernando Alves Aldeia, the colony's future looked brighter. A liberal-minded soldier and a compassionate man, Aldeia embarked on a campaign to build basic infrastructures throughout the country. Miles of water pipes were laid down, bringing fresh water to the remote villages for the first time. Schools were set up everywhere (though with enormous deficiencies) and basic medical facilities were brought to the villages. Aldeia himself was a political man and his constant trips around the country seemed also orchestrated to gain points back in Lisbon; however, the result was a brighter outlook for East Timor. Travelling on horse or in a four-wheel-drive vehicle, Alves Aldeia crisscrossed the country, visiting inaccessible villages never visited before by a white man or an educated East Timorese from the capital. Every village he visited gained something: a water pump, a well, a school, a few hundred agriculture tools.

However, no matter how compassionate and capable Alves Aldeia was, he represented an archaic system riddled with inefficiency and corruption. East Timor was filled with incredible stories of graft and greed. In the 1960s the Portuguese proudly opened the first and only bridge crossing over the Laklo River. Shortly after its inauguration, the bridge was washed away by floods. The chief architect of the bridge was fired. He found a job with the firm that was awarded the contract to rebuild the bridge. A few years later, the bridge was up—and collapsed again!

NOTES

1. Forman, Shepard. *Human Rights in East Timor.* Hearings in the House Sub-Committee on International Organizations, U.S. House of Representatives, Washington, D.C. June-July 1977.

2. Boxer, C.R. "Portuguese Timor, a Rough Island Story: 1515-1970", in *History Today* 10, No. 5 (1970).

3. Barbosa, Duarte, "Livro em que se da relacao do que viu e ouviu no Oriente", in *Coloquois sobre as provincias do Oriente*, Volume I, No. 80, Lisbon (1968), in the series Estudos de Ciencias politicas e sociais.

4. Pigafetta, António, in *"Perspectiv Historica de Timor"*, op. cit., p. 50.

5. Forman, Shepard. Supra note 1.

6. Dunn, James. *Timor, A People Betrayed*, The Jacaranda Press, Qld. (1983).

7. Ibid.

8. Araújo, Abílio. *Timor: os Loricos Voltaram a Cantar*, edição do autor, Lisbon (1977). Also, "Revolt in Timor: Government House Looted", *Argus*, Melbourne, February 19, 1912.

9. Sa, Artur Basilio de. *A Planta de Cailaco, 1727*, No. 122, Agencia Geral das Colonias, Divisao de Publicacoes e Biblioteca (1949).

10. Callinan, Bernard J. *Independent Company, The Australian Army in Portuguese Timor 1941-43*. William Heinemann, Vic. Australia (1984). Also Dunn, J. *Timor: A People Betrayed* (1983).

11. Wallace, Alfred Russel. *The Malay Archipelago*, MacMillan, London (1869).

3

The "Carnation Revolution"

According to the pre-1974 Portuguese Constitution, East Timor, known until then as Portuguese Timor, was an "overseas province," just like any of the provinces that made up continental Portugal. "Overseas provinces" also included Angola, Cape Verde, Guinea, Mozambique, Sao Tome and Principe in Africa; Macao in China; and had included Goa in the Indian sub-continent until Nehru's swift military invasion in December 1960. Colonies? No, the Portuguese argued. We were not "colonized people," as we were being called at the United Nations and in other international forums; we were as Portuguese as the whiter ones living in Lisbon.

In the 1970s, as international pressure mounted and the guerrilla war heightened, Angola and Mozambique, the two most important prizes, were elevated to the status of Associated States, though real power was vested in the Governor General appointed by Lisbon. The "Commonwealth State" (read colony) of Puerto Rico has more political and administrative autonomy *vis a vis* Washington than did Angola and Mozambique in regard to Lisbon.

East Timor existed in the Portuguese geography texts as the site of the highest mountain in the "Portuguese empire," or in the history classes with a few passing references. Dom Aleixo Corte Real—who fought the Japanese until the bitter end because he opposed the Japanese and not because he loved the Portuguese—was portrayed as "a martyr for the Motherland"—which of course was Portugal, not East Timor or his tribe, Ainaro.

The little rectangle on Europe's western edge was inflated with the area of all the "overseas provinces" in a map superimposed over Europe, extending beyond Spain, France and even Germany. Ironically, I recently found an official Indonesian publication with a map of the archipelago superimposed over Europe, stretching from Portugal all the way to the

Soviet Union. East Timor was, of course, added to the "Greater Indonesia" map.

The myth of empire crumbled in 1974. On April 25 of that year, a charismatic young army officer, Otelo Saraiva de Carvalho, who was born in Mozambique, engineered a bloodless coup bringing to an end a 50-year-old dictatorship. Faced with a three-front war in Africa that drained its meager financial resources and stagnated an already backward economy, Portugal was indeed in a dire situation. The military leaders who had fought in the wars in Africa hoped to rescue Portugal from certain military defeat and international ostracism. The beautiful tune of "Grandola Vila Morena," by poet Zeca Afonso, played over radio *Renascenca* set in motion a coup that was appropriately christened the "Carnation Revolution."

The coup paved the way for speedy decolonization of all Portugal's colonies, including East Timor. The five colonies in West and East Africa got their independence in 1974 and 1975. In Angola, the *Movimento Popular de Libertação de Angola* (MPLA) formed a government in Luanda, after routing its two rivals, the *Frente Nacional de Libertação de Angola* (FNLA) and the *Uniao Nacional Para a Independencia Total de Angola* (UNITA). FRELIMO (*Frente de Libertação de Mozambique*) had established itself, long before 1974, as the unchallenged political and military force in Mozambique, and the transfer of power there was relatively smooth. In Cape Verde and Guinea-Bissau, the *Partido Africano para a Independencia de Guine e Cabo Verde* (PAIGC), which had united the peoples of the two African colonies in the struggle against the Portuguese, took over smoothly from the defeated colonial power.* The *Movimento de Libertação de Sao Tome e Principe* (MSLTP) took over from the Portuguese in the two islands off the coast of Gabon. In Sao Tome and Principe, as well as in the Cape Verde islands, there was no armed opposition to the Portuguese. The Cape Verdean nationalists fought instead in the jungles of Guinea-Bissau in what they saw as the first and indispensable phase of the struggle for the liberation of their own country.

East Timor did not experience a war of national liberation. Nevertheless, there was growing discontent with Portuguese colonial practices. The young and educated were becoming frustrated and resentful over the lack of opportunities for education and promotion. In the early 1970s, an incipient nationalist organization began to take shape. The group, of which I was a member, along with many others in today's nationalist movement, began to

*Amilcar Cabral, founder of PAIGC, was assassinated by a close associate in 1972. One of the most inspiring and talented African thinkers of modern times, Cabral believed in and fought for the unity of Guinea and Cape Verde. He was succeeded by his brother, Luis Cabral, who became Guinea-Bissau's first President when independence finally came in 1974. Amilcar's dream of a united Guinea-Bissau and Cape Verde was shattered when Luis Cabral was ousted in a coup in December 1981. The two countries maintain close relations.

reach out for help in Indonesia—both because we were inspired by Indonesia's earlier independence struggle against the Dutch, and because of its geographic proximity. Indonesia was assumed to be sympathetic to any nationalist movement in East Timor. I was the liaison with the Indonesians through the Consul in Dili, E.M. Tomodok. I met with him on numerous occasions, usually in the middle of the night in order to avoid Portuguese police detection. With him I discussed our projects for studying and training in Indonesia. He was an enthusiastic supporter of our movement and encouraged us to cross the border into West Timor to seek support. I remember him saying: "There the military will be very sympathetic. Go, cross the border and you will find support there." Tomodok disliked the Portuguese and was eager to do anything to embarrass them. I could not help but be amused when I saw him in the Dili social circuit with the Portuguese colonial Governor, Fernando Alves Aldeia. Tomodok confessed to me his admiration for the charming and popular Governor, but at the same time, he did not hide his disdain for the Portuguese in general. He once told me: "The worst colonialism is the Portuguese. Second was the Dutch. Third, the French. The British were the best of the lot."

I was particularly happy with the news of the coup in Portugal because I had received orders to leave the country again. In January, I had been featured in an Australian paper, the *Northern Territory News* (Darwin), on conditions in East Timor and prospects for independence. I had just read Mondlane's *Struggle for Mozambique* (courtesy of Betsy Traub, a Harvard University Ph.D. candidate who was doing her field work in East Timor). Mondlane quoted an African saying: "When the whites came to our country, we had the land and they had the Bible; now, we have the Bible and they have the land."[1] In my interview in *Northern Territory News*, I applied that African saying to East Timor. It was amusing and powerful, but with little relevance to East Timor, where there were very few large properties, amounting to only a small percentage of the arable land. So, if I had quoted Mondlane's allegory to the villagers of East Timor, they wouldn't have understood, for they still had the land and only few knew the Bible!

The interview reached the desk of the Overseas Minister. The provincial governor, Fernando Alves Aldeia, was angry when he called me into his office. A liberal, he was mad because he felt I had betrayed his trust. He dutifully informed me that the matter was now in the Minister's hands, then asked, "What would you rather happen to you—go to jail or into exile?" I responded without hesitation. "Exile." It was going to be my second exile. I reached an understanding with the Governor that I would leave very discretely "to study overseas." A newspaper story was composed by me and edited by one of the Governor's aides announcing the "news" that I would be leaving the country to study journalism in Australia or in New York. However, word spread around Dili, small city that it was, that I was being exiled again. I began to pack and forwarded most of my luggage to Darwin; I bought a ticket and planned to leave by April 27. On April 26, the Governor called me into his office and told me, in a very relaxed manner: "You heard the news. You can stay now."

The coup changed everything. There was euphoria in Dili; an air of freedom and celebration prevailed for several days. When the euphoria subsided, the local elite began to wonder about the future. The conservative civil servants were worried about their jobs and the privileges that came along with them. The Chinese merchants were worried, because they feared they would suffer the most if there were to be political instability. As everywhere else in Southeast Asia, the ethnic Chinese had the monopoly of the import-export and retail business, and were the favorite scapegoats for the governments in times of crisis.

I know of few countries less prepared than East Timor to suddenly face a totally new political situation. The Portuguese fascist regime had never tolerated political dissent, let alone parliamentary democracy. In Portugal itself, the only party that emerged organized after the coup was the Communist Party (PCP). No other political parties ex'sted. For almost 50 years there had been no political debate in Portugal, and certainly not in East Timor. Yet, within weeks of the coup, the small Timorese elite began to ponder the various alternatives open to the country. A majority of the educated elite—the civil service sector, the traditional chiefs who had become identified with the colonial power, the handful of well-to-do Timorese families who could be considered landlords because they owned some coffee plantations—favored a continuation of Portuguese presence indefinitely. Some administrative reforms to make the system more liberal and efficient would have satisfied them. They were afraid of changes that might rock their placid lives. Their fears were understandable.

Another group, less numerous and influential, without any power base, also began to jockey for a role in the country's future. Our only assets were our youth, a more progressive vision for our country's future and a more realistic understanding of the meaning of the Portuguese "Carnation Revolution." We knew that the Portuguese would be leaving soon, and that we should prepare ourselves for one alternative: independence. The only other alternative was integration with the Republic of Indonesia. Unlike the first group, we had no special privileges under the Portuguese, no properties, no emotional ties to the metropole.

A third group of individuals without any significance in the capital, let alone in the countryside, favored a union with Indonesia. In Dili, this group could not count on more than ten extended families.

NOTE

1.   Mondlane, E. *The Struggle for Mozambique*. Penguin African Library, Harmondsworth (1969).

4

Politics in East Timor

The *Uniao Democratica Timorense* (UDT) was the first political association to be announced after the *"Revolucao dos cravos"* in Lisbon. More by coincidence than by design, I participated in UDT's creation. That evening, almost the entire Dili "who's who" was there, at Domingos de Oliveira's residence. An ex-seminarian, Domingos Oliveira was respected for his intellect, though this was never demonstrated anywhere, in writing or in any other form. We shared hours of discussion on his veranda in the years before the coup. His favorite topics were theology and philosophy.

Domingos was silent through most of the meeting. The obvious leader of the group was Mario Carrascalao, an agriculturist, one of the half-dozen university graduates the Portuguese were proud to show off after 500 years of their backward colonization of the island.

Ironically, Mario was the only politician in the whole country with any experience whatsoever. Until the "Carnation Revolution" he was the Chairperson of the East Timor branch of *Accao Nacional Popular* (ANP), a sort of fascist action group, the only political party allowed in Portugal. Watching Mario's new role as the leader of a "progressive" group suited to the new times, I could not but be amused by his flexibility. His father, *Senhor* Carrascalao, was a well-known Portuguese anarchist, a bomb-thrower in his youth until Salazar shipped him off to exile in East Timor. With time, he changed into a respectable legislator in the local rubber stamp assembly, and later became Mayor of Dili.

Today, Mario has completed the circle. Since 1981, he has been Indonesia's obedient "Governor" of occupied East Timor.

That evening Mario proposed the creation of a political association to be called *Uniao Luso-Timorense*, a name that proclaimed the group's desire to cling to a Portugal that was breaking apart and whose leaders were anxious to leave as quickly as possible. Yet, not everything was negative in

Mario's proposal. I found some of his words progressive and encouraging: "We want self-determination under the Portuguese flag. However, we must also have our feet firm on the ground. We shall not jump into the sea if they (the Portuguese) want to abandon us." Mario Carrascalao had been matured by his experience under the Portuguese, even though he could not be proud of his political record. He was a realist; he did not discard the independence option, but he wanted to tie down the Portuguese as long as possible.

There was no debate; no questions of any depth were asked. Augusto Mouzinho, the mayor of Dili, who later became UDT Vice Chairman, asked just to be polite: "*Senhor engenheiro*, could you explain what democracy is all about?" As Mario hesitated, Domingos Oliveira, who enjoyed philosophical explorations, began to explain the Latin roots of the word, "demos" meaning people . . . etc.

I was too self-conscious about my unwelcome presence in the gathering to offer any suggestions. However, I could not help voicing my reservations about the politically out-of-fashion name of the association. "Couldn't you think of something more in tune with the present political atmosphere? For instance, Popular Democratic Union or Democratic Union . . . ?" The suggestion took hold, and as easily as they had adopted the initial name proposed by Mario Carrascalao, everybody opted for *Uniao Democratica Timorense*.

Because of its conservative origins and a platform that showed allegiance to Portugal, UDT won the automatic allegiance of a number of "traditional" chiefs. Most of these had been created by the Portuguese to replace the truly traditional tribal leaders. UDT's major strength was in areas such as Maubara, ruled by *liurai* Gaspar Nunes, a native chief notorious for his devotion to Portugal; Maubisse, also ruled by pro-Portuguese chiefs; Laklubur, ruled by Moniz; and Ainaro, the chiefdom of Dom Aleixo Corte Real who the Portuguese propaganda machine portrayed as a "Martyr for Portugal." However, while the old chiefs supported UDT, their sons supported FRETILIN; as in colonial Africa, where tribal rulers who were puppets of the colonial regime lost their power when independence came, the so-called Timorese "traditional" chiefs saw their fortunes fading within months of the Lisbon coup.

One important fact about UDT is that it *never* advocated integration with the Republic of Indonesia. In fact, most of its leaders were more virulently anti-Indonesia than FRETILIN leaders. UDT leaders even spread rumors that some elements in FRETILIN were pro-Indonesia; I personally was a victim of accusations of that sort.

UDT evolved from a group of privileged individuals who could not conceive of an independent East Timor, to a UDT that clearly favored independence as a goal, by early 1975. This evolution was compelled by two factors: in East Timor itself, the UDT leaders could sense that the idea of independence was gaining ground fast, and was identified with FRETILIN. In Portugal, there was a determination on the part of the radical army officers to grant independence to all the African colonies by the end of 1975. East Timor, an inconsequential issue in the decolonization process, would be disposed of one way or another. The UDT leaders began to feel that their Portuguese brothers were not going to stay on much longer. Mario Carrascalao made an emotional statement in Dili in May 1974, during a meeting between East Timorese political leaders and two Portuguese senior army officers. In response to a comment by a pro-Indonesian demagogue, Mario said, "In my view, integration with Indonesia would be a treason! Portugal is the only country with which we have cultural affinities!" I joined Mario in denouncing Osorio Soares, leader of *Apodeti*.

Mario was not the titular UDT leader. In fact, his title was President of the *Comissao Organizadora* that was preparing the ground for the creation of the party. In view of his fascist background, Mario was discouraged by the Portuguese army officers in charge of the decolonization process from being in the forefront. Another leader was selected. He was Francisco Lopes da Cruz, a brother of the ferocious *mestre* Jaime, a native of the village of Soibada where I grew up. Like most Timorese with any ambition, Lopes da Cruz went to the Jesuit seminary, but never finished his training for the priesthood.

Lopes da Cruz was a perfect example of a figurehead. He never made any contribution to the party he was supposed to lead. At meetings he remained silent for hours. He simply could not formulate a coherent thought or idea. Before the "Carnation Revolution" he was an NCO in the Portuguese army and served in Mozambique, in the colonial war against FRELIMO. In East Timor, he gained notoriety as a basketball player. That was the *curriculum vitae* of the UDT leader. I remember his amazing silences during meetings with the Portuguese in the initial stages of decolonization. Not once did Lopes da Cruz utter a word. João Carrascoalao, intelligent and stubborn, was the UDT spokesperson.

The nominal second-in-command in UDT was Augusto Cesar Mouzinho, then mayor of Dili. He was one of the few Timorese who managed to reach seniority in colonial Timor. He was ambitious, hard-working, and basically honest. Politically, Mouzinho was an arch-conservative with no grasp whatsoever of parliamentary democracy, which was anathema to him.

The man who emerged as the brains behind UDT was Mario's younger brother, João Carrascalao, a land surveyor. In the early stages of the political liberalization process, João was studying in Switzerland. Upon his return to East Timor early in 1975, he basically assumed command of UDT to the consternation of Lopes da Cruz—and the Indonesians. Lopes da Cruz was by then a target for Indonesia's efforts to bribe and coopt UDT leaders. João was the only UDT leader with any real leadership qualities, a conservative with a larger vision of politics. His major problem was that he was stubborn. It was impossible for anyone to have a sensible argument with him, and to change his position.

Associacao Popular Democratica Timorense (APODETI) never had any popular appeal and was anything but democratic. APODETI was founded by Jose Osorio Soares. Its initial name was *Associacao para Integracao de Timor na Indonesia,* a straightforward title that described its goal, the integration of East Timor into the Republic of Indonesia. It brought together a "who's who" of corrupt incompetents and marginals. The figurehead of the group was the elderly Arnaldo dos Reis Araujo, the only Timorese to be given a prison sentence for war crimes. Araujo had led gangs of Timorese from the border region against Australians during World War II. Their targets were also Portuguese officials, their families, and Timorese who were active in the resistance to the Japanese occupation. These *"colunas negras"* (black columns) were responsible for the brutal deaths of hundreds of helpless Timorese in the Aileu, Maubise, and Same region. They burned down entire villages, and confiscated cattle and jewelry that were turned over to the Japanese forces.

The intellectual force behind APODETI was Jose Osorio Soares, a Portuguese colonial official who had been fired over a rape charge. Moving to Dili, Osorio was given a minor administrative job and again fired after three years because of fraud. Osorio claimed to have been framed by the Portuguese authorities because of his pro-Indonesian sympathies. I suspect there was some truth to this. I knew Osorio rather well. He was intelligent, arrogant and uncompromising. During the initial period of the formation of the political associations, I tried to win over Osorio to our group. I offered a number of concessions: I would accept that the Indonesian language be adopted as a compulsory subject in our school system; that Indonesian "realities" be taught: and most important, that integration with the Republic of Indonesia be considered—but only *after* the independence of East Timor, and *after* our people had learned about the realities of such an integration.

Osorio seemed amenable to these concessions and was present at the first meeting I called to discuss the formation of a political association. He chaired the meeting with myself and Francisco Xavier do Amaral, who became FRETILIN's first president. However, Osorio was in close touch with his mentor, the Indonesian Consul in Dili, Mr. E. M. Tomodok, who advised him not to deviate from a straightforward pro-Indonesia platform. Tomodok assumed direct control of APODETI strategy in our country and was responsible for the climate of intrigue, uncertainty and fear that began to prevail in East Timor in early 1975. An extremely corrupt individual, Tomodok had no moral restraints to hinder him in gathering a fortune and gaining more political clout back in Jakarta. It was through Tomodok that I learned about Indonesian realities and politics and became convinced that independence was our only realistic option.

While FRETILIN (and to a lesser extent, UDT) "stumped" the country trying to win the hearts and minds of the Timorese, APODETI leaders did not seem to worry about building an electoral bloc. They did not venture out of their Dili homes. On more than one occasion, Osorio told me, half serious, half joking: "I cannot understand you. Timor is going to be Indonesian whether you want it or not! You are killing yourself with all this bullshit for nothing." At other times, he would try to persuade me to join with him "before it is too late!"

APODETI's favorite tactic was intimidation. Rumors were planted that Indonesian warships were already landing troops somewhere on the island, and that anyone who opposed integration would be "disposed of." The campaign was not limited to rumors. APODETI began recruiting Timorese along the border with Indonesian West Timor for military training in Atambua. Sent back to East Timor, they began to burn houses, kill at random, and coerce people to move to West Timor. This was part of a calculated campaign by Jakarta.

Another sinister APODETI personality was the powerful chief of Atsabe, Guilherme Gonçalves. One of the wealthiest chiefs in the country, Guilherme was a despot who had acquired his fortune through ruthless exploitation of his people. Thousands of men and women were forced to pick his coffee every year and carry it on their backs to storage miles away. Thousands were forced to work his rice fields. With my parents, I lived for seven years in Atsabe and grew close to the Gonçalves family. I saw with my own eyes some of the atrocities committed by his two sons, Lucio and Tomas, both of whom served jail sentences later for rape, arson and murder. One incident I never forgot: I was ten and was enjoying the long summer break in Atsabe. Lucio had a huge vicious dog called *Oriente*. One evening, I was playing with Lucio when we saw the night guard arriving to take up his post. Lucio whistled to the dog and incited him to attack the guard. He was laughing hysterically as the dog jumped the poor man, threw him to the ground and tore at him. The servants heard my cries and rushed to rescue the poor man. He was rushed to the local pharmacy, bleeding profusely. I was traumatized by the incident and became very afraid of Lucio. I dislike dogs to this day.

This sadistic behavior went unpunished because Guilherme was a loyal chief protected by the PIDE. Only in the early 1970s when a young, aggressive state prosecutor took up the job, were the father and two sons sent to jail in spite of the Governor's and PIDE's intervention.

Not surprisingly, Guilherme and his sons saw no future with UDT or FRETILIN. With profound resentment, they joined APODETI and were instrumental in the terror campaign in the border region in 1974-75.

These were the people Indonesia used to form the APODETI party: rapists, murderers and incompetents. Not surprisingly, Arnaldo Araujo and Guilherme Gonçalves, who became the first "governors" of East Timor after 1975, were removed from office one after the other because of corruption and incompetence. Even for the Indonesians, among whom corruption is a way of life, Guilherme and Arnaldo were too much!

Having attended the first UDT gathering at Domingo's home, I was positively impressed with its draft platform and Mario Carrascalao's explanation that independence would not be discarded as an option. I had strong reservations about the politics of most of the group's founders; their love for Portugal was distasteful to me. However, I thought I could work within the group to steer it to the right course.

I conveyed my impressions and ideas to a number of my old buddies. Unlike the group that formed UDT, we had already gathered a nucleus of nationalists before the Portuguese coup. Though we were not an organized political force, we shared an aversion to the backwardness of the Portuguese colonial system. We all felt strongly that an independent East Timor could be a manageable economic unit. "Look at the job they have been doing for all these years; we could do just as well or better"—this was a common observation among our group.

The group consisted of myself; Mari Alkatiri, an articulate radical of Arab descent whose grandparents had come from Southern Yemen some 200 years before; Justino Mota, part Timorese, part African and part European, bright and most antagonistic toward the "metropole"; and a dozen other youthful schoolmates who faded away by 1974. Though not a frequent participant in our group's meetings, Nicolau Lobato was perceived as the leader. The eldest son of a minor school teacher from Soibada (where I met the Lobato family and *mestre* Narcizo, the father who became my godfather), Nicolau attended the Jesuit seminary in Dare, on the hills overlooking Dili. Finishing high school, he dreamed of going on to study law in Portugal, but could not get a scholarship or money to pay the fare. Besides, his father was ill and retired and his 14 brothers and sisters needed him to look after them. So, he found a job in the civil service. A serious intellectual, very ambitious, with an enormous appetite for reading, Nicolau inspired respect very early on.

Francisco Xavier do Amaral, a prominent Timorese intellectual some ten years older than Nicolau, was another promising leader. Xavier had studied in the advanced Jesuit seminary in Macao; he had completed his priesthood training, but was never ordained. Xavier and Nicolau were among the most serious intellectuals in East Timor, and the only two gifted with leadership qualities.

My tentative proposal for a merger of our nucleus with the UDT group was turned down. Justino Mota refuted my argument that we could steer UDT to the right course with one of his matter-of-fact remarks that did not encourage much discussion: "Are you naive or are you just kidding? They are the ones who will end up controlling us." The others supported Justino's position and we moved ahead with plans to set up our own party.

We were all clear about the ultimate goal, and were aware of the complexities of the decolonization process; however, none of us had any coherent ideological vision beyond independence. Marxism was far from our minds. None of us, except Nicolau Lobato and I suppose Alkatiri, had read a single word of Marx or Lenin. The only revolutionary writings with which we were familiar were those of Amilcar Cabral, the great African thinker and revolutionary leader of Guinea-Bissau and Cape Verde.

I was one of the least disposed to what I usually called the "abstract extravaganzas" of Marx and Lenin. Social democracy to us, and to me particularly, seemed closest to the ideal. It stood for social justice, equitable distribution of the wealth of the country, a mixed economy and a democratic political system.

There was much discussion of the draft manifesto that I proposed before it was adopted unanimously as our platform. It was rather vague and conservatively worded. We called for independence without a time frame. We thought then of a period of about 10 years before the country could be adequately prepared for political independence. The 10-year period would be a time of basic administrative, judicial, and economic reforms; acceleration of the formation of an elite capable of running the country; and the establishment of international contacts in the areas of commerce, economic aid and cooperation. We hoped that Portugal would assist us, but we counted on Australia above all.

The *Associacao Social Democrata Timorense* (ASDT) was announced on the evening of May 20, 1974. It immediately attracted widespread support from the young educated and the low wage earners; and "conditional" support from Timorese university students pursuing studies in Lisbon, whose reservation was that social democracy was a bourgeois doctrine that did not represent the real interests and aspirations of the common people.

Xavier do Amaral was hesitant about accepting the leadership role. He phoned the printing house one morning to withdraw his name from the list of the "Organizing Committee." A Portuguese director of the government printing house phoned me about Xavier's request to delete his name. I panicked, because ASDT could not get off the ground without his name on the list. Although Nicolau Lobato was committed to our project and was undoubtedly a potential leader, he was an unknown figure. We desperately needed an older person with some intellectual standing to give our group an air of respectability and maturity. Our patriarchal society had no respect for a bunch of young people.

I phoned Xavier at his office in the Dili Customs House, where he held a senior position, and pleaded with him to leave his name. "It is just a temporary thing, *Senhor* Xavier," I said, deliberately misleading him. After a few minutes of my pleading and flattery, Xavier finally accepted the role of "president of the Organizing Committee."

Nicolau was the second on the list. Again, I had included his name without consulting him. When he came to my office to pick up a copy of the daily *Boletim*, of which I was an editor, I sensed his surprise at seeing his name. I told him, "Nicolau, we couldn't do anything without you. You and Xavier are indispensable." Nicolau, always reserved and quiet, did not raise any objections, but knew that I had left him no alternative. There was no disagreement on anyone's part about the choices of Xavier and Nicolau as our leaders.

Xavier do Amaral was Osorio Soares' brother-in-law. Xavier married one of Osorio's younger sisters, Lucia, a crude, talkative woman who often complained about our long meetings at their house on the outskirts of Dili. Lucia cheated on her husband by sleeping with one of Xavier's adopted "nephews." Xavier, who was already suspicious of his wife, left with me for a campaign to the country; returning earlier than she expected him, he caught them both in the act. Our opposition did not hesitate in using this scandal to humiliate and discredit our leader. "If he cannot rule at home, how can he rule the country?" became a favorite question that was played on the radio again and again.

Xavier survived the ordeal. His popularity increased in spite of the incident. He and Nicolau provided ASDT with a unique combination of two charismatic leaders. Xavier was immensely popular, an orator who knew how to move the crowds, using his profound knowledge of the common people's problems, aspirations, and way of thinking, embellished with the oratorical skills that are part of a preacher's training. Nicolau was less known, not a great orator but an impressive organizer, tireless and methodical. Together, they provided the key elements for a successful leadership.

I helped both Nicolau and Xavier with my journalistic skills. I drafted most of Xavier's speeches and almost every single ASDT press release, communique, letter, radio propaganda text, etc. I travelled frequently into the countryside with Xavier or Nicolau or both. A handful of us did all the work. It was a most trying and exasperating period, with most of the paperwork falling on my shoulders.

In July, 1974, a movement started within ASDT to change our name and platform into something broader. In the meantime, the UDT leaders, alarmed by reports that the Australian Prime Minister, Gough Whitlam, favored East Timor's integration with Indonesia, sought us out to form a common front. I was in Baucau with Nicolau Lobato when Domingos Oliveira and other UDT leaders showed up in a chartered plane, looking for us. They were shaken by Whitlam's statements. Upon our return to Dili, we began exploring the possibilities of a merger of the two parties. A large meeting was held at my mother's humble palm tree house on the outskirts of the city. Because it was unbearably hot under the tin roof, we met in the shade of a tree in front of the house. It was an informal and friendly discussion. There was receptivity on UDT's part for a merger. The meeting was adjourned and a second one scheduled for a week later.

The same reservations that had blocked my proposal to join with UDT in the early stages surfaced again. I detected some receptivity from Xavier; less from Nicolau; and outright opposition from Mari Alkatiri. Over the next few months, Mari and I found ourselves always voting opposite positions, with Justino invariably siding with Mari. Yet, we remained close friends, and this was the case among all other FRETILIN cadres.

When the next meeting was supposed to be held, Domingos Oilveira had gone to Gleno Valley to inspect his rice plantation. ASDT's abrupt decision to move ahead without UDT because of such a minor incident reflected our collective immaturity. I was disappointed but did not fight hard for a change in ASDT's attitudes, because I simply lacked the courage and the numbers to succeed.

In September 1975, we announced the formation of the *Frente Revolucionaria de Timor Leste Indepentente* (FRETILIN). The proclamation text was drafted by Borja da Costa, a writer and poet who had just returned from Lisbon. The manifesto's preamble was extremely rhetorical with little relation to the reality in East Timor. Borja had been influenced by a radical group of Timorese students in Lisbon, and the preamble reflected their interpretation of East Timor's colonial situation. There was no debate and the new platform was unanimously approved. I managed only to sneak into the manifesto our continuing adherence to social democracy.*

When the text reached Lisbon, it caused a furor among the Timorese radical students. Social democracy was in sharp contradiction with everything else stated in the new platform, it was argued. In one of our endless debates on the question, I raised something that had been boiling in my head for some time. I said, "Communism means the control of the means of production by the state. It means the nationalization of private enterprise. I cannot see what a country like ours, without any industry, would have to nationalize! In the land sector, there are almost no landlords." This began another round over "dogma" and applying Marxism-Leninism to the "concrete conditions" in each country. Though there was no attempt to push FRETILIN towards a Marxist-Leninist line, the theoretical discussions went on among the "leftist intellectuals." There were about a half dozen who argued among themselves because nobody else

---

*Social democracy was then and has been my conviction; I was inspired from the very beginning by the Swedish success story. However, I was also fully aware of the need to look into our own historical and cultural realities instead of just trying to emulate the Swedish model. I began therefore to concoct our own version of social democracy by coining the word *Mauberism*—from Maubere, a common name among the Mambai people that had become a derogatory expression meaning poor, ignorant. Though vaguely defined without any serious theoretical basis, *Maubere* and *Mauberism* proved to be the single most successful political symbol of our campaign. Within weeks, *Maubere* became the symbol of a cultural identity, of pride, of belonging.

understood their high-sounding phrases. Many of us simply dozed off. Once in a while, I would encourage Alarico Fernandes, a ferocious anti-communist, to raise a point that I didn't want to raise myself for fear of being ridiculed by the "communists," as we began to call them. Alarico was even less prepared than I, from a theoretical point of view, to argue with the left, but he had more guts. Every time he raised a point, he was devastated with a barrage of words. After such a meeting, Alarico finally said to me: "You son of a bitch, you always push me to challenge the communists and then leave me to their mercy! Next time, do it yourself. I am not going to be a fool again." We all cracked up laughing.

It has been claimed that it was the Timorese students from Lisbon that inspired the change from ASDT to FRETILIN. That is not true. We resented this claim because it seemed to attribute to the Lisbon students all the innovation and dynamism in FRETILIN's strategy in 1974-75. The need for a change in name and tactics was seen and discussed by the ASDT founders without any connection with the Lisbon group. When we drafted the manifesto, none of the group was present. By coincidence, FRETILIN was announced the evening of the arrival of the students. As it turned out, they had their own plans to create a broad front; however, when they learned of our decision that afternoon, just hours before we were going public, they endorsed it without question.

They began to influence the movement toward a more radical outlook. This was to the good. They were instrumental in our campaign for mass support. It was largely as a result of their *trabalho de base* (grassroots work) that FRETILIN gained influence and popularity by mid-1975. Without them, FRETILIN wouldn't have exploded into such a mass movement within such a short period of time.

The group was made up of Abilio Araujo, an economist and a gifted musician; his wife, Guilhermina, also an economist; Antonio Duarte Carvarino (commonly known by his *nom de guerre*, Mau Lear, after a famous robber, a sort of Timorese Al Capone); Vicente Sah'e; and Joao Soares, an agriculturalist. A few others arrived later, among them, Helio Pina, also an agriculturalist.

FRETILIN leaders and cadres crisscrossed the country in an energetic campaign to rally the people behind the cause of independence. Our theme was simple. We spoke the language of the people: "Are we human beings or a sack of potatoes to be sold away to another country? Should we crawl after the *malae* (foreigner)? Aren't we men enough to govern ourselves? Why should we remain as horses, first of the Portuguese and tomorrow of the Indonesians?" The Timorese, fiercely independent and proud, responded enthusiastically to the cry for independence. The people didn't need fancy explanations about the right of self-determination and the UN Charter.

FRETILIN mobilized students to take part in the grassroots work, the campaign for *consciencializacao politica* (political conscientization). A literacy campaign based on Paulo Freire's method was launched; student brigades taught children and adults to read and write in their own languages for the first time ever. They helped the people build schools and health centers, where they were taught nutrition and hygiene; para-medics were mobilized for a vaccination campaign on behalf of FRETILIN. Nicolau Lobato inaugurated the cooperative schemes that became so popular. All this differentiated FRETILIN from UDT and established our popularity in the remote mountain interior.

5

My Meeting With Malik

While concentrating our energies on the grassroots work, preparing ourselves for the ballot box verdict, we did not lose sight of the world surrounding us.

Indonesia, our giant, aggressive and militaristic neighbor, was uppermost on our list of worries. In one respect, Osorio Soares was tragically right: no matter what the people of East Timor, and that included UDT and FRETILIN, might wish for their beloved country, in the end, it would be Jakarta that would make the choice. The sad reality was that the fate of the Timorese would be chartered and manipulated by outside powers. Local politics and all the energy that went into the campaign for popular support seemed futile and irrelevant in the face of the overwhelmingly unfavorable geopolitical factors surrounding us.

Yet, we hoped that with some effort, appeasement and a prudent foreign policy, we might win Indonesia's blessings. In June, 1974, paying my own way to Jakarta, ostensibly on a private visit, I ventured into the treacherous Indonesian political waters. In Kupang, West Timor, I met with Governor El Tari. I had known El Tari before and he received me cordially. It was rumored then that he dreamed of a united independent Timor. He was decidedly sympathetic to an independent East Timor, which he saw as a first step towards the realization of his dream. However, ASDT or FRETILIN *never* coveted privately or publicly the Indonesian section of the island. It was never discussed even lightly in our meetings. We were satisfied with the colonial boundaries and endorsed Indonesia's, as inherited from the so-called Dutch East Indies.

El Tari provided me with an aide—his nephew, Louis Taolin—to accompany me to Jakarta. As it turned out, Taolin was a BAKIN official whose job was to monitor all my movements. He even explained to me his mission: "The *gubernur* likes you a lot. He told me to escort you so that you do not get manipulated by the communists." If there were any communists left from the 1965-66 bloodbath, I doubted that they would see any point in trying to escort me in Jakarta, let alone manipulating me. Taolin escorted me throughout my two-week stay in Jakarta. *Tempo*, the Indonesian equivalent of *Time* magazine, and the daily *Sinar Harapan* both featured me on their front covers. This helped me gain an interview with Adam Malik, then the Indonesian Minister for Foreign Affairs, a survivor of the Indonesian's bloody political wars.

Malik had served with Sukarno in various senior positions, including Ambassador to Moscow; yet, when Suharto took over, he switched easily to the winning side. Under Suharto, Malik climbed even further, becoming Minister for Foreign Affairs and Vice President of the Republic. In 19 /3, Malik was elected President of the United Nations General Assembly. I met Malik in his private residence, and his wife joined us. No one else attended the meeting, which lasted one hour.

I thanked Malik for the meeting and expressed the "respect and esteem of the Timorese people and of the ASDT leaders." After showering my host with adjectives, I proceded to explain current developments in East Timor and the various political options opened to us since the Portuguese coup. To my surprise, Malik responded that he had read the ASDT program and fully sympathized with our aims.

I assured Malik that an independent East Timor would seek a close relationship with Indonesia, and cooperation in all areas and at all levels, including foreign affairs and security. "We will always bear in mind Indonesia's interests," I said. Malik raised the issue of East Timor joining ASEAN (The Association of Southeast Asian Nations). I responded positively without hesitation. This would become a point of controversy within ASDT/FRETILIN, where certain radicals regarded ASEAN as an "imperialist bastion."

Malik invited me for another meeting the next day. I arrived promptly at the hour he suggested. We sat down, and I offered him a silver-plated sword with bull horn carvings on behalf of the ASDT president as "a symbol of our respect and trust." (In fact, it was my personal souvenir which I treasured a great deal!) To my surprise, Malik handed me a bundle of money saying it was a donation for our activities. Later, I counted 50,000 rupiahs. That was not much then (about $300) and I later turned it over to the ASDT treasurer. As we were closing this second meeting, I raised with Malik the possibility of some of our cadres being sent to his ministry for diplomatic training. He agreed. I then touched on the most important part of my trip: a written assurance from Malik that the Republic of Indonesia would support our right of self-determination and independence.

"Mr. Minister," I said, "the people in East Timor have great esteem for you. Your name is widely known and loved there." (I was lying, of course.) "Our people and leaders will be very happy and honored to receive a message from you." I did not dare suggest the content of the message and just hoped that Malik understood what I meant to ask him. Malik promptly agreed to draft a message and invited me to return the next day for a final brief meeting and to take the letter.

The next day, I went to his home for the third time. His private secretary was finishing typing the letter while we chatted. Shortly after, he signed it in front of me, and handed it over with a handshake. The letter was far better than I expected. It contained all the assurances I had hoped for.

Malik's letter, addressed to me, read in part:

> The Government of Indonesia until now still adheres to the following principles:
>
> I.   The independence of every country is the right of every nation, with no exception for the people of Timor.
>
> II. The Goverment as well as the people of Indonesia have no intention to increase or to expand their territory, or to occupy other territories other than what is stipulated in their Constitution.
>
> III. (. . .) whoever will govern in Timor in the future after independence, can be assured that the Government of Indonesia will always strive to maintain good relations, friendship, and cooperation for the benefit of both countries.

Malik's statement was widely circulated and read over the radio in East Timor, translated into Portuguese and Tétun. It calmed the fears of the Timorese community, for it was a clear affirmation of his Government's position on the question of East Timor. It went even further than I expected inasmuch as it seemed to favor independence over any other alternative. " . . . whoever will govern in Timor *after* independence . . . " seemed to preclude the two other options.

It wouldn't be long before I learned two things about Indonesia: 1) Malik was little more than a figurehead and what he said did not necessarily reflect the position of the military; and 2) the word of an Indonesian official, civilian or military, is meaningless. Promises can be broken as easily as they are made.

Next to Indonesia, Australia loomed largest in our diplomatic considerations. The major industrial democracy in our vicinity and a medium-sized power in world affairs, Australia was a magnetic word for the Timorese. We always thought that somehow Australia would support our independence, and that after independence we could count on millions of dollars in Australian aid. We also believed that an independent East Timor was in Australia's best interests. Since our country had been, in the 1940s, a "buffer zone" against the Japanese from the North, surely Australia would see the advantages of East Timor becoming a friendly independent neighbor.

In a later chapter, I will deal fully with Australia's role in the East Timor question.

6

Portuguese "Fado" —Our Tragedy

Without glorifying Portugal's colonial adventures, one cannot but be impressed by the enterprising spirit of the Portuguese missionaries and navigators of the 16th century. They braved unknown seas in fragile *caravelas* and reached the shores of Brazil, Benin, Congo, Angola, Mozambique, Mombaza, Aden, India, China and Japan. For a country of roughly one million, that was no small feat. Think of what Portugal was then—and what it had become by 1974. From an empire where the sun never set, it was reduced to an insignificant rectangle in southern Europe— the "South of the North" in the words of Prime Minister Pinto Balsemão, in a speech to the United Nations' General Assembly in the Fall of 1982.

"Portugal, Africa's only colony in Europe . . . By the early 1970s, it had become obvious that Portugal, at the head of Europe's last great overseas empire, had not so much succeeded in leaving its mark on Africa as Africa succeeded in leaving its mark on Portugal," wrote Robert Harvey of *The Economist*.[1] Unlike France and Great Britain, which remained major powers without their overseas empires, Portugal was reduced to the pitiful status of Europe's lone developing country by 1975.

Fado, which means "fate," is a sort of national anthem that best expresses the Portuguese soul. One can hear *fado* anywhere in Lisbon, in the centuries-old Alfama, Madregoa and Bairro Alto, or even in the large Portuguese communities of Paris and Newark. Men and women, dressed in dark clothing, sing to the sad notes of guitars the sagas of Portuguese sailors lost to the seas. Unlike their Brazilian brothers or their Spanish cousins, the Portuguese are neither expansive nor vibrant. They are as formal as the British. They may shout threats and insults as profusely as the Brazilians or Italians, but they are remarkably less violent.

The April 25th coup was bloodless, and it was appropriately called the *"Revolucao dos Cravos"* ("Carnation Revolution"). Fascist officials and

45

elements of the dreaded PIDE were spared. Many returned, after brief exile in Brazil, to resume normal life in Portugal. This remarkable Portuguese trait explains how the bitter wars in Angola, Guinea-Bissau, and Mozambique did not leave long-lasting scars. Unlike the French, traumatized by the Algerian war of the 1950s, the Portuguese were quickly reconciled with the new states. The vast majority of the Portuguese people, who did not gain or lose in the colonies, warmly welcome visiting delegations of their former foes. Samora Machel, the Mozambiquan President, regarded as the fiercest foe of the Portuguese, was the target of countless pejorative jokes; however, when Machel visited Portugal in 1983, he conquered the hearts and minds of millions of Portuguese.

East Timor was always last in Portuguese priorities. This was also the case when the new regime took over in 1974. The new leaders had little thought for their Far Eastern colony. The African colonies, Angola and Mozambique particularly, were uppermost in their agenda. Arnao Metello, a senior Portuguese army officer, told me during an interview in his Lisbon residence: "At that critical time, we wanted to assure Angola's independence under MPLA. That was our big concern before we were toppled from office. So, I lost contact with the Timor process." Following the coup, Metello emerged as *de facto* strongman of East Timor. His senior in the army, Governor Alves Aldeia, was Commander-in-Chief in the colony, but Metello, part of the Armed Forces Movement (MFA), was the man who represented the new regime. Soon after, Metello was recalled to Lisbon to take up higher posts.

Alves Aldeia had committed a tragic mistake on the eve of the coup. Having learned of a previous abortive coup, he called the coup plotters a bunch of "undisciplined" soldiers. He tried to suppress publication of that speech, but it was too late. He remained in office for only three months. In his place came Colonel Niveo Herdade, an arrogant officer who had served as an aide to Spinola in Guinea-Bissau. Herdade had arrived in Dili with a mandate to insure that East Timor would not follow the path of Angola and Mozambique. It was to remain with Portugal as an "Associated Territory" or a "Federal State." Spinola had the same objective for Sao Tome e Principe, off the coast of Gabon. Having lost Angola and Mozambique, Spinola was determined to keep East Timor and Sao Tome.

However, by September 1974, Spinola had been ousted. "If he had not been ousted, you would have been in trouble. Spinola had a real dislike of FRETILIN," I was later told by Major Jonatas, a leading MFA officer who was appointed in 1974 to help oversee the decolonization process of East Timor.

The first moves to decolonize East Timor actually began some six months after the coup. The appointment of a new governor to oversee the decolonization process ran into some embarrassing obstacles. The first Army officer nominated for the job was Colonel Garcia Leandro, who had served in East Timor in the early 1970s as the colonial governor's *chef de cabinet*. Unfortunately, Leandro had left behind in 1972 some questionable dealing which tarnished his image, and his name was soon withdrawn.

Nivio Herdade aspired to the job as well as to the command of the local Portuguese garrison. He didn't last long. In the few months of his stay in East Timor, he managed to antagonize everybody with his dictatorial manner and ultra-conservative views. He orchestrated a "spontaneous demonstration" in Dili in support of his appointment as Governor. Only about 200 civil servants showed up. Shortly after, he left.

Lisbon finally picked Colonel Lemos Pires, a liberal, decent and bright officer who had served in Guinea-Bissau. Pires arrived in Dili in November 1974, with a group of army officers. The two most salient elements of his team were Majors Jonatas and Mota, both of whom had served tours of duties in East Timor in the 1960s and had knowledge of and attachment to the country and the people.

The decolonization of the remote Portuguese colony began.

Lemos Pires had hoped to recruit as one of his senior aides, none other than a young Lieutenant-Colonel Eanes, who had been his subordinate in Guinea-Bissau. Eanes was then the MFA delegate in charge of *Mass Media* and could not take the offer. Had Eanes gone to East Timor with Lemos Pires, history would have been different in 1975, for it was Eanes who masterminded the successful November 1975 coup which prevented a complete take-over of Portugal by the radical left. Eanes served two five-year terms as President and became Portugal's most popular leader.

The prevailing sentiment in Portugal in late 1974 was that East Timor would never achieve independence. There were two schools of thought. One, a conservative group of senior civil servants who had spent time in East Timor, favored continuing Portuguese presence. The other school, socialists and communists, believed that East Timor would inevitably be absorbed by Indonesia. For this group, the only question was how this would come about. In their view, Indonesia should be allowed to take over East Timor without loss of face for Portugal; an appearance of legality and legitimacy was all that mattered.

The independence option was dismissed in Lisbon as "atrociously unrealistic" by one leading member of the Socialist Party. Another senior member of the MFA told a group of Portuguese journalists: "Timor doesn't justify more than a few lines." Pro-Moscow elements in the government, Generals Costa Gomes and Vasco Goncalves, also dismissed the independence option. The Soviet Union had excellent relations with Suharto's Indonesia, and East Timor was subordinate to its regional strategic interests.

Lemos Pires and his aides arrived in East Timor with all these considerations in mind. They were certainly skeptical about the ability of the Timorese political leaders to assert themselves as true representatives of their people. I cannot criticize them for this skepticism, since there had been no visible and credible independence movement on the island. However, after traveling extensively in the country, they reached the conclusion, beyond any shadow of doubt, that the overwhelming majority of the educated, as well as the common people in the mountain interior, were strongly opposed to integration with the Republic of Indonesia.

With little backing from Lisbon, Pires and his two aides, Jonatas and Mota, tried as best as they could to implement the MFA decolonization program in East Timor. Reforms were introduced in the civil services, education, and army. Timorese with years of experience in the bureaucracy, but until then restricted to minor responsibilities, were justly promoted to senior posts. Directorship posts, until then an exclusive domain of Europeans, began to be occupied by Timorese. The Portuguese-oriented educational system also was the target of profound reforms. I could not but be impressed with the dynamism and dedication of the Portuguese army officers and other experts who were part of the monumental task of preparing East Timor for the future. In a year, much was accomplished in spite of the enormous difficulties. This impressive improvement only highlighted the neglect and shortcomings of the fascist regime.

The local army experienced dramatic shake-ups that were to prove disastrous. From a high of almost 3,000 troops in 1974, European army personnel was reduced to about 200 by the summer of 1975. This troop reduction took place at a time when the country was undergoing a delicate and unpredictable phase of the decolonization process. Next door, Indonesia saw with relief the diminishing Portuguese military presence in East Timor.

During one of my trips to Australia, I tried to convey a different picture of East Timor's defense posture. In a conversation with a *Canberra Times* military analyst, I played up the fact that the Portuguese were re-equipping and retraining the local army and that combat helicopters were being unloaded in Dili. However, this was said in an effort to discourage the Indonesian generals. Meanwhile, a Portuguese army officer, Captain Ramos, asked by an Australian journalist if the Portuguese army in East Timor would resist an Indonesian invasion, responded: "We would tell them . . . come in!" When I confronted him with this, he confirmed the statement.

In my view, the troop reduction was the single most damaging error committed by the Portuguese in 1974. It was argued that the leaders in Lisbon did not have much choice. In the aftermath of the "Revolucao dos Cravos," the army's discipline and cohesion began to crumble. The soldiers, tired of the wars in Africa, demanded their repatriation. Those stationed in East Timor were no less anxious to pack and leave.

There was no real effort to prepare to defend East Timor against what was then already clearly an impending Indonesian invasion. It couldn't be otherwise when the policy-makers in Lisbon had their own misgivings about a continuing Portuguese presence in East Timor or independence for the half island. The troop reduction was simply part of the policy to facilitate an Indonesian take-over.

Had the central government in Lisbon taken a strong position in favor of an independent East Timor, it could have rallied several thousand volunteers. Four battalions of commandos and paratroopers, backed by the thousands of Timorese who were anxious to serve in the army, could have maintained internal stability during the volatile period of 1975, and equally important, discouraged any Indonesian attempt to intervene. The Indonesian army, as the war with FRETILIN was to prove, would be no match for the battle-tested Portuguese and Timorese troops.

A campaign of *"consciencializacao politica"* was undertaken by the Portuguese in order to educate the people about the MFA program and the choices they would have to make. *"Grupos dinamizadores"* of the army crisscrossed the country to prepare the people for local elections in a first step towards elections for a Constituent Assembly that would determine the future status of the territory.

The MFA was invariably accused by UDT, FRETILIN and APODETI of favoring one side or the other. There were individual army elements in the lower ranks who favored FRETILIN, as there were others whose sympathies were with UDT. APODETI was simply absent in the countryside. There were very strong sentiments against APODETI. Its leaders didn't bother travelling into the interior to run the risk of being beaten up by local villagers. However, between 1974 and mid-1975, there was very little violence. Whatever disturbances occurred in that period were nothing compared with the violence in New Caledonia in 1984-1985, or in other colonial situations in the 1960s. The "instability" in East Timor was an exaggeration, and in many instances, an outright fabrication of Indonesia's propaganda machine.

Governor Pires and his aides Jonatas and Mota, tried to maintain impartiality in the decolonization process. Jakarta's accusations that they favored FRETILIN were false, and we better than anyone else knew it. UDT also accused the three of supporting FRETILIN. UDT's unhappiness with the MFA was inevitable. Having relied on the colonial machine and the traditional chiefs, UDT saw this base being undermined as the process of decolonization was implemented. The colonial officials (*chefes de posto* and *administradores de concelho*) who along with the "traditional chiefs" were the base of UDT's support were either removed or voted out of office.

During the first half of 1975, the Portuguese organized elections throughout the territory at the village level. This was the first democratic exercise ever in East Timor's history. The villagers were invited to elect their chiefs. Though these elections were not conducted on a party basis, each of the three political groups tried to have its supporters elected, since this would greatly influence the elections for a Constituent Assembly. The results were heavily in favor of FRETILIN and UDT. APODETI won only one delegate out of several hundred.

The election results, more than anything else, alarmed the Indonesian military rulers who realized that APODETI would have no chance at all in a free, open contest for the future of East Timor. This was also the feeling of the Portuguese, as Jonatas told me later in an interview in Lisbon.

NOTE

1. Harvey, Robert. "Almost There, Portugal: A Survey," *The Economist*, June 14, 1980.

7

Coalition and Civil War

In January 1975, after weeks of negotiations, FRETILIN and UDT reached an historic agreement and formed a coalition for national independence. More than anyone else within FRETILIN, I had labored for this coalition. Unity of all nationalist forces was vital for our success. Though Xavier and Nicolau took part in most of the discussions with the UDT leaders, the painstaking work of softening up individual FRETILIN leaders who were suspicious of any alliance with UDT fell on me. I also had to persuade individual UDT leaders of the necessity of such a coalition.

At one point, the negotiations were bogged down and threatened to kill the whole project. The deadlock was caused by FRETILIN's insistence that two-thirds of any interim government to be formed would be filled by FRETILIN. We aimed for key positions such as economy, treasury, foreign relations, security, and defense. UDT, which would be left with only minor portfolios, was not to be outmaneuvered so easily, and the negotiations bogged down. I visited Governor Lemos Pires in his office one afternoon, and it was his intervention that saved the coalition. Pires drew my attention to the fact that we were dealing with issues that should be left until a later stage. What we should do now, he advised me, was concentrate on basic principles and objectives. I drafted a new text, submitted it to both FRETILIN and UDT leaders, and it was adopted without major changes. However, the text was a significant victory for FRETILIN, since the language was in a FRETILIN style rather than UDT's. This was a subtle way to convey to the public FRETILIN's political influence in the coalition.

The unity effort succeeded, at least for the time being. The coalition was praised by the Portuguese authorities and the general public as a demonstration of maturity on the part of the two organizations. Always with an eye on

51

Canberra, I hoped that the coalition would strengthen the position of our Australian friends who favored an independent East Timor.

The coalition represented almost the entire educated sector and the vast majority of the population. It was a serious blow to the Indonesians who were counting on divisions among the pro-independence factions and hoping APODETI might win by default. But, Indonesia did not give up. Bent on sabotaging the process of decolonization then in full swing, it stepped up its campaign. UDT leaders like Lopes da Cruz and Mouzinho were the targets of outright bribes.

The coalition brought more benefits to FRETILIN than to UDT. It opened the terrain for FRETILIN activists to carry our grassroots campaign into UDT strongholds that were blocked previously. UDT supporters were always less solid, more easily swayed than FRETILIN supporters, who were more politically conscious.

By April 1975 an internal split began to shake the UDT leadership, with Lopes da Cruz leading one faction that wanted a rupture with FRETILIN, and Mario and João Carrascalao leading a more liberal faction opposing a rupture. The split within UDT was not caused simply by FRETILIN's "radicalism." Lopes da Cruz was by then already leaning toward the Indonesians.

At the end of May 1975, following a trip to Jakarta by Lopes da Cruz and Mouzinho, the UDT leadership met one evening at Lopes' residence. The discussion centered on FRETILIN's violations of the coalition provisions barring political ideological and physical attacks. This, however, was simply the excuse Lopes da Cruz needed, since the coalition had created a number of joint commissions whose task was precisely to resolve such problems.

Lopes da Cruz managed to rally enough support to vote for the termination of the coalition. Just as its formation in January had been a political setback for Jakarta, UDT's unilateral decision to terminate the coalition could not but benefit the Indonesians. Some in FRETILIN were delighted with this tragic event; for them it was a vindication of their suspicions of UDT. I remember seeing Vicente Sah'e jumping with joy when he learned the news.

I was worried. I could see unfolding before me a chain of tragic events: increasing tension with verbal and physical assaults between the two independence groups; APODETI enjoying the spectacle of its rivals fighting each other; more intereference by Indonesia to exploit and exacerbate the political rivalry in East Timor. I feared the break would hurt my efforts to win Australia's support.*

Dispatched to Australia, I met with Andrew Peacock, who told me that he, like everybody else, thought the end of the coalition was due to the radicalization of FRETILIN. This was not entirely false. The radical wing of FRETILIN had gained some influence and my own position was becoming more and more difficult. However, there was not a remote possibility that FRETILIN could turn into what the Indonesians were claiming—a "communist front." Xavier and particularly Nicolau remained strong and were backed by the vast majority of FRETILIN's supporters. The radical group had no power base.

The Macao talks took place while I was in Canberra. Over the phone and by letter, I kept in touch with events in East Timor through Alarico Fernandes, FRETILIN's most conservative leader. The Macao talks had been arranged by the Portuguese in an effort to bring all three parties together to agree on a timetable for elections to decide the future status of East Timor. These talks, held in Macao during the last week of June 1975, were boycotted by FRETILIN over my vehement protests. My comrades' argument was that APODETI's presence rendered any discussion of decolonization meaningless, because APODETI represented nothing but Indonesia's interests. This was true, but Indonesia was watching menacingly every move we made and any false move was a gain for them. Our failure to attend the Macao talks was politically costly, fueling our enemies' propaganda machine, which portrayed FRETILIN as a group of communist radicals. Having urged FRETILIN's participation, it was left to me to explain to the press in Canberra our absence from Macao. This was one of

*The afternoon after we received UDT's letter informing us of its decision to terminate the coalition, I went to see Governor Lemos Pires in his office. I expressed my deep concern about the sudden development and asked his help. My idea was that with his intervention, both FRETILIN and UDT could remove our respective "radical elements" and restore the coalition. Lemos Pires, always astute and prudent, but sympathetic to an independent East Timor, answered: "I'll put them in the plane and send them to Portugal"—but only after we took the necessary action; he would not intervene unilaterally. I then approached my "moderate" allies within FRETILIN who supported the idea. However, we would not move if the UDT moderates would not move against their own extremists of the right. I approached João Carrascalão on this subject and his hesitation was most disappointing. While considering this "internal coup," I also realized then that the so-called "radicals" were our best cadres; much was owed to their enthusiasm and ideas. However, I was prepared to move against them for the sake of tranquility in East Timor during that crucial period. Relations between myself and the "radicals" were deteriorating rapidly and the idea of cleaning up the mess was therefore even more urgent. But things did not turn out as I had hoped. Following a Central Committee meeting, I was assigned to go to Australia. I advised Alarico Fernandes, the leading conservative element in FRETILIN, to handle the situation and pursue the idea with João Carrascalão. On our part, I knew we could have neutralized the radical left without any difficulty and, more important, without violence. We could have achieved it in a Central Committee meeting since I had secured the support of Xavier do Amaral and Nicolau Lobato. However, this "palace coup" never took place simply because the UDT wasn't prepared to do likewise with their own "radicals" of the right.

our tactical political errors for which I could never find an intelligent explanation.

A Voz de Timor, usually with a pro-FRETILIN bias, hailed the Macao talks as a victory for UDT and criticized FRETILIN's absence. However, the Portuguese negotiators were well aware of FRETILIN's importance in any formula and timetable for East Timor's future. Though FRETILIN boycotted the talks, in the end there was a consensus within our leadership in support of the basic agreement contemplating the appointment of a Portuguese High Commissioner and five assistants, of whom three were to be from East Timor; and the election of an Advisory Council representing the people. General elections were to be held in 1976 for a Constituent Assembly that would draft a Constitution and decide the future status of the territory. We were confident that the outcome of any free election would be heavily in our favor. For this reason, we agreed immediately with the basic provisions of the Macao agreement and set out to intensify our grassroots work in the countryside.[1]

But the UDT was already preparing to cut us off at the pass.

On August 11, 1975, as I was preparing to drive to the Darwin airport for the one-hour flight to Baukau, the news of a coup was broadcast over the radio. I immediately suspected that FRETILIN had staged it. However, within a few hours, it was clear that the coup was the work of UDT and the leader was João Carrascalao. All flights were cancelled, and I was stranded in Darwin.

In the next few days, reports began to circulate about an orgy of killings, massacres, bashing of babies and women. Refugees, mainly UDT supporters and families, began arriving in Darwin by boat. I had to endure the horror stories that were front page news every day. Each refugee had a story of FRETILIN "atrocities."

The UDT coup had proceeded in classic fashion: a street "show of force," take-over of the radio station and the international communications system, airport, police, etc. It was a neat operation. However, UDT fatally underestimated FRETILIN's capacity to react. Carrascalao and his colleagues were counting on a general uprising against FRETILIN and its break-up into factions—some supporting the coup, others opposing it. But FRETILIN leaders, having learned of the UDT plans well in advance, quietly retreated into the rugged mountain interior. From there, they began to plan a counterattack while calling for peace talks. FRETILIN leaders imposed a number of conditions for talks, among them that all UDT forces be disarmed. João Carrascalao refused to lay down his arms.

Since the departure of the European troops, the bulk of the Portuguese-controlled army was made up of Timorese conscripts who overwhelmingly sympathized with FRETILIN. Of the hundred or so sergeants, perhaps half were UDT sympathizers, but they could not rely on the rank-and-file soldiers who identified with FRETILIN. When efforts for negotiations failed, the FRETILIN leadership issued a call to all "patriots of the Army" to crush the "UDT reactionaries." The Timorese troops, who had until then been kept in their barracks by their European officers, broke out and placed themselves under FRETILIN command.

A bloody civil war broke out, with the leaders on each side losing control over the behavior of their supporters. By and large, the UDT leaders behaved with restraint and humanity during their control of the capital. The several hundred FRETILIN supporters under detention were properly treated. However, in the interior, a number of senior UDT cadres orchestrated the cold-blooded murder of eleven students, among them a brother of Nicolau Lobato. Numerous other acts of violence were reported; the largest part could be traced to personal vendettas among rival families and tribes, using the civil war to settle old accounts.

When FRETILIN gained the upper hand, hundreds of UDT leaders, cadres and supporters were made prisoners. It was time for revenge. The UDT leaders, largely innocent, were blamed for the killings in the countryside, and those who were unfortunate enough to have been captured by FRETILIN forces took severe beatings. I visited FRETILIN prisons in Dili and Aileu, and for the first time I was confronted with the ugliness of the war. I was dismayed at how we had turned against each other overnight, we who had been friends, neighbors and relatives, just yesterday.

The civil war did not last more than three weeks. The total casualty figure was between two and three thousand, according to a survey carried out by the International Committee of the Red Cross (ICRC). In contrast with the Indonesians after 1975, the FRETILIN leadership complied in full with the Geneva Conventions. The ICRC team was allowed free access to all prisons and to any part of the territory. I was the FRETILIN leader who dealt with all NGOs and the ICRC as well as the foreign press and governments. We did not restrict foreigners in East Timor. Their biggest problem was getting an Australian permit and a Portuguese visa to depart Australia for East Timor. There wasn't a single case of FRETILIN refusing entry into East Timor. We wanted as many journalists and NGOs in the territory as possible. We have nothing to lose and much to gain from their presence.

FRETILIN gained complete control of the territory by mid-September 1975. Quickly we set out to form a provisional administration, which in spite of our shortcomings was functioning reasonably well. What motivated people to work hard, to volunteer their labor, was the euphoria of the victory and the prospect of a free and independent East Timor within a short period of time.

I returned to Dili in the second week of September. The capital had been secured by FRETILIN forces. An aircraft was chartered by the Portuguese chief negotiator, Almeida Santos, who had asked me to sound out my comrades' position on peace negotiations with UDT. I landed in Dili and was met there by a number of FRETILIN leaders. One brother, Nuno, was there, too. He had been a prisoner of UDT. His head had been shaved and showed fresh scars. His back showed signs of even more severe beating. He was very bitter and anxious for revenge.

A few days later, I was witness to another heartbreaking scene. A truck drove past the FRETILIN military barracks, and I spotted my brother Arsenio among some thirty UDT prisoners. Arsenio was an innocent bystander. A resident of Australia, he had come to East Timor for a vacation against my advice. On August 11, he was stranded in Dili when all the flights in and out of the country were canceled. He decided then to go to the nearest camp . . . which was the UDT's. Thus began his ordeal. In prison, along with the UDT leaders, he was beaten by a drunken FRETILIN military commander.

The beatings stopped only when Nicolau Lobato personally intervened at my urging. I was shocked when I visited a prison and saw the frightened expressions of the prisoners, most of whom I knew by name. "Nicolau, this has to stop, or I'm calling the foreign journalists and the ICRC to denounce this situation," I told Nicolau in his home when he invited me over for lunch.

Nicolau was a most humane person. His own brother had been brutally murdered by a UDT leader. Nicolau visited his brother's killer in the hospital after he was captured. Chico Oliveira had been a fellow worker of Nicolau, and when they faced each other in the hospital, Nicolau asked in a low voice: "Why did you kill him? You knew he was my brother." Oliveira did not respond. He knew he was now at the mercy of Nicolau. Nicolau then asked how he was feeling and touched his hands. Oliveira was almost blind from beatings he had suffered in the head and face. It was a very moving scene. It revealed the ugliness of the war, of any war, and the greatness of Nicolau Lobato.

Carrascalao and other UDT leaders took a simplistic line that Indonesia would not invade East Timor if the threat of "communist" influence on the island were eliminated. They failed to understand that the Indonesian military were determined to incorporate the territory *regardless*.

NOTE

1.   For a detailed analysis of the Macao talks, see *A Voz de Timor*, No. 787, July 14, 1975 and No. 786, June 30, 1975, on file with the author.

8

Portuguese Inaction

Portuguese attitudes toward East Timor ranged from condescending paternalism to outright disrespect for the rights of the people of East Timor to self-determination. From early 1974, the preference in Lisbon was for handing over the country and its people to Indonesia, bearing in mind only the Portuguese image.

Though Lisbon was fully aware of Indonesia's campaign to destablize the country—and there was abundant evidence of this—Portuguese diplomacy failed to draw the United Nations into the affair. For example, the Special Committee on Decolonization (Committee of 24) which usually undertakes fact-finding missions to "Non-Self-Governing Territories" was not asked to visit East Timor. The then Chairman of the Committee of 24 was the Tanzanian Ambassador, Salim A. Salim, a forceful diplomat who would have supported a Portuguese request for a fact-finding mission to visit East Timor. Instead, the Committee met once in Lisbon in June 1974, and the Portuguese authorities did not invite or encourage the Timorese parties to travel to Lisbon to attend the meeting.

Nor was there any effort on the part of the Portuguese embassies to brief their host governments about the situation in East Timor. The Portuguese Ambassador in Canberra visited the country only once and was notoriously detached from the Timor conflict even when it reached tragic dimensions in the summer of 1975. The *chargé d'affaires* in Jakarta, a Doctor Girão, was inactive. I surveyed the United Nations archives and could not find a single Portuguese official report about the situation in the territory in 1974. At a time when East Timor was undergoing an energetic decolonization process, there was no report about the local elections or the administrative and educational reforms, let alone a "*note verbale*"* about Indonesian acts of interference.

During a period of about two months in 1975, I fired off more than 400 telegrams to the Portuguese and to some 20 other governments, including Australia and the ASEAN countries, as well as to the United Nations Security Council and a long list of newspapers around the world. The Portuguese government, in possession of the reports I sent (and of other, "more reliable" ones) nevertheless refused to act. Governor Lemos Pires had moved his seat of government to the offshore island of Atauro; from there, he sent repeated messages to Lisbon asking for instructions and help. There was no response. Finally, exasperated, he sent the 18th telegram, pleading with Lisbon to answer "the 17 telegrams I sent earlier."

I was in constant touch with the Portuguese authorities on Atauro Island and with a team of negotiators that had set up office in a Darwin hotel, led by Almeida Santos, a senior cabinet minister. During my meetings with the Portuguese, including the notoriously aloof Ambassador in Canberra, I always stressed FRETILIN's willingness to resolve the conflict through negotiations. From the moment I arrived in Dili during the second week of September, the FRETILIN Central Committee issued a number of communiques consistently supporting *any* peace conference. On September 16 I drafted a communique which would serve as FRETILIN's basic position. My draft, unanimously endorsed by the Central Committee, made the following points:

1. The affairs of East Timor must be decided by the Timorese people within the national territory, without external pressures. FRETILIN recognizes Portugal's sovereignty over East Timor and seeks talks with the Portuguese government's representatives on September 30, 1975, in Baukau.

2. The Central Committee of FRETILIN would welcome a joint conference with representatives from Portugal, Australia and Indonesia, and the leaders of East Timor in order . . . to promote friendship and cooperation amongst the people of the region.

In a demonstration of FRETILIN's good will toward the Portuguese, its Central Committee, acting upon my recommendation, released without conditions several Portuguese officers and soldiers who had been detained

---

*The normal practice of UN member states is to send "*notes verbales*" to the General Assembly and/or the Security Council on issues that the governments deem necessary. These reports serve to build up dossiers that can be recalled later in support of a complaint. These documents draw the attention of the international community to an issue that requires attention.

when pro-FRETILIN troops rebelled. The prisoners were handed over to representatives of ICRC.

However, the negotiations never took place, with the Portuguese side always asking for postponements. The alleged stumbling block was UDT's refusal to come to the talks in Baukau or anywhere else but Bali, in Indonesia. Half of the UDT leadership had fled to Indonesia when their forces were routed by FRETILIN. There they were at the mercy of the Indonesian military, who dictated their every word and move. Not surprisingly, they were unable to return to Dili or to travel to Darwin, an alternate site I proposed for talks.

In Dili, I made contact with a number of UDT leaders who were FRETILIN prisoners, among them the Vice President of the party, Mouzinho. I explained to them the peace efforts underway and Indonesia's own efforts to sabotage the talks. I urged them to take a stand and disavow their comrades' position since they were acting under coercion. The UDT leaders agreed and issued a communique in which they claimed to represent the true ideals and platform of the party. FRETILIN assured them that they would be released once the details for the talks were finalized, and would be free to travel anywhere.

To the FRETILIN leadership's consternation and growing impatience, the Portuguese, playing into the Indonesian strategy, continued to stall the negotiations. Early in October, Lemos Pires himself sent a memorandum to his superiors in Lisbon, expressing his own uneasiness over the continuous postponement of the negotiations. Pires stressed:

> . . . the existence of a FRETILIN that proposes negotiations while we are running out of excuses. Though I agree that any solution in the region must pass through negotiations with Indonesia, it is a fact that FRETILIN declares to control most of the territory, and has been seeking negotiations for a while now, and these have been postponed because of the prevailing situation.

In the country, Portuguese symbols were being respected. The Portuguese flag continued to fly on top of the government's palace; the governor's official Mercedes was not used; the bank remained locked. There was strict respect for Portuguese official properties, and the same went for the Indonesian Consulate in Dili, not to mention the Taiwanese Consulate, in spite of the fact that FRETILIN was receiving verbal support from Beijing.

While the Portuguese authorities failed to respond to FRETILIN's repeated calls for talks, Melo Antunes, the Portuguese Foreign Minister, met in Rome with Indonesia's professional double-crosser, Adam Malik. The Indonesians did not want an East Timorese involvement in the Rome talks and the Portuguese did not insist on it. The Indonesians did not want any United Nations involvement, and the Portuguese went along with that, too. As it turned out, the Rome talks were a Portuguese recognition of Indonesia as a principal party to the Timor question—a *more* principal party than the East Timorese themselves! The two parties discussed the civil war that had ended two months before and urged talks between "Portugal and all political parties in Portuguese Timor . . . aimed at ending the armed strife and bringing about a peaceful and orderly process of decolonization in Portuguese Timor." At the time of the Rome meeting the "armed strife" between UDT and FRETILIN had long since ended; the "armed strife" referred to in the Portuguese-Indonesian communique could only have been the border incursions by regular Indonesian army units started as early as mid-September! These border incursions escalated into larger assaults involving hundreds of marines, helicopters and tanks. Batugade fell to Indonesian troops on October 7 in a major assault involving 100 special troops supported by an amphibious task force; Balibo fell on October 16 to a force of 400 Indonesian commandos.Before they moved on to Balibo, 400 other Indonesian troops had taken Maliana. In the Balibo assault, two Australian, two British and one New Zealand newsmen were murdered by the invading troops. (In another chapter, I shall return to Indonesian operations against East Timor during this period.)

Meanwhile on the beaches of Atauro, Lemos Pires and his staff were lounging in the tropical sun. I would hesitate to say that Lemos Pires was oblivious to the fighting, since Pires was a man of moral and political integrity. But the sad irony was that two modern Portuguese frigates were anchored off Atauro. They never sailed to the coast as a reminder of Portuguese sovereignty and a warning to Indonesia. The ships' crews were also sunbathing on the Atauro beaches, while a few miles away aggression was being carried out against a small nation with which Portugal had maintained a relationship for almost half a millenium!

9

Indonesia's View of East Timor

Indonesian nationalism has long been a deep and powerful force, sufficient to sustain the country through over thirty years of political, and five years of armed struggle against Dutch colonialism. At no point in that long struggle for independence; nor under the liberal parliamentary regime of 1950-1959 when freedom of expression was virtually complete for all groups; nor under President Sukarno's Guided Democracy of 1959-1965, with its commitment to militant anti-colonialism; nor during the first decade of General Suharto's regime, did *any* significant group express the slightest interest in Portugal's remote Southeast Asian colony. Only when this 400 year old colony threatened to free itself from colonialism, thirty years after Indonesia's proclamation of its own independence, did a Jakarta government decide to intervene. This historical record shows that it is utterly false to claim that the "annexation" of East Timor is a response to deeply-felt, long-standing ties of national brotherhood. (And one might add that if Jakarta's "brotherhood" claims are to be accepted at face value, there are at least as good so-called ethnic grounds for annexing East and West Malaysia, some of the southern provinces of Thailand, Papua New Guinea, and most of the Philippines.)
    —Ben Anderson, Professor of Government and Politics at Cornell University, New York, speaking to the Fourth Committee of the United Nations General Assembly on October 29, 1980.

I tried to establish in an earlier chapter, "Colonial Beginnings," the unique historical identity of East Timor, and to demonstrate the absence of any valid Indonesian claims to that island, even in the period prior to the arrival of the Europeans. It is now necessary to review briefly Indonesia's own emergence as a modern republic, and the views and motivations of the decision-makers in Jakarta concerning the Portuguese half of the Timor Island.

What is today known as the "Unitary Republic of Indonesia" is only some 40 years old. It is a mosaic of ethnic groups and languages. "Bahasa Indonesia," the official national language, is a convenient adaptation of Malay, introduced by Sukarno as a unifying vehicle for the more than 250 ethnic groups that form the Republic. Some 300 languages are spoken throughout the vast archipelago of 13,000 islands, of which 3,000 are inhabited. In Java itself, the most populated island, containing half of the total population of more than 160 million, "Bahasa Indonesia" is secondary to the many Javanese languages.

The Indonesian Republic is the result of Dutch administrative efforts to lump together the disparate ethnic groups of the so-called "Dutch East Indies" into a single unit for the purpose of facilitating their administration. If the British or the French had had the same bureaucratic inspiration, all of Southern Africa would be today a single political unity, and the same would have happened to the French-speaking countries of the Sahel region. It would have made life easier for Henry Kissinger, who complained when he became Secretry of State in 1974: "How can an African policy be formulated for some 50 different countries?"

Conversely, it can be argued that if the Dutch had respected the ethnic, linguistic and cultural identity of the various people of their East Indies, the Republic of Indonesia would not exist today, with the numerous secessionist movements that threaten its artificial "unity in diversity." Instead, at least a half dozen nation states would have emerged in a more cohesive and stable form.

Kissinger wrote about Indonesia in his 1959 bestseller *Nuclear Weapons and Foreign Policy*:

> Indonesia, for example, was nothing but a geographic expression until the Dutch found it more efficient to unite the islands of the Indies under a single administration.

> The collection of islands called Indonesia is meaningful only in terms of the history of the Dutch role; its frontiers follow the frontiers of the empire, and so does its national consciousness. Because West New Guinea was part of the Dutch East Indies, Indonesia has laid claim to it, although it is inhabited by people as different from the Polynesian stock of Indonesia as the Dutch themselves.[1]

West New Guinea was the first flagrant act of land-grabbing carried out by the Indonesian generals. Then as today, Indonesia, because of its vast natural resources and strategic location, encompassing such vital sea routes as the Malacca Straits and the Ombai-Wetter deep-water straits, managed to win the acquiescence of major powers to its empire-building. The United

States under Kennedy supported Indonesia's 1963 take-over of West New Guinea partly because of Kennedy's laudable anti-colonial sentiments, and partly to placate the mercurial Sukarno lest he jeopardize the overall geopolitical equilibrium in the region. The Soviet Union and its allies saw in Sukarno's adventures a legitimate anti-colonial and anti-imperialist crusade worthy of their support.

West New Guinea should have become an independent country or should have joined with the other half of the world's largest island, then under Australian administration, which became independent as Papua New Guinea (PNG). However, because both East and West decided for their own ideological and strategic reasons to placate Sukarno, the helpless people of West New Guinea saw their fate decided by forces alien to their race, culture, and aspirations! The United Nations played then a most shameful role in according legitimacy to Indonesia's take-over of West New Guinea.[2]

The West Papua affair is a sad reminder of the opportunism of the left. Because Sukarno was then regarded as a progressive Third World leader, his claims over that former Dutch colony were enthusiastically endorsed by the left in Australia and Europe, who thought little of the indigenous inhabitants of the island. Today the Left is in the embarrassing position of having to take up the West Papua case, symbolized by the *Organizasi Papua Merdeka* (OPM), as yet another demonstration of Indonesian expansionism and brutalities. The Right was ironically on the right side: not of course out of love for the indigenous peoples of West Papua, but out of desire for an independent state with a pro-Western government.

West Timor became part of the Indonesian Republic because it, too, was a part of the Dutch East Indies. The Dutch and the Portuguese agreed on the boundary separating East (Portuguese) Timor and West Timor in the 1880s, and it was formally ratified at the 1913 Hague Round Table Conference.

Portuguese Timor was initially spared the Indonesian empire-building process because it was not part of the Dutch East Indies. There were passing thoughts about adding East Timor to the rest of the empire, but there was no real debate on the subject. The Indonesians were certainly aware that any claim to Portuguese Timor would hurt whatever valid argument they had for claiming West New Guinea and the other Dutch territories.

As the Indonesians were pushing their case for the annexation of West New Guinea at the United Nations, the Indonesian Foreign Affairs Minister stated before the General Assembly's Fifteenth Session in 1960:

> (We) are declaring the right of the Indonesian people to be sovereign and independent within all the territory formerly covered by the Netherlands East Indies. We do not make any claim at all to territory

such as that in Borneo or Timor which lies within the Indonesian archipelago, but was not part of the Netherlands East Indies.[3]

Three years earlier, during the Twelfth Session, the Indonesian Representative had made a similar statement: "Indonesia has no claims on any territories which had not been part of the Netherlands East Indies. No one should suggest otherwise or advance dangerous theories in that respect."[4]

To emphasize his respect for Portuguese colonial sovereignty over Timor, Sukarno even visited Lisbon, a visit which caused bitter resentment among the African nationalists who were then fighting the Portuguese. Sukarno, the self-proclaimed anti-colonial and anti-imperialistic leader of the emerging Afro-Asia block, was lavishly entertained by the Portuguese ultra-colonialist dictator, Doctor Oliveira Salazar.

As I explained earlier, Indonesia was uppermost in the minds of FRETILIN leaders. It was with this awareness of Indonesia's importance in the Timor question that a few weeks after the formation of ASDT, I travelled to Jakarta to meet with Adam Malik, the Indonesian Minister for Foreign Affairs.

Not everything was as smooth in Jakarta as it appeared from my successful meeting with Malik. Shortly after the Lisbon coup, the deputy speaker of the Indonesian rubber-stamp "House of Representatives," John Naro, had called on the government to begin working towards the "return of East Timor to the fold of the Republic." During my visit to Jakarta in June 1974, I sought a meeting with Naro. We met over lunch in the company of six other Indonesian officials. Toward the end of our meeting, I raised the issue of self-determination for East Timor, and he agreed that the people should be able to choose their future "just like in Irian Java." He added that of course he was certain that the people of East Timor would choose to "rejoin their brothers in Indonesia."

Naro was a nonentity in the power elite of Jakarta, an opportunist who wanted to be the first on record to have fought for the incorporation of East Timor into the Republic. The problem was that he was certainly speaking the mind of others in the military. When I met with Malik, I mentioned Naro's statements, which were in contradiction to Indonesia's official policies. Malik responded that it was he who represented Indonesia's foreign policy, not Mr. Naro, and promised to talk to Naro about it.

My optimism about Malik's support for ASDT did not last long, for there were powerful forces in Jakarta who did not agree with Malik's views. In the mind of the generals around Suharto, the incorporation of the Portuguese colony into the Republic was simple common sense: the western half of Timor was already Indonesian, so why not Portuguese Timor? Its absorption would complete the archipelago and would preempt future problems. Why allow a small, independent country in the midst of the

Republic—a potential base for the remnants of the outlawed Indonesian Communist Party (PKI)—as an inspiration for the separatist sentiments in West Timor, the Moluccas, West New Guinea and Aceh Sumatra? Jakarta's top generals—Ali Moertopo (now deceased), regarded as Indonesia's master strategist; Benny Murdani, a hawkish rising star; and Pangabean, then Defense Minister—all lobbied with Suharto for their strategies. Moertopo favored a diplomatic and political approach. Murdani, a Catholic in a land of Moslems who had always to prove himself a loyal servant and executioner of the regime, favored a strike against Dili and outright annexation. Pangabean favored Murdani's position.

Suharto supported Moertopo's approach, which was peaceful absorption through a fifth column, APODETI. Unlimited funds were set aside for this operation. Money was given to APODETI leaders for their personal use and for bribing other Timorese. Portuguese and Timorese officials were invited to Jakarta and lavishly entertained. Propaganda about the wonders of Indonesia and its military might was broadcast over Radio Kupang. Colonel Sugyanto, Economic Advisor to Ali Moertopo, disbursed funds for air fares, hotel accomodations in Bali (usually at his own Peneda View hotel in Denpasar) and Jakarta, as well as cash for "personal expenses." A minor flaw in this campaign was that Sugyanto and his aides, particularly a BAKIN agent, Louis Taolin, pocketed millions of dollars intended for UDT and FRETILIN leaders, Timorese personalities such as the *liurais* and Portuguese officials.

General Marpaung, the current Indonesian Ambassador to Australia, told me in New York: "Many people got rich out of East Timor. One was Sugyanto!" Marpaung, then the Indonesian deputy Representative to the United Nations, is a charming, very able man and one of the few Indonesian officials one might classify as clean. He did his best to lure me into working with the Indonesians. The offers were generous, including the governorship of East Timor!

There were mounting signs of Indonesia's destabilization campaign. Radio Kupang was engaged in strident nightly propaganda in Portuguese, Tétun and other Timorese languages. The theme was no longer simply the wonders and advantages of Indonesia, but included threats of force against "communists" in East Timor, and expressed Indonesia's determination that the people of East Timor would be able to enjoy a new future within the Republic, etc.

The situation in East Timor was relatively quiet through 1974. However, in December of that year, 100 Indonesian commandos were sent to West Timor as part of the first phase of a campaign to destabilize East Timor. This information was confided to me by an Indonesian journalist when I visited Jakarta the second time, in April 1975. This visit on which I was accompanied by Alarico Fernandes, who by then had been elected

FRETILIN's Secretary-General, was perceived differently by us and by the Indonesians. We saw the visit as a chance to clear the air, they saw it as a chance to further divide us.

The FRETILIN-UDT coalition was still intact then, and it would have made sense for us to travel together, since UDT's President Lopes da Cruz and Vice President Mouzinho had also been invited by Sugyanto to visit Jakarta. I approached the UDT leaders in order to coordinate our trip and work in Jakarta. However, Lopes da Cruz made some excuses, and the Indonesians deliberately arranged the tickets and meetings in Jakarta at different dates, thus effectively separating our two delegations. Alarico and I arrived first, with Lopes da Cruz and Mouzinho arriving only toward the end of our visit. The UDT delegation was taken to a different hotel. Knowing their whereabouts through an Indonesian journalist, I took a taxi one evening to the hotel where they were staying. I found them in the lobby waiting to be taken to a meeting. Their Indonesian escorts could not disguise their surprise and annoyance at seeing me there.

Alarico and I met with Ali Moertopo and explained to him our position on independence and our foreign policy principles. We specifically assured Moertopo that Indonesia should rest assured that an independent East Timor would not harbor PKI remnants nor would it support separatist groups in Indonesia. Meanwhile, we were "honored" with a special brochure profusely illustrated with photographs of our meeting with Moertopo and our numerous visits to assembly lines, museums, etc. We shared the four-page paper with Queen Elizabeth, who had just recently visited Indonesia. Hundreds of copies were sent to Dili and a copy was displayed at the Indonesian Consulate in a glass box on the street for the benefit of the passers-by. The purpose of all this was rather obvious: It was to demonstrate Indonesia's "good will" and to discredit Alarico and me in the eyes of the public. Neither APODETI nor UDT visiting delegations were "honored" with such publicity.

This, my second and last visit to Jakarta, dissipated any illusions about Indonesia's intentions. Their intention was clearly to incorporate East Timor, and a complex machine had been put in motion to achieve this aim. My discussions with Liem Biau-Kie, a Chinese Catholic with the Center for Strategic and International Studies (CSIS), a think-tank of Moertopo's, confirmed my fears. I tried to convince the CSIS group that Indonesia had a chance to win the hearts and minds of the Timorese if it would cease all hostile clandestine operations, and concentrate instead on projecting a positive image of Indonesia. My hope was that if military intervention could be delayed, we would have time to make East Timor a focus of international attention. Only this could prevent an Indonesian invasion.

However, all of our assurances of friendship, cooperation, membership in ASEAN, a foreign policy that was tantamount to Finlandization of East Timor—all fell on deaf ears. In retrospect, I cannot see what assurances and concessions we could have offered to buy our own survival. The Indonesians realized that time was running out for them. APODETI had proved to be irrelevant and ineffective in promoting Indonesia's interests. The Indonesian military decided then to step up their destabilization campaign to subvert the decolonization process.

NOTES

1. Kissinger, Henry. *Nuclear Weapons and Foreign Policy*. W.W. Norton & Company, Inc. New York (1969).
2. See *Report of the Special Representation of the Secretary General on the West New Guinea Act of Free Choice* contained in United Nations GAOR, 2 Annexes, United Nations Doc. A/7723.
3. 15 UN GAOR (888th Plen. Meeting) 431, 451, UN Doc. A/PV.888 (1960).
4. 12 UN GAOR, C. 1 (912th Meeting) 243, 247, UN Doc. A/C.1/SR.912 (1957).

10

Intervention ·

Ali Moertopo spared no efforts in 1974 and 1975 to win over the Portuguese to Indonesia's position. In October 1974, he visited Lisbon at the same time as the Portuguese minister in charge of decolonization, Almeida Santos, visited East Timor. In Lisbon Moertopo met with President Costa Gomes, Prime Minister Vasco Goncalves, Foreign Minister Mario Soares and other MFA officers. During the discussions with Costa Gomes, Ali Moertopo was encouraged by the latter's comment that independence was "nonsense," a view expressed earlier by Almeida Santos. Subsequent to this meeting, a telegram was sent to Almeida Santos in East Timor, instructing him to "abstain in public statements from giving emphasis to or even reference to the independence solution on a plane with other solutions."

Costa Gomes and Vasco Goncalves were very receptive to Moertopo's persuasions. On the other hand, Mario Soares was unequivocal on the question of self-determination. "I was surprised that Mario Soares took such a firm position, knowing how unprincipled and malleable he is," a former Portuguese cabinet minister confided to me during an interview in Lisbon.

A second meeting was held between the Portuguese and the Indonesians, this time in London, early in March 1975. The Portuguese delegation consisted of Almeida Santos; Major Victor Alves, Minister without portfolio; Jorge Campinos, Secretary of State for Foreign Affairs; Doctor Castilho; and Major Mota from the staff of Governor Lemos Pires. Moertopo led the Indonesian delegation.

A Portuguese source whom I consider reliable because he stands at the opposite end of the political spectrum from Santos, assured me that Almeida Santos and particularly Jorge Campinos "behaved correctly" during the exchange with Moertopo. According to my source, whose information I verified with other accounts of the London meeting, Ali Moertopo tried to maneuver the Portuguese side into accepting the following points:

I.   The only guarantee of stability in the region is Timor's integration with Indonesia.

II.   The creation of a joint Portuguese/Indonesian administration that would advise the Governor and persuade the local population to accept integration with Indonesia.

III. Portugal should not internationalize the Timor problem.

According to a confidential memo on the London talks, Moertopo reminded the Portuguese delegation of the positions taken by Costa Gomes and Vasco Goncalves, that independence was "irrealist" and that continued Portuguese rule was against the MFA program, thus also unacceptable.

James Dunn, in his *Timor: A People Betrayed*, wrote: "The Portuguese appear to have told the Indonesians that integration was an option for which there was little support in the colony . . . " The Portuguese delegation also rejected Indonesia's suggestion for a joint Portuguese/Indonesian administration of the territory.

Ali Moertopo, a master of brinkmanship, tried to intimidate the Portuguese by saying that his government was under pressure from "the people of Indonesian Timor, some of whom were prepared to invade the colony." This was an outright bluff. East Timor did not represent for the Indonesian people and intellectuals a nationalist "cause celèbre," as was the case with West New Guinea. The only people crying for military intervention were Murdani, Pangabean, and their immediate circle of ambitious officers, who saw in East Timor an easy expedition with rewards of rapid promotion and loot.

While individual Portuguese negotiators in the London meeting might have stood firm against the most outrageous demands by Ali Moertopo, the final communique revealed Portuguese vaccilation. A confidential report from Governor Pires to Portuguese President Eanes, released in 1981, provided a clear denunciation of the London meeting:

> Of the London meeting, one can read that Indonesia was very explicit in its intentions, always aiming the integration (of East Timor). Portugal maintained an attitude of indefinition inasmuch as it tried to reconcile two contradictory facets:
>
> —the will of the people, by necessity and coherence with Portugal and international public opinion;
>
> —Indonesia's position, to which it suggested forms of operating in such a way to win over the will of the people.[1]

I personally believe the Portuguese negotiators in London were trying to prevent an Indonesian armed intervention by assuring them that Portugal would not object to an Indonesian political campaign within East Timor. I was to try the same tactic in April in Jakarta at the CSIS meeting. The problem with the Portuguese position was that it never considered internationalizing the problem, even when it was clear at the London meeting that Indonesia would stop at nothing to bring about the integration of East Timor.

In spite of repeated promises of non-interference in East Timor, the Indonesians prepared for invasion. UDT's decision to unilaterally terminate the coalition with FRETILIN in May 1975, played right into their hands. It was a fatal wound for the independence cause. From then on, events began to unfold rapidly.

Hundreds of Timorese from the Atsabe region, who had gone over to the other side with APODETI leaders Tomas and Lucio Goncalves, were sent back into East Timor. They had received military training in camps at Atambua from Indonesian commandos and began to attack villages, looting and burning in the Atsabe region. These acts of banditry, orchestrated by Indonesian special units, were immediately picked up by the Indonesian offical ANTARA news agency and distributed around the world. Meanwhile, Indonesian diplomats flooded foreign embassies with reports of "open warfare" among the Timorese, "communist harassment of APODETI supporters," etc. A scenario was being prepared to justify armed intervention. Anyone living in Dili in early and mid-1975, hearing foreign radio dispatches on the civil strife, killings and total chaos, certainly thought these reports referred to some other country!

UDT was decisively beaten by mid-September. When its leaders and their defeated rag-tag army entered West Timor, they became prisoners of the Indonesians, with the exception of Lopes da Cruz. He managed to reach West Timor where he was lavishly entertained by the Indonesian military. "While we were starving, his tent was full of food and drink provided by the Indonesians," Joao told me.

According to Joao, UDT elements rarely took part in the incursions into East Timor. "After the fall of Balibo we were ordered to occupy the town," Joao said. His information is confirmed by a series of CIA briefings on the Timor situation during the period of FRETILIN control, from September till the invasion in December. These CIA briefings were on the American President's desk each morning in 1975, revealed Dale Van Atta, an associate of Jack Anderson, who together with Brian Toohey of the Australian *National Times*, collected and published the reports.[2]

On September 10, the CIA briefing to the President stated: " . . . serious fighting between the factions evidently ended." In this same paper, the CIA acknowledged an important act which has been largely ignored by FRETILIN critics:

Meanwhile, the leftists [i.e. FRETILIN] have publicly abandoned their demand for immediate independence and are calling for a gradual decolonization program similar to the one announced by Portugal in June.

On September 18, the CIA reported:

Indonesia continues to follow a two-track approach toward the Timor problem. Publicly, Jakarta denies any intention of unilateral intervention and calls on Lisbon to move faster in arranging talks between the Timorese parties. Privately, Jakarta has stepped up covert military operations inside Timor, including use of Indonesian special units . . .

The CIA September 26 briefing was revealing in three aspects: FRETILIN's ability to fend off Indonesian attacks; the inability of the UDT forces to defend positions once the Indonesian troops were withdrawn; the involvement of Malaysia in providing arms for Indonesian operations in Timor. It also reported that "Indonesian special forces have taken casualties in recent fighting in Portuguese Timor . . . Some Indonesian soldiers have been captured." The CIA report added that FRETILIN's "efforts to stir up an international outcry by publicizing Jakarta's involvement have evoked little response."

In mid-September, 30 Indonesian commandos had been ambushed and killed or wounded by FRETILIN forces in the Bobonaro region. Among the captured Indonesians was a corporal who was taken to Dili and produced for the foreign press. I advised the ICRC of our willingness to release the Indonesian prisoner to ICRC for repatriation. However, the Indonesian authorities refused to acknowledge the existence of a POW with FRETILIN, because this would be a formal admission of their involvement in the conflict.

October 1975 marked a dramatic escalation in Indonesian intervention in East Timor. I took charge of our media campaign to publicize Indonesia's involvement in the conflict and a "*carte blanche*" policy was adopted for foreign correspondents wishing to visit East Timor. I cabled invitations to newspaper offices around the world. (I even sent an invitation to ANTARA, which did not accept because their correspondent was on "another assignment.")

Sometime around October 12, I went to Dili airport to pick up two British nationals working for Australian *Channel 9*—Malcolm Rennie, 28, and Brian Peters, 29. We departed the same day for Balibo, a small abandoned town some eight miles from the border with Indonesian West Timor. Three other journalists were already there: Greg Shackleton, 29, a television correspondent for Melbourne HSV7; Tony Stewart, 21, his sound man; and

Gary Cunningham, 27, a cameraman from New Zealand. They wanted to "film some action," as they put it, and verify our charges that regular Indonesian troops were involved in the fighting. That evening I ventured into the town to chat with FRETILIN troops. I could not believe what I saw. A group of FRETILIN fighters were trying to set up an 81 mm mortar, but could not figure it out. They had never seen one before and asked me for help. Me? The only weapon I knew how to handle (and with some considerable skill, I might add) was an air rifle; now, they were asking me to help with a sophisticated mortar! There were no more than 60 FRETILIN fighters in Balibo, not one a regular soldier.

After "inspecting" our position, I joined the journalists in an abandoned Chinese shop in Balibo. They were sipping Portuguese *tinto* (red wine) that they had brought from Dili. I was exhausted and layed down next to them on the dirty floor. Mosquitos were zooming like jet fighters and I began to have visions of Indonesian aircraft diving toward our house, "I am going to get the hell out of here by tomorrow," I decided. Brian Peters interrupted my thoughts to ask whether they could go a bit closer to the border in the morning. I answered, "yes, but be careful!"

We got up early the next day. After a bite of bread and cheese, I asked the militia commander to arrange an escort for the journalists to travel a few miles to the hills overlooking Indonesian West Timor. A large Indonesian frigate had been positioned in Indonesian waters very close to the border. I felt compelled to accompany the journalists, since I had been told by Nicolau to stay with them at all times. But after less than 500 meters, I excused myself, claiming I wasn't feeling well, and stayed behind sitting on a rock in the bush. I was too conscious of the dangers to follow them. After an hour or so they returned safely. Back at Balibo, I told them I would be leaving that afternoon, and would like them to do likewise, because the Indonesians were going to attack at any time. They objected. I left.

That was the last time I saw them alive. The next day, 400 Indonesian special forces and commandos attacked Balibo after several hours of shelling. The five newsmen were taken prisoner and shot. The Indonesians were determined to "teach a lesson" to the Australians, as Radio Kupang boasted that same evening. The newsmen had gathered evidence of Indonesian direct involvement in the fighting, an involvement which was already known to the Australian and American governments, but which Jakarta continued to deny.

Indonesian officials tried to justify the journalists' deaths with allegations that they were wearing FRETILIN uniforms. Not true. Greg Shackleton was wearing shorts and the same shirt shown in his last report from Maliana. They had arrived in Balibo in casual civilian clothing. Never for one instance did they touch a gun or wear an army uniform.

Back in Dili, when I heard of the fall of Balibo, I immediately called a meeting of the Central Committee, and won approval for a proposal that I put forward: FRETILIN would release 100 UDT prisoners, as well as Indonesians, in exchange for the journalists. I had some hope that they were still alive, and I sincerely hoped they would return to Australia and show on TV the truth of what was going on in our little island. But they died and the truth died with them . . . at least temporarily.

NOTES

1. This and other information on the responsibility of Portuguese officials in the Timor crisis may be found in a detailed report ordered by President Eanes and released in 1981, on file with the author. Other information consisting of original materials is also on file with the author.
2. Atta, Dale Van, and Toohey, Brian. "The Timor Papers," *The National Times*, May 30-June 5, 1982.

11

Australia: Betrayal

Australia could have made a positive impact on the Timor decolonization process. Only 364 miles separate our two countries, and Timorese know more about Australia than about any other country. Australian commandos fought a heroic guerrilla war in the mountains of East Timor against the Japanese army, with the help of Timorese civilians who sheltered, fed and fought alongside them. This wartime relationship endured in Timorese minds, becoming part of our mystical beliefs: *Australians will return one day to help us.* Sure enough, they came—as tourists, in small numbers, spending as little as possible. Partly because of the colonial authorities suspicion of Australian intentions, partly because of Australia's own lack of interest in the island, there was not one penny of Australian aid to East Timor after World War II.

A war memorial built by the Australian veterans of the East Timor campaign, in the hills behind Dili, was dedicated to "The Portuguese, from Minho (a Northern Portuguese Province) to Timor." The memorial was intended for native Timorese who gave their lives for the Australians, but the inscription did not mention the word "Timorese" because all Timorese were supposed to be Portuguese subjects. So the Timorese who fought and died during World War II had to be content to be classified as Portuguese on the war memorial.

Australia became the focus of our attention and efforts soon after the Portuguese coup. There was no other alternative. Our closest neighbor, a significant power in regional politics, enjoying historical, cultural, political and diplomatic ties with the United States and Western Europe, Australia was our single most important *potential* asset.

Soon after my first Jakarta trip I left for Australia in July 1974. I had no contacts then with any Australian politician, academics, or political activists. I arrived in Darwin without a penny and had to beg a loan from my brother, Arsenio. (It has been more than 10 years since, and I still haven't repaid the

$500!) Jim Dunn, a former Australian Consul in East Timor, had been to Dili on a fact-finding mission in June 1974, and offered me accommodation in Canberra. It was Jim who introduced me to Australian politicians and academics. He was my mentor in those early days. A specialist in Indonesian affairs, he had served in several overseas posts. His wife, Wendy, was always a perfect hostess, never showing any displeasure when I accepted Jim's invitations to stay with him. Christopher and Murray, their two sons, became very attached to East Timor through their father's work.

I was discouraged by Australia's official reception to my visit. Gough Whitlam had been elected Prime Minister in the early 1970s, breaking the Liberal-Country Party monopoly of the executive office for about two decades. Whitlam was regarded as a man dedicated to chartering a new, more independent course for Australia. He succeeded in fostering a more assertive foreign policy, much to the annoyance of Washington. Under Whitlam, Australian forces were withdrawn from Vietnam, and Canberra took a more progressive stand on the colonial issues on the United Nations agenda.

Nancy Viviani, a senior advisor to Whitlam's Foreign Minister, wrote about the Prime Minister:

> [Gough Whitlam] had an undoubted capacity for the broad vision, well-matched by rhetoric, and a confident grasp of the problems of balance of power relations among the great powers. He conceived a new role for Australia in international relations, and he wanted Australia to emerge from the shackles of past fears and parochialism and share his vision. He delighted in the untrammelled nature of the power involved in foreign policy-making—he would not consult his cabinet on foreign policy issues generally, and he did not on Timor, and he was loathe to have such issues raised in Caucus. [1]

Indonesia, the fifth most populous nation in the world, endowed with vast reserves of oil and other minerals, became an obsession for Whitlam in his quest for a more visible role for Australia in the region's affairs. In the face of Japan's highly visible and competitive presence in Southeast Asia, it seemed only rational that Australia should launch a more aggressive diplomatic strategy in the region. Gough Whitlam did what is common in Asia, Africa, and even Europe: he befriended the regional strongman—in this case, Suharto. By the time he was confronted with the Timor issue in 1974-1975, he had already cemented Australia's new relations with Indonesia through his "batik diplomacy."

Whitlam's position on East Timor was also influenced from the outset by his paternalistic and condescending view of "mini-states." Andrew Peacock, Australia's most talked-about politician who often made the covers of women's journals, took a more positive position. Speaking to the Australian Parliament, Peacock said in 1974:

The Labor Government says that the people of Portuguese Timor cannot be self-sufficient. It ought to tell that to the Nauruans, the Tongans, the Samoans, or the Papua New Guineans . . . So far as Portuguese Timor is concerned, we would prefer to see Portugal remain in control and assist with a program for self-determination. It would then be up to the Timorese to determine their own future in a program that they can work out.[2]

I met Peacock during my first visit to Australia and was impressed by his personal charm. His position, as outlined in his parliamentary speech, coincided with the position of all Timorese political parties then. I called on Peacock on numerous occasions.

Whitlam kept a firm hold on his party and brushed aside criticisms or innovative approaches to the Timor issue. The Labor MPs who did not agree with Whitlam's decisions on Timor policy grew in number; however, they could not muster enough clout to challenge their leader backed by the powerful pro-Indonesia lobby in the Foreign Affairs Department. Unlike the American system, which gives Congress significant power in foreign policy decisions, the Australian system leaves foreign policy to the discretion of the executive branch. This, in turn, is very dependent on a deeply entrenched foreign service bureaucracy.

As the Timor issue became more popular in Australia, Whitlam became more virulently anti-FRETILIN. Of Timorese leaders, he had this to say:

Political parties emerged there for the first time in May 1974 . . . They were led by mestizos . . . who seemed to be desperate to succeed the Portuguese as rulers of the rest of the population.[3]

And on another occasion:

I myself hesitate to accept at face value the claims of the political personalities who have emerged in the first year of political activity in Timor. They have sprung from what appears to have been a political vacuum under the Portuguese. Most appear to represent a small elite class—the educated, the government officials, and various other Westernized elements.[4]

Whitlam ignored the historical fact that the "educated" have always led liberation struggles everywhere in the world, for this is their historical and moral responsibility. In his vindictive drive against East Timor's independence, Whitlam tried to discredit the entire leadership with labels such as *mestizos*. One is tempted to ask how many aborigines are in the Australian government? For anyone aware of the fate of the original inhabitants of Australia, and the present living conditions of those who survived the head-hunting pogroms of the 19th century, Whitlam's professed preference for a more racially pure Timorese leadership was an intellectual travesty—to say the least.

One of the issues I repeatedly raised with the Foreign Affairs Department in Canberra and with Australian MPs was the importance of an Australian consular presence in East Timor. The Australian Consulate in Dili had been phased out in the mid-1960s and never reopened. With the developing situation in East Timor, we believed that reopening of the Consulate would be of enormous value. It would send a signal to Jakarta about Australia's interest in monitoring the situation in the territory. It would be a restraint on Indonesian covert operations. The Portuguese government also pleaded with the Australians on the same subject. The Australian response was pathetic: it would offend the Indonesians!

The prime backer of Whitlam's "batik diplomacy" was Richard Woolcot, a refined diplomat and arch-pragmatist, who could have filled in for Machiavelli as the tutor of the Prince if he had lived in the 15th century!

Soon after the UDT-instigated civil war had started, there was a proposal to Whitlam by some of his advisors that he convey to Suharto Australia's opposition to the use of force in East Timor. In April 1974, Suharto and Whitlam had met in Australia, and Suharto had given his personal assurance that Indonesia would not use force against Portuguese Timor. Richard Woolcot opposed such a reminder to Suharto because, he reminded Canberra, there was a "settled Indonesian policy to incorporate Timor." According to Woolcot, Suharto would not be happy with such a letter, which "he might regard as a lecture or even a friendly caution." Woolcot's Machiavellian stand on the Timor issue and almost blind obsession with Indonesia led him to recommend that:

> . . . [Australia's] policies should be based on disengaging ourselves as far as possible from the Timor question; getting Australians presently there out of Timor; leave events to take their course and if and when Indonesia does intervene act in a way which would be designed to minimize the public impact in Australia and show privately understanding to Indonesia of their problems . . . I know I am recommending a pragmatic rather than a principled stand, but that is what national interest and foreign policy is all about.[5]

Fall 1975 was marked by a political crisis in Australia. Gough Whitlam was dismissed by the Governor General, and with the Labor Government out of office, a caretaker liberal government filled the vacuum. President Suharto, who reportedly was wavering on the invasion of East Timor because of his personal assurance to Whitlam, now apparently felt released from his oath.

There is no doubt in my mind that if Australia and the United States had cautioned Suharto against intervening unilaterally in East Timor, the invasion wouldn't have taken place. A CIA analysis confirms this view:

President Suharto himself is ambivalent. Personally he would probably prefer military action, because he has an overwhelming fear of communist subversion in Indonesia. He is also concerned about his international image, however, and does not want to revive the ghost of adventurist foreign policies practiced under former President Sukarno. Suharto is also concerned about the impact on Indonesia's bilateral relations with Australia and the United States. In both cases, he is worried about the loss of military assistance, which he badly wants to improve Indonesia's outdated equipment.

Suharto has apparently relied heavily on this argument in counselling caution to his military commanders and is now showing some concern that if substantial aid is not forthcoming, there will be severe political repercussions for himself. In trying to balance off his various advisors, Suharto has appeared to blow hot and cold on Timor. When meeting with military advisors, he has emphasized his willingness to authorize an invasion should Indonesian security require it. In meetings with his political and diplomatic advisors, he has stressed the need to get a new agreement with Lisbon that will settle the Timor problem.[6]

Because of Peacock's public record on East Timor, the Indonesians were somewhat more concerned with the caretaker Liberal-Conservative coalition government. However, Peacock soon reassured the Indonesians that a liberal government would be sympathetic to their position even if they were to take military action against East Timor. Peacock's about-face was most painful to me. But a few years later, in May 1977, the extent of Peacock's double-talk on East Timor was revealed to the press in Australia. Peacock, in his capacity as opposition foreign affairs spokesperson, had visited Bali in September 1974, and met with Liem Bian-Kie of Ali Moertopo's CSIS. According to the record of their conversation later leaked to the press, Peacock

> . . . said his party would not protest against Indonesia if Indonesia was forced to do something about Portuguese Timor, for example to go in to restore peace there. He recommended that such Indonesian action be given open support by the ASEAN nations, in order to provide "moral cover" for it. Indonesia was forced to go in. At the maximum, he would criticize Whitlam and his government for hesitating to join in solving the Portuguese Timor problem, thereby forcing Indonesia to act militarily . . . Basically, he respects Whitlam's policy in this Portuguese Timor problem, and he personally is of the same opinion.[7]

With Whitlam out of office, FRETILIN representatives were barred from entering Australia; radio facilities set up in Darwin by Australian supporters of East Timor were confiscated and a Timorese who was part of the group was deported; faint efforts by aid agencies to ship medical supplies to East Timor were thwarted by the coast guard, and the perpetrators arrested and charged with drug smuggling and illegal arms export (they had medical supplies and a shortgun on board for self-defense). Within a year, Frazer extended *de facto* and *de jure* recognition of Indonesia's incorporation of East Timor in exchange for Indonesia's concessions on the Timor Sea boundary dispute. At the same time, in a display of hypocrisy, Frazer withdrew recognition of the Baltic states as part of the USSR.

As reports of Indonesian brutalities, mass killings and starvation began to reach Australia and the rest of the world, the Frazer government and the Foreign Affairs Department bureaucrats dismissed them as "unsubstantiated" or "exaggerated." At the United Nations, with Woolcot as the new Australian Permanent Representative, Australia dropped all pretense of "neutrality" on the Timor issue and began lobbying openly for Indonesia.

As the opposition leader in 1981, Bill Hayden was very critical of what he described as Australia's "servility" toward Indonesia. However, what Bill Hayden said in 1981 as the opposition leader, and what he told the ALP National Conference in Canberra in July 1984, after he became Minister for Foreign Affairs, made me wonder if Hayden was suffering from "split personality" syndrome. Sitting in the diplomat's section of the auditorium, I saw the Indonesian Ambassador also listening attentively to Hayden's harangue against FRETILIN. The thrust of his speech was that to "offend" the Indonesians with a resolution would be a disservice to the Timorese themselves; and it would jeopardize Australia's efforts to gain Jakarta's support for the Indochina peace initiative, Hayden's pet project.

As soon as the Australian Labour Party (ALP) was elected into office in 1983, Foreign Minister Bill Hayden had jumped onto the bandwagon of "peace initiatives" in Indochina. Hayden told the ALP National Conference in July 1984, that Indonesia had been very cooperative in the search for a negotiated solution of the Cambodian conflict. If Australia's initiative were to succeed—Hayden argued—Indonesia's continuing cooperation was indispensable. Therefore, a strong ALP resolution on East Timor would compromise his peace efforts. The essence of Hayden's message was that East Timor was a small price to pay for his grand diplomatic schemes. I tried to counter Hayden's absurdities by explaining to the ALP delegates that Indonesia had its own strategic interests in Southeast Asia, and that long before Hayden got his first taste of world diplomacy, Indonesia was already playing the role of "moderate" within ASEAN in regard to the Cambodian conflict. Indonesian Foreign Minister Mochtar Kusumaatmadja was in fact infuriated by Hayden's initiative, which he saw as a self-serving exercise that would rob him of the credit and limelight.

Almost ten years after the invasion of Timor, and in the face of mounting evidence of a tragedy of enormous dimensions next door to Australia, Bill Hayden wrote to an Australian MP in February 1985:

> The Government is aware of various reports from Amnesty International and other resources concerning human rights abuses in East Timor. The Government does not have sufficient or enough substantial information with which to confirm these reports.[8]

To say that Hayden's statement reflects ignorance of the true situation in Timor would be an understatement. The fact is that the Foreign Affairs Department does have "sufficient and substantial" information about the killings, systematic use of torture against detainees, and forced deportation of thousands of Timorese to the Atauro Island and other remote islands in the archipelago. It also has information about the armed resistance to Indonesia still active almost ten years after the invasion. However, these facts would rock the boat if they were to be publicly acknowledged.

While Hayden refrained from making any reference to Indonesia human rights abuses in East Timor, presumably because of "lack of information," he was very outspoken in his harangue against FRETILIN. Listening to Hayden at the ALP Conference, I wondered whether it was FRETILIN that had invaded Indonesia, and set out to kill and burn people and villages in Java and elsewhere!

I met with Bill Hayden in his office in Canberra in June 1984 while I was in Australia for a six-week campaign aiming at the ALP National Conference. Hayden received me unwillingly essentially as a move to deflect criticisms from the ALP left. I put forward to Hayden our peace plan, for which we asked Australia's support. The idea was for Australia to host or to help arrange a meeting involving the United Nations, Portugal, Indonesia and FRETILIN, as well as other Timorese, *without preconditions* and *without* a formal agenda, in an effort to resolve the Timor problem.

Hayden rejected the proposal, arguing that Indonesia would object to it; and saying that "FRETILIN is reduced to a small band of terrorists who are desperate, pillaging villages, murdering people." It was therefore inappropriate for Australia to raise the issue.

I was offended by Hayden's blatant distortion of the facts, attributing to FRETILIN the responsibility for the tragedy in East Timor. It was like telling the French resistance or the Yugoslavian partisans during World War II that they were responsible for the Nazi retaliation raids against civilians. It is like blaming the Blacks in South Africa for apartheid's brutalities.

Another blatant distortion is Hayden's moralistic lectures about the legacy of Portuguese colonialism, as if the Portuguese were responsible for what happened in Timor after 1975. Even if one were to compare the two evils, the Timorese would prefer a million times the backward Portuguese colonial rule, to the daily nightmare and terror of Indonesian occupation. However, any such comparison misses the point. The Timorese have been fighting for the past ten years and will be fighting many more years if necessary, regardless of the style of the oppressors, be they more benevolent than the Portuguese, or be they more brutal.

Hayden visited Portugal in early September 1984, the first such visit ever by a senior cabinet member from Australia. This, if nothing else, reflected the strong body of opinion within the ALP and Australia in regard to the Timor problem. In Lisbon, Hayden lost no time in again attacking FRETILIN while refraining from uttering the slightest criticism of Indonesia. In an exchange with journalists in his hotel, Hayden said:

> Officially, the situation is that the FRETILIN (*sic*) are in a beleaguered situation. They are badly broken up and bottled-up. They are reduced to pillaging East Timorese villages. The villagers are reacting to this with hostility. The FRETILIN [*sic*] are now in a position where, if they had hearts and minds support from any significant number of East Timorese, this has been badly damaged and markedly reduced.

The truth is turned upside down. The Indonesian troops, an alien occupation force that has perpetrated wanton killing and destruction, become forces of law and order, engaged, as Hayden put it, "in construction, development." A sort of Peace Corps. FRETILIN, an indigenous movement carrying on a legitimate armed resistance, becomes, in Hayden's Orwellian logic, "reduced to pillaging East Timorese villages".

After boasting that his government's information on the Timor situation was "as reliable as anyone is getting and more reliable than most," Hayden was questioned by a journalist about the claims by Timorese refugees that "the Indonesian Army is conscripting the Timorese civil population to assist in the fighting, including school children . . . "

Hayden responded:

> Well, I don't know. I don't think I would be prepared to swear my life away that this is correct at this point. It may be, but I don't have any evidence of it . . .

It was pathetic and grotesque to see Hayden, who rightly deplored Australia's subservience towards Indonesia in 1981, now going even beyond servility to outright dishonesty.

One of Hayden's actions in pleasing the Indonesians was to appoint as Australia's Ambassador to Jakarta, Mr. Bill Morrison, a Defense Minister under Whitlam. Lacking Whitlam's intellect and international standing,

Morrison nonetheless outdid his boss in supporting a pro-Indonesia policy in 1974-1975.

During the ALP State Conference in Sydney, early in June 1984, I had the unique opportunity of witnessing Morrison's hysterical tirade against FRETILIN, blaming all the killing and atrocities on the Timorese themselves, as if the country was not occupied by a foreign army. Gesturing and shouting like someone who had just come out of a pub at four o'clock in the morning, Morrison went on a verbal rampage against the Timorese. Not a word about Indonesia!

Bill Morrison led a parliamentary group to visit Indonesia in July 1983. East Timor was included. As expected, Morrison concluded that the Indonesians had brought development and progress to Timor. The delegation "saw no evidence" of human rights abuses. (It probably was expecting the Indonesians to put a show of torture techniques for the benefit of the politicians!) The delegation also asserted that they saw no military activity. This was indeed the case, because there had been in effect since March 1983, a ceasefire agreed to by FRETILIN and the Indonesian military command.

When Morrison's delegation traveled by road to the eastern sector of the island, they were intercepted by a guerrilla unit carrying an invitation from the FRETILIN regional leader to visit their camp. Morrison asked for the details of their whereabouts but refused the invitation! Shortly after his delegation's departure, Indonesian troops attacked the FRETILIN camp and massacred its inhabitants. Morrison had betrayed the confidence of the FRETILIN group and passed information to the Indonesian military. This story was reported by an East Timorese now living in Australia who was a member of the FRETILIN delegation that intercepted Morrison's party.

In another *volte face* in the Labor government's position on Timor, Prime Minister Hawke announced unexpectedly in Jakarta in August 1985, that his government recognized Indonesia's sovereignty over East Timor and the inhabitants of the island as "Indonesian citizens!" Another nail was put in the Timor coffin. The Indonesians rejoiced. Coming at a time when the negotiations involving Lisbon and Jakarta were moving to another stage, the discussions on self-determination, Hawke's announcement could only strengthen Indonesia's position. The Portuguese President and Prime Minister Soares took a surprisingly tough stand, condemning Hawke's position and recalling their Ambassador to Canberra. The Timorese refugee communities in Portugal and Australia, usually divided, took a common stand in denouncing this most recent Australian act of betrayal and cowardice.

The debate over Timor and Indonesia will not go away, as much as the likes of Whitlam, Morrison and Hayden might wish it. For the armed resistance continues unabated in East Timor, as does Indonesia's terror campaign. In 1975, it was hoped in Canberra that the issue of East Timor would fade away within months of the invasion. Almost ten years later, in July 1984, East Timor was the most hotly debated issue at the Australian Labor Party's National Conference.

The continuing border violations and armed incursions by regular Indonesian troops into Papua New Guinea's territory is a reminder of the danger of Australia's appeasement policies in regard to a regime that, by its very nature, is brutal, arrogant and militaristic. Papua New Guinea, a country that has been an economic and diplomatic appendix of the Australian Foreign Affairs Department, is becoming increasingly aware of the danger of its dependence on Australia. In the last two years or so, there are visible signs that Papua New Guinea's diplomacy is gearing up for a more visible posture in the United Nations, the Non-Aligned Movement, and for more diversified bilateral relations with other countries.

As the armed rebellion in West Papua increases in intensity, and as the emotions of Melanesian brotherhood and solidarity drive the Papuans to support their oppressed brothers on the other side of the island, Papua New Guinea will find itself in the same boat as East Timor in 1975, and West Papua in 1963. The only deterrence against an Indonesian invasion is for Papua New Guinea to have a visible international posture, diversification of its international relations, and some serious military preparedness through mass mobilization.

New Zealand, under its feisty Prime Minister Robert Muldoon, took a strident anti-East Timor stand long before Indonesia invaded the territory. Muldoon spoke about "another Cuba" in the region and Indonesia's "legitimate interests." After the invasion, his government voted with Indonesia on every United Nations resolution on East Timor and not once expressed concern about the human rights situation there. In 1983, Muldoon, nicknamed "Pork Pie" (I must say, with justice), was replaced by David Lange, a well-fed Anglican preacher. Lange gained instant notoriety, thanks to his government's stand against visits to New Zealand ports by American nuclear-armed vessels. He was praised by the Euro- and American-centered anti-nuke movement, and was even proposed for the Nobel Peace Prize.

Long before Lange joined the anti-nuke bandwagon, Prime Minister Lini of Vanautu had already opposed port calls by American nuclear-armed vessels. However, the white Anglo-Saxon peace movement in New Zealand and Australia did not propose Lini for the Nobel Prize. This tells a bit about the peace movement's agenda: the survival of the Anglo-Saxon species. Conventional wars, fueled by the mammoth transfer of weapons to Third World countries, have killed millions since the end of World War II. Wars are going on at New Zealand's and Australia's doorsteps, in the Gulf region, Central America and Southern Africa. Yet, there has been no serious effort on the part of the peace movement in the Western world to face these situations. The reason is simple: whites are not being killed, and thousands would enter the unemployment lines in Europe and the United States if arms exports were to be drastically reduced.

Lange's stand on the nuclear issue is commendable. However, his stand on the on-going conflicts in East Timor, New Caledonia and West Papua betray the hypocrisy of his government's diplomacy. On East Timor, Lange opposes self-determination. On New Caledonia, he supports the French. Along with Hawke of Australia, he blocked a South Pacific Forum plan to bring the New Caledonia issue to the United Nations General Assembly in 1985. On East Timor, Lange said: "Quite simply, I do not believe that keeping alive the issue of independence will do anything to help the East Timorese people." On December 12, 1984, in a radio interview (New Zealand Radio, *Checkpoint* program), Lange claimed that the situation in East Timor had improved in comparison with Portuguese rule. His claims were supposedly based on a report by his Ambassador to Jakarta who had just concluded a brief visit to the territory. However, as it was revealed later by Gordon Campbell of *The New Zealand Listener*, Ambassador Michael Powles' report was more critical of the situation in Timor than Lange made it appear to be. Where Ambassador Powles said that his delegation was "not in a position to investigate allegations of human rights violations," Lange claimed that there was "a very marked development" in the human rights situation. Where Powles said, "We . . . could not confirm that there had been some acquittals" of prisoners, Lange chose to assert: "People are now being put on trial, given effective legal aid . . . and there have been acquittals."

NOTES

1. Viviani, Nancy. "Australians and the Timor Issue," in *Australian Outlook 30*, No. 2 (1976).
2. Commonwealth Parliamentary Debates, House of Representatives, Canberra, A.C.T., October 30, 1974, p. 3135.
3. Whitlam, E.G. "Indonesia and Australia, Political Aspects: the Indonesian Connection," seminar held at the Australian National University, November 30, 1979. Canberra, A.C.T.
4. Whitlam, E.G. Letter to Senior Arthur Gietzelt (NSW), dated April 22, 1975.
5. Walsh and Munster, *Documents on Australian Defense and Foreign Policy*, 1968-1975. This book was banned by a court order and withdrawn from circulation.
6. Atta, Dale Van, and Toohey, Brian. "The Timor Papers," *The National Times*, May 30-June 5, 1982.
7. *The National Times*, May 2-7, 1977.
8. Hayden, William. Letter to Robert Ticker, MP, Member for Hughes (NSW), dated February 14, 1985.

12

Washington: Pragmatism

Today, freedom-loving people around the world must say, "I am a Berliner. I am a Jew in a world still threatened by anti-Semitism. I am an Afghan, and I am a prisoner of the gulag. I am a refugee in a crowded boat floundering off the coast of Vietnam. I am a Laotian, a Cambodian, a Cuban, and a Miskito Indian in Nicaragua."

—President Reagan's address on May 5, 1985, during his speech in Germany on the 40th anniversary of VE-Day.

"The essence of Ronald Reagan was exposed at Bitburg," wrote Anthony Lewis of *The New York Times*. "Confronted by the most profound questions of man's nature and responsibility, he responded with narrow ideology and warped history."

Reagan, like his predecessor, Jimmy Carter, politicized human rights and used them as an ideological tool against socialist and progressive countries. Reagan, like Carter, ignored the plight of black South Africans who languish under a system of institutionalized terror and racism; the widespread and systematic use of torture in Chile and Guatemala. They not only ignored, but actively supported the mass murder of the Timorese women, men, and children, orchestrated by their friend and ally, General Suharto of Indonesia. Under Carter, there were crocodile tears for the oppressed; under Reagan, there hasn't been even a pretence of concern for those in East Timor, Chile, Paraguay, South Africa.

1975 was a bad year for the United States. The world's greatest economic and military power suffered its first defeat ever, humiliated by a Third World peasant army. Vietnam, Cambodia and Laos were "lost" to the communists. That same year, Angola, endowed with oil and diamonds, became independent after a long guerrilla war against the Portuguese. The United States tried to stop the Marxist *Movimento Popular de Libertacao de Angola* (MPLA) from gaining power by supporting two pro-Western factions, and enlisting racist South Africa in its crusade against "communism" in Angola. It lost the confrontation. Mozambique also became independent under a movement that did not fit the criteria of the United States. A year earlier, America's longest reigning ally in Africa, Emperor Haile Selassie of Ethiopia, was overthrown by a group of radical officers, almost in the same manner as the Portuguese officers disposed of their own dictator. Kissinger's assessment in 1969 that "there is no hope for the blacks to gain political rights through violence" proved to be wrong.

It was in the midst of international changes which seemed to prove Lyndon Johnson's "domino theory" that President Ford and Kissinger visited Jakarta and conferred with Suharto on the Timor problem. With the wounds of Vietnam still fresh, it wasn't difficult for Suharto to persuade his American patrons that military action against East Timor was necessary to stamp out another "communist" enclave. The Indonesian propaganda machine fabricated stories of Chinese and Vietnamese generals arriving in Timor to train FRETILIN forces.

Suharto had resisted an earlier invasion of East Timor for a number of reasons. One was his concern about a negative American reaction, with possible Congressional action to cut off military aid. The Indonesian army was going through a modernization program and was dependent on United States generosity. Australian Ambassador Woolcot acknowledged this in a report to Canberra:

> The United States might have some influence on Indonesia at present, as Indonesia really wants and needs United States assistance in its military re-equipment program. But Ambassador Newsom told me last night that he is under instructions from Kissinger personally not to involve himself in discussions on Timor with the Indonesians on the grounds that the United States is involved in enough problems of greater importance overseas at present. The State Department has, we understand, instructed the Embassy to cut down the reporting on East Timor.[1]

Certainly, Henry Kissinger, known for his contempt for "mini-states"* was not very interested in East Timor. His Ambassador to Jakarta, Newsom, certainly reflected Kissinger's thinking when he commented to

---

*In his book, *From the Congo to Soweto: U.S. Foreign Policy Toward Africa Since 1960* (Quill, New York, 1984), Henry F. Jackson offers an insight into Kissinger's contempt for African countries: "Kissinger's indifference verged on contempt in his treatment of African Ambassadors in Washington. He refused continually to receive the diplomats of individual missions and deigned to see them infrequently only en masse."

Woolcot, "If Indonesia were to intervene, the United States would hope they would do so effectively, quickly, and not use our equipment."[2]

While it is not clear that the Ford administration actually *approved* the invasion, the highest Washington officials knew for months about Indonesia's intentions and covert action leading up to the invasion. These Washington officials also knew that Indonesia could not make a move without using American weapons, supplied under various titles: 1) The Military Assistance Program (MAP), which provides grants of arms, ammunition, training, and technical support; 2) the Foreign Military Sales Program (FMS), which provides war material listed in MAP, paid for in hard cash or credit through the FMS Financing Program; and 3) the International Military and Education and Training Program (IMET). In addition to these official channels, large amounts of arms had been sold to Indonesia by United States arms producers through regular commercial transactions.

Indonesia's use of American weapons was in violation of the 1958 United States-Indonesian Mutual Defense Agreement, which states:

> Any weapon or other military equipment or service purchased by the Government of Indonesia from the Government of the United States shall be used by the Government of Indonesia solely for legitimate national self-defense . . .

Lest the word "self-defense" allow for wrong interpretations, the agreement narrowed the meaning of the term:

> . . . it is self-evident that the Government of Indonesia, as a member of the United Nations Organization, interprets the term 'legitimate national self-defense' within the scope of the United Nations Charter, as excluding an act of aggression against any other state.

A 1963 telegram marked "secret," sent from the American Embassy in Jakarta to the US Secretary of State, summed up *then* what would be the American position on the Timor question 15 and even 20 years later! The telegram, now declassified, first made the argument that "Portuguese Timor (was) not economically viable," then went on to suggest that the "United States should urge Portugal to take steps in Timor now to cut losses in darkening future." Warning of a possible Sukarno intervention in the future, the telegram said further:

> Communist countries would, of course, exploit in Indo any military confrontation between Western country and Indo and this in turn would have adverse effect on United States position here. We think effort should be made to convince Portugal it is in their interest to anticipate confrontation and deal with it peacefully.

Then as now, the United States' relation with Indonesia overrode any considerations of the rights of the Timorese themselves. Portugal, then under Salazar's iron rule, was not the least impressed with American suggestions to relinquish East Timor to the Indonesians or to grant independence to Angola. As soon as Kennedy was elected to office, Salazar passed word through Foreign Minister Franco Nogueira, that the American facilities in the Azores would be in jeopardy if Kennedy were to insist on Angolan independence. The old Portuguese accountant/dictator forced the charismatic young president of the mightiest country on earth to back down![3]

In 1958 the CIA tried to overthrow Sukarno and failed. The Americans then pursued a different strategy. The US continued to supply arms to the regime as well as military training to its officer corps, ingratiating themselves with the conservative military elite. This proved to be a farsighted CIA strategy, as the 1965 coup revealed. Former Assistant Secretary of Defense Paul Warnke defended United States military aid to leftist Sukarno, saying its aims were "not to support an existing regime" but "to preserve a liason of sorts with the military of the country, which in effect, turned out to be one of the conclusive elements in the overthrow of that regime."[4]

Following the coup, Suharto inaugurated his "New Order" with an open door policy for Western capital investment. The 1967 Foreign Investment Law paved the way for increasing United States corporate control of the Indonesian economy. Japan, West Germany, France and Holland also benefited tremendously from the 1965-1966 bloodbath. By 1973, foreign interests controlled 96% of capital invested in mining; 59% in forestry; 47% in hotels and tourism; 35% in industry; and 33% in agriculture and fisheries. By 1981, United States exports to Indonesia amounted to $1 billion per year. Investments outside the petroleum sector stood at $600 million, and American oil companies were expending $1.5 million per year in the country.[5]

I followed with interest the Carter-Ford race for the White House in 1976. That was my first taste of American democracy, having left the jungles of tropical East Timor a few weeks earlier. The mind-boggling publicity blitz, covering every step and word of the Presidential contenders, impressed me a great deal. I wondered what Carter would do if he took office. His human rights pronouncements were a fresh departure from Nixon-Ford and Kissinger's approach to Third World problems.

Soon, my hopes and illusions were shattered. Within a year of Carter's election, military assistance to Indonesia doubled. In 1977, with the Indonesian military inventory depleted by its invasion of East Timor, the Carter Administration increased the State Department's original request for $25 million in FMS sales to more than $100 million. A year later, during Walter Mondale's visit to Jakarta, an offer was made for the sale of 16 A-4

"Skyhawk II" jet attack planes to Indonesia. Included in the FMS package were 16 Bell UH-1H "Huey" helicopters.

The United States arms transfer to Indonesia in that crucial period included 16 OV-10 "Bronco" aircraft, 3 Lockheed C-130 transport aircraft, 45 Cadillac-Cage V-150 Commando armored cars. The "Bronco" aircraft has been the key weapon used by the Indonesian army in its counterinsurgency operations against FRETILIN forces. Used against FRETILIN were also the "Skyhawk II" aircraft which is capable of spraying wide areas with weapons-fire and high explosives.

Like the Australian Government and other Western governments, the Carter administration engaged in a crude campaign to cover up the tragic situation in East Timor, for the truth would have seriously damaged its moral standing. In the media and Congress, it tried to discredit Timorese sources of information with buzz words such as "exaggerated," "unfounded allegations," etc. To touch a sensitive chord in Congress, the State Department's Indonesia Desk described the Timorese resistance as the "Marxist FRETILIN."

Carter's Deputy Assistant Secretary for East Asian and Pacific Affairs, Robert B. Oakley, claimed that "the number of total casualties, civilian, military, everything else, is probably under ten thousand ... most of violence in which there were major losses of life or wounded, took place during the period between August, 1975, and March, 1976." Oakley thus suggested that it was the UDT-FRETILIN civil war, which did not last more than a month, that was responsible for most of the casualities, Oakley erred, I believe deliberately, on all accounts. By 1977, the casualty figures had surpassed 100,000. The total casualties of the brief UDT-FRETILIN strife did not exceed 3,000 according to ICRC's own investigation in October, 1975.

On a political and legal plane, the Carter administration's position on the Timor issue was ambiguous and contradictory. It acknowledged that:

> ... as a matter of legal theory, when a people has a right to self-determination which is generally acknowledged and which we have acknowledged, that right cannot be extinguished except through an act of exercise of that right of self-determination, which I think has not occurred in this case. Therefore, what I am saying is that, as a legal matter, the right of self-determination continues to exist.

This statement was made by George Aldrich, a State Department legal advisor, during hearings on Timor in the House Subcommittee of the Committee on Appropriations in June 1981. However, the actions of the Carter administration in the United Nations General Assembly contradicted this stand since it voted against all General Assembly resolutions on East Timor.

The Carter administration had the same strategic views of Indonesia as did Richard Nixon and Ford. It was this strategic consideration that far outweighed the issue of human rights in East Timor. Richard Holbrooke, Carter's Assistant Secretary for Asia and Pacific Affairs, summed up in June 1980, his administration's views on Indonesia and East Timor:

> The situation in East Timor is one of the number of very important concerns of the United States in Indonesia. Indonesia, with a population of one hundred and fifty million people, is the fifth largest nation in the world. It has the largest Muslim population in the world, is a moderate member of the Non-Aligned Movement, is an important oil producer—which plays a moderate role within OPEC—and occupies a strategic position astride the sea lanes between the Pacific and Indian Oceans. President Suharto and other prominent Indonesian leaders have publicly called for the release of our hostages in Iran. Indonesia's position within the Association of South East Asian Nations—ASEAN—is also important, and it has played a central role in supporting Thailand and maintaining the security of Thailand in the face of Vietnam's destabilizing actions in Indo-China. Finally, Indonesia has provided humane treatment for over fifty thousand Indo-Chinese refugees and taken the initiative in offering an island site as an ASEAN refugee processing center. Indonesia is, of course, important to key United States allies in the region, especially Japan and Australia. We highly value our cooperative relationship with Indonesia.[6]

Disillusioned with Carter, I watched with great interest Ted Kennedy's race for the Democratic nomination in 1980. The Kennedy family's history fascinated me. This fascination goes back to my childhood when John F. Kennedy captured the world's imagination. I remember the day when our high school teacher announced to the class the news of Kennedy's assassination. There was sadness in everybody's face and a somber mood took over. Most of us had never seen even a picture of Kennedy, but somehow he exercised on us, as on millions in America and all over the world, a magnetic appeal. The last of the Kennedys also attracted my admiration, and I couldn't have been happier, seeing him challenging the man who I felt had betrayed our hopes. A senior aide to General Ali Moertopo had been in New York in the Fall of 1981, instructed by Moertopo, so he told me, to invite me to Indonesia for the possible post of Governor of East Timor. In the course of our conversation, he expressed to me the Indonesians' concern with a Kennedy victory. I played up Kennedy's chances and his "positive stand" on East Timor. "We hope Carter wins," my interlocutor told me, "but we are worried about Kennedy." Ted Kennedy lost to Jimmy Carter and Jimmy Carter to Ronald Reagan.

Sometime later, I received a letter from Moertopo's aide which said sarcastically, "Your friend lost. We won big. So think it over. The door is still open for you to return and join us."

He was right. The Indonesian military regime and all military regimes around the world won big with the election of Ronald Reagan.

Both the Carter and Reagan administrations had a free ride with their policies on East Timor. However, members of Congress began to take a closer look into reports of gross human rights violations in East Timor. They began to question the official line that reports of human rights abuses there were "unverified allegations."

Congressman Harkin, Democrat of Iowa, was one of the early advocates of the rights of the people of East Timor. Unlike many other issues where members of Congress have to respond to a particular ethnic constituency, the Timor issue is among the least known in the United States. No politician has to worry about a Timorese electorate in his or her district. In 1975, when not a single Timorese refugee or leader had set foot in the United States, Tom Harkin introduced a resolution in the House calling for a cut in military aid to Indonesia because of that country's invasion of East Timor. The motion was defeated.

In subsequent years, a number of Congressmen began also to take an interest on East Timor. Former Congressman Donald Fraser, then Chairman of the House Subcommittee on International Organizations, sponsored a full hearing on East Timor in March 1977. A series of hearings followed in subsequent years with growing interest. However, it was not until 1982 that there was a more consistent interest in the Timor tragedy by members of the United States Congress.

On the Senate side, former Massachusetts Democrat Paul Tsongas spearheaded the investigation into the human rights situation in East Timor. Interest was also shown by Republican Senator Dave Durenberger of Minnesota. Letters were addressed to President Reagan and Secretary Schultz, as well as to visiting foreign government leaders. These letter campaigns have proven to be effective in drawing the President's attention to the problem and in encouraging media coverage.

In view of Indonesia's dependence on Congress for economic and military assistance programs, the Indonesian leaders have been nervous about the growing interest in Washington in the Timor issue. When Secretary Schultz visited Jakarta in July 1984, for the ASEAN meeting, a record number of House and Senate members urged him to raise the Timor issue. So Schultz did—something that no senior official of the Carter administration had done! During Reagan's visit to Lisbon in May 1985, after his troubled summit meeting in Bonn, 133 United States Congressmen used the occasion to again raise the Timor issue in a letter to the President.

Congressman Tony Hall, who was a Peace Corps volunteer in Thailand, took an early interest in the Southeast Asian region. His aide, Marty Rendom has been to Lisbon to interview Timorese refugees living in miserable camps. Trained in a Jesuit seminary and as a lawyer, Marty is extremely meticulous in amassing detailed and verifiable information from refugees, church officials, human rights organizations such as Amnesty International and others.

Late in April 1986 Reagan visited Bali on his way to the Tokyo summit of the industrialized countries. The tour, labeled "Winds of Freedom" (supposedly blowing in Asia), turned out to be a public relations fiasco for the Indonesians. Even Knowlton & Johnson, the giant New York PR firm that was contracted by the Indonesian government to handle the Reagan visit for a $600,000 fee, did not help much. *The New York Times* correspondent, Barbara Crossette was stopped at Bali Airport and expelled from the country because A. Rosenthal, her boss, had included Indonesia in his "Journey Among Tyrants" article in *Times* magazine and accurately stated that, compared with Suharto of Indonesia, Marcos looked like a Jeffersonian democrat! Crossette is an inoffensive lady whose articles on Indonesia and East Timor have invariably been very positive toward Indonesia. Foreign Minister Mochtar Kusumaatmadja came to her defense and stated publicly how much a true friend of Indonesia (read, of the Suharto regime) she had been. Two Australian journalists traveling on the press plane to cover Reagan's visit were also expelled from the country because of an article published in *The Sydney Morning Herald*, charging the Suharto family with amassing a fortune estimated to be between $2 to $3 billion. The Indonesian dictator was reportedly angry and personally ordered the retaliation, not only against the journalists, but also against Australian tourists arriving in Indonesia, who found their visas cancelled as they arrived.

About 150 American legislators, among them some of the most influential Democratic and Republican Congressmen and Senators, had addressed a letter to Reagan urging him to raise the Timor issue with Suharto. That did not impress Reagan, while Qaddafi's "terrorist" activities were much discussed. "Winds of Freedom" became a tempest against freedom in Indonesia.

The United States Congress is certainly not a humanist institution devoid of hypocrisy, double standards and corruption. However, the US Congress is unique among the Western democratic institutions in that it does scrutinize government policies and check the awesome power of the President. It can be blamed for a number of foreign policy disasters, such as the American intervention in Vietnam, but in the field of human rights, it has proven to be influential in shaping the administration's policies.

NOTES

1. Cited in Dunn's *Timor: A People Betrayed* (1983).
2. Walsh and Munster, *Documents on Australian Defense and Foreign Policy* (Sydney, 1980). Banned by court order.
3. Richard D. Mahoney, *JFK: Ordeal in Africa*, Oxford University Press (1983), Chap. 8, p. 203.
4. US Assistance Programs, p. 96. Cited in Noam Chomsky, and Edward S. Herman. *The Washington Connection and Third World Fascism*, South End Press, Boston (1979).
5. Flora E. Montealegre, *"Background Information on Indonesia, The Invasion of East Timor, and US Military Assistance,"* Institute for Policy Studies, Washington, D.C. (May 1982).
6. *"Foreign Assistance and Related Programs-Appropriations for 1981"*, Hearings before the Sub-Committee on Asian and Pacific Affairs and on International Organizations, 96th Congress, Second Session, 1980.

13

The Security Council Fails To Act

I was in Canberra during the last two weeks of November 1975, calling on the Portuguese, Brazilian, Chinese, Russian, Canadian, British, Dutch, German and Swedish Ambassadors, to inform them about the growing Indonesian intervention in East Timor, and of the possibility of a Unilateral Declaration of Independence (UDI) by FRETILIN. Two factors were pushing us toward the UDI: one, the Portuguese failure to respond to our appeals for talks; two, Indonesia's military escalation. Atabai, a strategic mountain base, once considered an impenetrable FRETILIN fortress, had fallen to some 400 Indonesian troops. The FRETILIN garrison, led by Commander Aquiles, a valiant professional soldier trained by the Portuguese and son of a prestigious chief of Kelikai, fought back; but he was forced to retreat in the face of a more powerful Indonesian assault force, involving tanks and air cover. The loss of Atabai was a crushing blow to our morale. I got the news in Canberra by telephone from Alkatiri. He tried to appear unshaken, but it was obvious to me that things were turning ugly.

The tentative date for the UDI had been set for December 1, 1975. December 1 was a symbolic date. It was on that day in 1640 that a group of Portuguese noblemen overthrew the Felipes dynasty and thus ended Spain's 60-year domination of Portugal. Though I disagreed with the idea of a UDI, at least at that stage, my mission was to canvas support for such an eventuality. The fall of Atabai only hastened my comrades' resolve to proclaim East Timor's independence, and the date was moved to November 28. I discussed with Jim Dunn the prospects of the UDI, and I remember him suggesting that if we had to proclaim our country's independence unilaterally, we should wait a few more months. Jim was aware of the grave political and legal implications of a UDI. I took his words seriously and flew back to Darwin en route to Dili, determined to persuade my comrades to wait at least until January 1976.

On November 28, 1975, I was in Darwin. That evening after a relaxed meal, I learned via an ICRC radio communication that FRETILIN had made the UDI and established the Democratic Republic of East Timor (DRET). I flew to Dili the next day in a chartered aircraft. On my arrival I was informed that I had been named Minister for External Relations and Information in the new, and first ever, cabinet of an independent, free East Timor. I was 25 years old, probably the youngest and the least experienced cabinet minister in the world!

I accepted the post without great enthusiasm, resenting the fact that I had not been consulted. What I wanted most then was to go back to journalism. A driver had been sent to pick me up, and I asked him to take me along the bay. I needed to contemplate the ocean, inhale the fresh breeze from the sea, and absorb the beauty of the mountains beyond Dili, the Fatukama hills to the east. I wanted to retain, with a last look, the magic beauty of my beloved island. It seemed as if I already knew I was going to lose it. What an irony! I had dreamed and fought for this day; and yet Dili did not have an air of festivity. There were no ceremonies marking the birth of our new nation. I could not help remembering that just a couple of years earlier, almost the whole town of 30,000 would turn out on the Square of Henry "The Navigator" to watch the ritual Sunday afternoon of the lowering of the Portuguese flag. Now Dili was deserted. No foreign dignitaries had been invited to attend the UDI. Adam Malik, the Indonesian Foreign Minister, was conspicuously absent. He had told me: "I'll come to Timor for your independence celebrations!" in June 1974, when we had met at his home in Jakarta. *"Que grande filho da puta"* (what a son of a bitch), I thought out loud, and the driver turned around wondering who I was talking about. Lest he think I was referring to one of our leaders, I explained to him that the subject of my thoughts was Adam Malik and his government.

Looking toward the island of goats, Atauro, some 15 miles across the channel, I thought of Governor Lemos Pires and his troops, all waiting for orders to abandon the last overseas bastion of Portuguese sovereignty. They knew it was only a matter of days before the Indonesians would launch their long-expected invasion. The words of Captain Ramos, the Portuguese intelligence chief in East Timor, echoed in my mind. He had been asked by an Australian journalist about the Portuguese response to an Indonesian intervention and had answered nonchalantly: "Come on in!" Were all Portuguese civilian and military leaders that insensitive, and irresponsible? I knew Lemos Pires well enough to think highly of him, but his hands were tied by his bosses in Lisbon, President Costa Gomes and Prime Minister Vasco Goncalves, who had already demonstrated their negligence towards the whole Timor drama. Almeida Santos, chief architect of the East Timor decolonization process, had told me one evening in October 1975, in his hotel room when we were reviewing the situation in East Timor: "The Indonesians might kill 500 or so FRETILIN elements . . . this would resolve the problem."

Dili was strangely quiet that afternoon. The streets were empty. What had happened was simple: many people had gone to the mountains, looking for protection in the tropical forests. Dili's strange, oppressive emptiness smothered the joy of our historical hour, the hour we severed the umbilical cord that for centuries had tied us up to a backward colonial power.

I was taken to the hotel "Turismo" to be on hand for the journalists and NGO representatives. I left our humble palm tree house for the classy hotel a few yards from the beach; this kept me away from mother and the rest of the family, a situation that aroused in me feelings of guilt.

I put on the same navy blue suit I had worn when I left for Mozambique in 1970, and rushed to the colonial mansion that used to be the residence of Portuguese governors. The mansion had not been occupied by FRETILIN until that time, nor were other Portuguese or foreign properties seized. It was our mark of civility in the midst of our revolution. Apart from the anarchy that reigned in the first days of the civil war in August 1975, violence, looting and inter-tribal fighting were absent on independence day. There was not one case of looting, even in the remotest mountain villages. There was no power vacuum and no anarchy, contrary to Indonesian propaganda. After the civil war caused by UDT's August coup, FRETILIN had managed to establish a functioning, stable administration throughout the country. Foreign governments that wanted proof that such a "backward, primitive people" could stand on their own feet needed only to look at the period of FRETILIN interregnum, between September and November 1975.

The swearing-in ceremony was probably the most low-key, somber and modest of any such ritual anywhere in the world. Because of the threat of an Indonesian invasion, only a handful of foreign correspondents were still around. I saw Michael Richardson, by far the best Australian reporter covering Southeast Asia; Jill Jolliffe, a militant Trotskyist working as a stringer for a number of Australian newspapers; and David Scott, representing Australian NGOs. David inspired confidence in me and all FRETILIN leaders the moment we met him. Time only reinforced our first impression of that mild-mannered, good-hearted, wonderful man. The only foreigner who could be mistaken for a Western military attache was our old friend, Samuel Kruger, proudly wearing his medals earned in battles 30 years back. A Jew of German extraction, Samuel fought in Guadalcanal during World War II, and chose East Timor for quiet retirement.

One after another, we all read the oath of allegiance to the people, the Central Committee of FRETILIN and the new Constitution. A few hundred people looked on and applauded without great enthusiasm from the gardens of the palace. After the ceremony, we celebrated with a modest banquet. Xavier do Amaral, FRETILIN and DRET first President, was driven in the Portuguese Governor's official black Mercedes. That was the first time we took possession of Portuguese properties. Xavier, a humble man of modest origins and habits, looked uneasy in the limousine.

The next day, the newly formed DRET cabinet held its first meeting in the *Palacia das Reparticões*, our version of the State Department. The meeting was presided over by Nicolau Lobato in his role as Prime Minister. Xavier had not been asked to the meeting, since the Constitution did not require the Head of State to attend meetings of the Council of Ministers. However, Xavier's absence was also a clear indication of his declining importance. Nicolau was the unquestioned leader by then, even though Xavier was still immensely popular. The meeting dealt with four pressing items: (a) the deteriorating military situation and the pending Indonesian invasion; (b) measures to be taken for the evacuation of the remaining civilian population; (c) the defense of the city in order to slow the enemy progress into the interior; (d) the urgency of sending a delegation to the United Nations and the world at large to gain support for DRET.

It was decided that Mari Alkatiri, State Minister for Political Affairs, Rogerio Lobato, our quixotic Defense Minister, and myself, should leave the country and join three other FRETILIN leaders already overseas: Abilio Araujo, a Lisbon-trained economist who had been appointed State Minister for Economic and Social Affairs; his wife, Guilhermina, also an economist, appointed my Deputy for Economic Relations; and Roque Rodrigues, a psychologist, Ambassador-designate to Mozambique.

To me fell the task of arranging for our departure. This proved to be a challenge. The Australian government, forewarned of the invasion by the Indonesians, had ordered the evacuation of all Australians and banned all flights from Darwin to East Timor. I phoned an Australian charter company that had inaugurated flights between Dili and Darwin. We had given them exclusive rights and they were happy with us. However, they had received orders not to make any more flights to Dili, though they told me they were willing to fly us out if we could secure the necessary clearance. I phoned the Foreign Affairs Department in Canberra and explained the whole problem. They asked: what kinds of passports were we travelling on? How long did we intend to stay in Australia? What was our next destination?

I entertained little hope that we would be able to leave the country, and thus began to make preparations for the mountains. I donned fatigues and boots, checked the formidable "G3," packed cameras with loads of 35mm film, gathered note pads, malaria tablets, etc.

When all foreign nationals were evacuated at the end of November, Roger East, an Australian free-lance reporter, refused to leave. Roger had come to East Timor at my invitation in October, leaving behind a well-paid job as Public Relations Officer.

I had told Roger about my idea of starting up a news agency, to be called "East Timor News Agency" or simply ETNA. I viewed such an agency as an indispensable instrument of our struggle, especially since ANTARA, the Indonesian news agency, was flooding the world with misinformation and outright lies about the situation in East Timor. I gave Roger *carte blanche* to run the agency, and secured for him access to all FRETILIN leaders and daily briefings on the military situation, as well as off-the-record analyses of our plans to deal with the coming invasion. To launch ETNA, I worked out a simple scheme: I arranged an exclusive interview for Roger with six FRETILIN soldiers who had been in Balibo and actually witnessed the fall of the town and the killing of the five Australian newsmen by Indonesian troops. No other journalist had such a privilege, and Roger scooped everybody else. The next day, his bylines were featured front-page in most Australian newspapers, and ETNA began to be quoted. The Reuters boss in Sydney fired an angry telex to his stringer in Dili for missing the story! The stringer justified her failure with the charge that ETNA was a semi-official agency for FRETILIN. Within days, newspapers that had already commissioned Roger to work for them sent telexes terminating his contract. Reuters mounted a campaign to discredit Roger and our agency. I remember seeing Roger visibly hurt by this setback, particularly since the back-stabbing was carried out by a fellow journalist. In retrospect, I believe the whole incident could have been avoided had I acted more sensibly by inviting the Reuters stringer to the interview.

In the days before the invasion, when all other foreign correspondents had left the country, Roger was flooded with requests for stories. Even the Sydney bureau chief for Reuters phoned Roger, pleading with him to be their special correspondent. I was with him at the time and heard him saying: "I will file for you, but I am doing it for the Timorese, not for you." Roger was driven by a profound sense of a mission. He was not a FRETILIN partisan as his detractors claimed. He cared about the Timorese and felt very strongly that the Australian public ought to know the truth. He was angry at his government's cowardice and connivance with Indonesia.

When I was preparing for what I thought would be my trip to the mountains, I suggested to Roger that he take along a rifle for his own protection. He refused, and holding his pen told me with a smile: "This is my gun. It's more powerful than this gun of yours. Gee, Jose, be careful, you might hurt yourself." And he cracked up with laughter.

Finally, a plane landed in Dili on December 4, 1975. Alkatiri, Rogerio and I left for Darwin.

Roger was not so fortunate. He was killed on the first day of the invasion. The circumstances of his death have never been clearly established, but I managed over the years to reconstruct his murder through interviews with people who actually witnessed the invasion. According to these sources, Roger was caught in the Radio Marconi building trying to send dispatches to Australia. He was handcuffed and dragged into the street, beaten with rifle butts and taken to the harbor, where many other people, mainly women and children, were being held. Nicolau Lobato's wife was among the 50 or so captives lined up along the harbor's edge. Always shy and withdrawn, she was never involved in her husband's politics. Her arms were tied and she was praying, staring at the blue sky. One after another, the women, men and children were shot, their bodies falling into the sea. According to my informant, who is still in Jakarta, an Indonesian officer shot Roger point-blank in the head from very close range. The officer was so close that Roger managed to spit in his face, my source told me. The next day, the bodies washed up on the beaches. The murder of Roger was never investigated by the Australian Government, nor by his fellow journalists.

The invasion took place while my travel companions and I were in the air, somewhere between Asia and Europe. We landed in Lisbon on the afternoon of December 8, 1975. Uncle Armando, whom I had heard about but never actually met, since this was the first time I had set foot in the capital of the empire, met us at the plane. He greeted us with a formal Portuguese "nicety": *"Os filhos da puta invadiram"* (the sons of bitches invaded), my uncle announced with a sad look on his face.

In Lisbon Abilio and I applied for US visas at the American Embassy. There was a delay of a few days, and in that tense atmosphere, we were inclined to think that the delay was a CIA "dirty trick" to delay our arrival in New York for the Security Council meeting on East Timor. I cabled Ambassador Salim A. Salim of Tanzania, then Chairman of the Special Committee on Decolonization, and pleaded with him to intervene. The next day we got the visas. In New York, we were told by the representative of a friendly country that had there been further delay, the matter would have been raised on the floor of the General Assembly.

Abilio and I arrived in New York City on December 11, 1975. I had never seen snow in my life, except in Christmas cards, or in my local church decorations in the tropical forest of Soibada during the Christmas season. A driver from the Permanent Mission of Guinea-Bissau picked us up at JFK airport. He took us to our hotel room and checked the locks, closed the door and tried to force it open, checked the windows, looked outside, under the beds to make sure there were no wires or bombs. This was our welcome to New York.

1975 was an eventful year. It seemed that a revolutionary tide was sweeping away the last vestiges of colonialism. American influence around the world had been severely weakened. In the United Nations, the Non-Aligned Movement, the Organization of African Unity and the progressive camp had gained considerable influence. A few issues clouded our collective optimism. King Hassan II had taken upon himself the mission of recreating a Greater Morocco at the expense of the Saharawi people, and sent some 300,000 unarmed subjects marching into the desert of Western Sahara to reclaim it for the throne.

The Indonesian invasion of East Timor set off violent demonstrations in Holland, the home of some 50,000 South Moluccans who had their own grievances against the "Javanese colonialists." A campaign of terror was unleashed against Indonesian diplomats; the Embassy at The Hague was occupied by radical separatists; a train was hijacked; innocent Dutch school children were taken hostage. In Port Moresby, students burned the Indonesian Embassy's flag. In Australia, dock workers refused to service Indonesian vessels or vessels carrying goods to and from Indonesia.

Guinea-Bissau was the first of the former Portuguese African colonies to set up a Permanent Mission in New York. It was headed by Gil Fernandes, a charming man, well liked by everyone, particularly the ladies. His deputy was Arnaldo Araujo: young and bright, and like Gil fluent in six languages. The Guinea-Bissau Mission became operational headquarters for Abilio and me during the Security Council debates.

Gil and Arnaldo were helpful, providing us with logistical support, introductions to government delegations and thorough briefings on the workings of the UN. What impressed me the most was their strict respect for our own independence, as they scrupulously avoided interference in our work. Arnaldo was at pains to avoid being seen as directing our activities, and was very sensitive about how we would be perceived at the UN. One afternoon when Abilio and I were meeting with Chinese Permanent Representative Huang Hua, Arnaldo signaled to us that another meeting was awaiting us. However, that was not the case. We had been with Huang Hua for over an hour, and Arnaldo was worried that the Russians might notice such an intimate relationship.

The Mozambiquans impressed us with their strict observance of discipline, and treated us with real warmth and deference. Armando Panguene, Shafurdin Khan and Carlos Lobo were among the Mozambiquans we met in New York at that time. Khan was an old hand at the UN, having been FRELIMO's Representative for many years in the 1960s and early 1970s. Khan gave the impression of being a "liberal," while Panguene appeared to be a militant Marxist. A code of ethics verging on puritanism was the mark of FRELIMO leaders and cadres.

The Guinea-Bissau Mission also housed the staff of the Cape Verdian delegation, led by a tall, elegant diplomat, Amaro da Luz. There I also met Elisio de Figueiredo, the MPLA Representative who later became Angola's Permanent Representative to the United Nations. The Mozambiquan delegation found a provisional work space in the Tanzanian Mission. Tanzania was FRELIMO's rear base during the liberation struggle. When Idi Amin's troops invaded Tanzanian territory in the late 1970s, Mozambiquan troops joined their Tanzanian comrades when Nyerere ordered the retaliation which eventually led to the ouster of that African monster. In Zimbabwe, Mozambiquan troops fought alongside ZANU forces against Ian Smith's army. Now, in the 1980s, when Mozambique is engulfed in a war of destabilization fomented by South Africa, Tanzanian and Zimbabwean advisers and troops come to the aid of their ally. Such solidarity is rare indeed!

The five Portuguese-speaking African countries have a special understanding of the Timor problem. Critics on the right take the simplistic view that only ideological affinity between FRETILIN and FRELIMO explains Mozambique's staunch support for East Timor. This ignores the fact that Mozambique—and for that matter all five former Portuguese colonies— supports equally other anti-colonial struggles. Having fought for their own independence, the newly-independent countries have not forgotten that their victories owed a lot to international solidarity.

It was behind prison walls that some Angolan leaders first learned about the plight of their brothers in East Timor. Following a bloody rebellion against the Portuguese in East Timor, in June, 1959, leaders of the rebellion were shipped off to exile and prison in Angola and Mozambique. Some Timorese found themselves in the same prison as Angolan rebels who are today members of the government in Luanda. It was this common suffering and struggle against the same oppressor that brought the liberation movements in Portuguese Africa emotionally and politically close to the struggle of the Timorese.

Our relations with ZANU were forged under similar circumstances. We found sanctuary in Mozambique for our overseas operations after the invasion of East Timor. ZANU found in Mozambique the same kind of rear base. In Maputo we crossed paths a million times with ZANU leaders and cadres. We did not hesitate then to choose ZANU as our natural ally instead of other groups. Mugabe and other ZANU leaders and cadres learned a great deal about our struggle during the years of their presence in Mozambique.

The same relationship is being forged between FRETILIN and other liberation movements in Africa. With SWAPO of Namibia, the ANC of South Africa and the POLISARIO FRONT of Western Sahara, we strive to build solid relationships based on our common struggle. In our geographic region, we have fraternal relations with the New Peoples' Army (NPA) in the Philippines and with the independentist Kanaky Party in New Caledonia, as well as with the indigenous minority peoples of Australia and New Zealand. Before Vanuatu's independence, FRETILIN had long established links with the *Vanuaku Pati*, led by Rev. Walter Lini.

Five days before the invasion, opening the debate in the Fourth Committee of the General Assembly, the Portuguese Representative took issue for the first time with the introduction into East Timor of "highly sophisticated military equipment" and stated that his government "strongly repudiates and condemns any military intervention in the Territory."[1] The Australian Representative also addressed the issue with an appeal for talks between the political parties and Portugal as offering "the best hope of bringing the conflict to an end." He did not have the courage to point the finger at the Indonesians who were poised for the invasion. Speakers in the Fourth Committee ignored mounting evidence of Indonesian interference in the political process in the territory, and escalating armed intervention across the land border. Fighting in East Timor was still attributed to the local political parties—even though FRETILIN was in full control of the situation, and the only fighting taking place was along the border, involving regular Indonesian troops and the nationalist forces. The People's Republic of China and Mozambique made strong denunciations of Indonesian preparations for the invasion. Speaking in the General Assembly, the then Minister for Foreign Affairs of Guyana, Fred Wills, also sounded the alarm.

The Indonesian Representative entered the debate in the Fourth Committee with a speech that was indicative of what the next Indonesian move would be. He talked at length about "geographic proximity and ethnic kinship" and his country's "concern about peace and stability in Portuguese Timor, not only in Indonesia's interests, but also in the interests of Southeast Asia as a whole." He went on to paint a classic scenario for a "humanitarian" intervention:

> As a result of the fighting, Indonesia is confronted with serious difficulties: thousands of refugees have to be fed and cared for; people favoring integration are being terrorized and are demanding that Indonesia act to protect them; and incursions by armed bands into Indonesian territory have made it necessary for Indonesia to take appropriate action to prevent territorial violations and the harassment of its people.[2]

The Indonesian Representative was constructing a case of distortions, exaggerations and outright lies reminiscent of Hitler's pretext for the *blitzkrieg* against Poland.

On December 7, 1975, Indonesia invaded East Timor. The next day, as the Fourth Committee continued consideration of the Timor question, it had before it a Portuguese official communique denouncing the invasion:

> . . . On 7 December, Indonesian naval, air and land forces launched offensive actions against Portuguese Timor, and against the town of Dili, where naval bombardment had taken place and troops had been landed.[3]

The Portuguese Council of Ministers decided to break diplomatic relations with Indonesia, and asked for an urgent meeting of the Security Council.

As members of the Fourth Committee continued to review the Timor situation, a number of draft resolutions began to circulate. Some countries allied with Indonesia made frantic efforts to soften the impact of Indonesia's actions. Most active in this group were India, Japan and Malaysia. Their draft ignored the invasion that had just taken place and attempted to place the blame on Portuguese negligence and lack of unity among the Timorese political parties. However, the pro-Indonesia lobby was forced to withdraw their text. Another draft, cosponsored by Algeria, Cuba, Guyana, Senegal, Sierra Leone, Tanzania, and Trinidad and Tobago, became the only text put forward for a vote in the Committee. It was adopted by a roll-call vote of 69 to 11, with 38 abstentions. Not satisfied with their first clumsy effort to dilute criticism of Indonesia, Mauritania, Saudi Arabia, the Philippines and Thailand made a last minute attempt to introduce amendments to the Algerian draft. However, the Committee rejected the amendments.

The Committee report was forwarded to the General Assembly, which began consideration of the Timor issue on December 12, and adopted the Algerian draft that same day with a vote of 72 to 10, with 43 abstentions. A separate vote was taken on operative paragraph four, which "strongly deplores the military intervention of the armed forces of Indonesia in Portuguese Timor." The result of this separate vote was indicative of the hypocrisy of most of the Arab bloc and Western nations.

In the United Nations lexicon, each word has its own political dimensions. To "condemn" requires more courage than to "deplore." Member States do not associate themselves with resolutions containing the words "condemn" or "deplore" if the targeted country is a friend and ally, no matter how serious its actions. The invasion of East Timor by Indonesia was a clear-cut act of armed aggression, contrary to the UN Charter and International Law. Yet, the invasion was only "deplored." The Algerian draft avoided the stronger word "condemn" in an effort to win over as many votes as possible. Still that was not mild enough for the Western countries, Japan, the ASEAN bloc and the Arab group, who would have preferred a complete silence on the matter. Faced with a blatant act of armed aggression by a Moslem country that is at the same time an anti-communist regime with close economic ties to the West, 59 countries voted to "deplore" the invasion, while 11 voted no, and 55 abstained. The main culprits were the Western industrialized countries, notably the US, Japan, Canada and the EEC members. Being major trading partners of Indonesia, and the regime's main source of economic aid as well as military hardware, the West could have had a significant influence had they chosen to support UN action against Indonesia. The Arab group, with the notable exceptions of Algeria and Democratic Yemen, displayed their double standards by siding openly with a fellow Moslem country. The Algerian draft was mild compared with the countless anti-Israel motions introduced each year in the General Assembly by the Arab group.

The Algerian draft was adopted as G.A.Res.3485(XXX). It called on the Security Council to "take urgent action to protect the territorial integrity of Portuguese Timor and the inalienable right of its people to self-determination." In pursuance of this important provision and the Portuguese complaint, the Security Council began consideration of the Timor question on December 15, a week after the invasion. I requested a couple of days delay because Abilio and I had just arrived in New York and had had no time to prepare a statement to deliver before the Council.

Though the General Assembly vote was discouraging, this was nevertheless the first time that a leading member of the anti-colonial bloc in the UN found itself the target of attack. Indonesia was, for the first time in its more than 30 years as an independent country, singled out for the attacks usually directed at Portugal, Israel, South Africa, etc. This was politically embarrassing for the Suharto regime, but it was no more than an embarrassment, since Indonesia knew that it still could count on the US, Canada, Japan, the EEC countries and the conservative Arab group for support. The Indonesian army's weaponry, ammunition, spare parts, transport vehicles, combat helicopters and planes, plus economic assistance for its sagging economy, came all from the West. Thus, the Western decision to abstain, instead of condemning Jakarta's actions—even when the aggression was perpetrated against a territory still under the jurisdiction of a member of the NATO alliance—could not have sent a clearer signal to the hawks in Jakarta that whatever they wished to do in East Timor was their business.

An abstention in the General Assembly can send different signals. It can mean that a Member State is reluctant to take sides on a controversial issue involving two friendly or equally powerful countries; it can indicate a studied neutrality that might prove useful in future conciliation efforts; or it can signal a mild disapproval of the actions of a friendly country, and a desire to allow the resolution to be carried. When the US abstains on an anti-Israel motion in the Security Council or General Assembly, it means to show its anger or frustration over Israeli actions, and to safeguard its own interests and credibility with the moderate Arab camp. The Western abstention on East Timor was based on two basic considerations: a desire not to offend the pro-Western regime of Gen. Suharto; and, at the same time, not to offend their lesser European ally, Portugal. The Timorese people themselves and their rights did not enter into the diplomatic equation.

In the meantime, back in East Timor, fierce fighting was raging in many parts of the country and in the streets of Dili. Contrary to what one read at that time in *The New York Times* and other Western publications, the territory had not been so quickly "pacified." At least 400 Indonesian paratroopers were shot dead before reaching the ground on the first day of the invasion. Many others fell into the sea and drowned. The FRETILIN military leadership had not planned a strategic defense of the city, but had left behind about 200 special troops to inflict as many casualties as possible on the enemy. Close-range combat took place in the streets of Dili, with Indonesian troops becoming easy prey of FRETILIN forces firing from inside the concrete buildings. There was also shooting between rival

Indonesian army units. Many others were too busy ransacking houses and Chinese-owned shops. A Timorese who actually witnessed the invasion and accompanied the invading forces, described what he saw on December 7:

> I just couldn't believe it. I was too terrified and shocked then to laugh, but thinking about it now I must say it was comic. I saw Indonesian troops ripping off windows and doors from the shops and houses and carrying them on their backs to the ships. They took everything they could find: radios, fans, air conditioners, refrigerators, canned food, beer, etc. . . . I saw many of them shot dead. They couldn't run or fight back because they had their hands full. I saw a FRETILIN soldier standing in the street, aiming his old Mauser in a very relaxed manner, and when a looting Indonesian soldier stopped, scared, he smiled and fired a single bullet into his head. Of course, it was not all looting and not all comic. More tragic things like rape, cold-blooded assassinations of women and children and Chinese shop owners took place before my eyes.

By Christmas, Dili was finally secured after the landing of 10,000 fresh Indonesian troops. By then, there were in all of East Timor some 30,000 Indonesian troops. The bulk of Indonesia's air force and navy, its tanks and armored cars, had been commited to the invasion and were now tied down in East Timor, poised for a long campaign against FRETILIN forces.

The day after our arrival in New York, Abilio and I met with the members of the Security Council to seek support for effective action against Indonesia. Third World members of the Council were generally favorable to our position; in December 1975 these were Costa Rica, Guyana, Iraq, Mauritania, Cameroun and Tanzania. Salim A. Salim of Tanzania and Jackson (now Minister for Foreign Affairs) of Guyana were our most effective allies. Other members we knew would lean to our side were China, France, Italy, Sweden, the Soviet Union and Byelorussia, and the United Kingdom—whose Ambassador, Ivor Richard, a fat chain-smoker lawyer, was President of the Council during the month of December. We were only worried about the US.

Abilio and I met frequently with Salim, Jackson and Huang Hua to discuss strategy. Huang Hua was acting on instructions from Beijing to give us the strongest possible backing. He treated us to lavish meals at the Chinese Mission near Lincoln Center, during which he would lecture us, not on Indonesia but on "Russian hegemonism." Time and again we would hear Chinese diplomats telling us: "Beware of the revisionists." They also counseled us against compromises with the Indonesians and advised us to persevere in the armed struggle as the most effective road toward our liberation. Whenever there was a suggestion for rewording of a certain paragraph or a particular word into a more palatable form, the Chinese would sound the alarm: "Beware of the social-imperialists. This is a Russian trick!"

There was, however, no Russian trick. The Russians simply wanted to keep a careful distance from the whole problem. Abilio and I met once with Yacob Malik of the Soviet Union. Unlike the hospitable Chinese, the Russians never invited our delegation to their Mission for a meeting, let alone for a meal. Malik received us in one of the rooms adjacent to the Security Council chamber. As had become customary, our talking points included a good deal of praise for our host and the role his country and people have played in the struggle for independence of colonial countries and peoples. After this introduction, Abilio and I would move on to the more practical goals of the meeting: in this case, to secure Soviet support. Yacob Malik was hardly listening. He was half-asleep, only occasionally opening his eyes to look at me for a moment before going back to his nap. In the end, our refined host woke up, and uttered a few words: "Well . . . we'll support you." Having said this, without even a polite handshake, he stood up and left the room.

Under rule 39[*] of the Security Council, I was invited to speak during the Council's deliberations. The Indonesians brought along their puppets: Mario Carrascalao, a former UDT leader; Guilherme Goncalves, the native chief of Atsabe and a prominent APODETI leader; and Jose Martins, leader of an obscure political party called KOTA.

Both Portugal and Indonesia addressed the Council. The Portuguese Representative Jose Galvao Teles made an excellent presentation which he concluded by urging the Security Council to:

> . . . first, condemn Indonesia for the aggression it has committed; secondly, demand the immediate cessation of all acts of violence and intimidation against the people of Portuguese Timor; thirdly, demand the withdrawal of all occupation forces from the territory of Timor; and fourthly, attempt to restore, through adequate processes and machinery and, in particular, by resorting to the good offices of the Secretary General—conditions to allow free accession by the people of East Timor to self-determination and independence.[4]

The Indonesian Representative Anwar Sani, a silver-haired former Dutch colonial official, did his best to portray his country's aggression as a sort of mercy endeavor to save the "backward people" of East Timor, and offered this simple logic for his government's actions:

[*]Rule 39 provides: "The Security Council may invite members of the Secretariat or other persons, whom it considers competent for the purposes, to supply it with information or to give other assistance in examining matters within its competence."

Portuguese Timor is part of the island of Timor; the other part is Indonesian territory. Timor is an island of the Indonesian archipelago.
The population of Portuguese Timor is of the same ethnic origin as the
population in the Indonesian part.[5]

Not surprisingly, the Malaysian delegation requested to speak during the
Security Council deliberations. The Malaysian Representative, Mr. Mo-
hamed Khir, tried to take precedence over us in the list of speakers, even
though we had submitted our request earlier and were an interested party. A
staff member of the Secretariat approached us in the Council chamber to
suggest that, if we didn't mind, Malaysia, as a sovereign state, should speak
before us. Abilio objected immediately and we remained firm in our
position, forcing the Malaysian Representative to stick to the original order
of speakers. Malaysia was an early supporter of Indonesia's clandestine
operations against East Timor in mid and late 1975. It supplied light
weapons that could not be traced back to Indonesia.

Malaysia's support for Indonesia's take-over of East Timor was calculated, for Malaysia itself coveted oil rich Brunei and was counting on
Jakarta's blessing. When Johari addressed the Council he knew he was
lying when he attempted to justify Indonesia's invasion of East Timor as an
act necessitated by "months of lawlessness and bloody fighting."[6] He
should have told the Security Council that his own government contributed
to the "months of lawlessness" in East Timor with its support for Jakarta's
clandestine operations in 1975 designed precisely to create a situation
favorable for an Indonesian invasion.

Australia, though not a member of the Security Council, felt compelled to
join in the debate. Australian Representative Ralph Harry should have been
decorated for his efforts to avoid offending his Indonesian friends. He never
called the invasion an invasion or called Indonesian troops by their real
names. Instead, he resorted to devious diplomatic language to explain that
his country was "confident that the Indonesian elements would withdraw as
soon as fighting between the political parties had ceased."[7] One needed
considerable poise to listen to such absurdities in silence. The Australians,
like the Americans and all other Western countries, knew in great detail
about the whole Indonesian campaign long before the actual invasion, and
did not have the slightest doubt that the whole conflict in East Timor had
been created by their Indonesian friends. Yet, Ralph Harry called
thousands of regular Indonesian troops "elements," and the vicious war
unleashed against the people of East Timor by the Indonesian army
"fighting between the political parties" of East Timor!

Salim of Tanzania made a brilliant speech after the vote. He said his
delegation would have preferred "a clearer and unequivocal resolution,"
but decided to support the text:

In the conviction that if fully implemented, the Council's decision would make an important contribution to the restoration of the conditions conducive to enabling the people of Timor to exercise their legitimate right to self-determination, freedom and independence in accordance with General Assembly resolution 1514(XV).[8]

Strong support for FRETILIN with strident denunciations of Indonesia came from Huang Hua of China. He accused Indonesia of "naked aggression against the Democratic Republic of East Timor" and stated that "Indonesia's acts constitute a gross violation of the purposes and principles of the Charter."[9] Soviet Representative Yacob Malik used milder language. He did not even mention Indonesia by name, and expressed his delegation's objection to "outside intervention" in the affairs of East Timor. He added that "the USSR would support any constructive measures of the Council which accorded with the Declaration on decolonization and with resolution 3485(XXX) which would be aimed at restoring a normal situation in the area and ensuring peace."[10] Malik outdid Ralph Harry of Australia in his efforts to spare Indonesia from any direct criticism, lest the generals in Jakarta get offended.

During the week-long Security Council debate, the Japanese delegation was conspicuous for its frantic activities in support of Indonesia. It was clear that Japan, a leading investor in Indonesia and a major importer of Indonesian oil, was more interested in currying favors with Jakarta than in serving the cause of peace in East Timor. I watched with growing frustration the Japanese movements around the Council chamber as they lobbied different delegations on behalf of Indonesia. On December 22, as the Council was closing the debate on East Timor, I requested a second hearing to supply additional information. I could not resist the temptation to use the occasion to vent my anger at the Japanese delegation by touching on the wounds of World War II, and said:

> May I tell the Government of Japan that in helping to put and end to the conflict, it could repair the damages and loss of lives, estimated at 40,000, suffered by the people of East Timor in the course of World War II.

Mr. Saito of Japan immediately exercised his right of reply:

> I would like to make a brief statement in regard to the remarks made by the Representative of FRETILIN. First of all, he said that 40,000 Timorese had been killed in the course of World War II. Since I don't have evidence of this figure, I cannot admit it. I reserve therefore the right to know whether this is true or not.

Secondly, today's Japan is a peaceful nation. We do not have armed forces for this kind of war. Therefore, even if Mr. Horta persists in what he said that the Japanese army had done, the Japan of today has nothing to do with it.

Thirdly, even if his remarks are based on statistics, they have nothing to do with the question that we are examining at this moment . . . [11]

Mr. Saito's response was clumsy. It is one thing to reject *criminal* responsibility for crimes committed by a regime some 40 years ago; but quite another to dismiss a nation's collective *moral* responsibility. In any case, my remarks were unnecessary and raised questions about my tact, to say the least.

The US delegation maintained a low profile during the entire debate. It did not want the issue to get any bigger and was at pains to avoid offending either of its allies. Indonesia had invaded a Portuguese territory with American-supplied weapons. Ford and Kissinger had been in Jakarta conferring with Suharto just hours before the invasion. Daniel P. Moynihan, one of the more liberal American Senators, was the US Chief Delegate to the UN at that time. In his book *A Dangerous Place*, published in 1978, Moynihan wrote:

> The United States wished things to turn out as they did, and worked to bring this about. The Department of State desired that the UN prove utterly ineffective in whatever measures it undertook. The task was given to me, and I carried it forward with no inconsiderable success. [12]

To hear Senator Moynihan, years later, castigating the UN for hypocrisy, one feels like reminding him of his own actions. Moynihan deserved credit indeed for the massive abstention in the General Assembly when the Algerian draft was voted on December 12. However, in the Security Council, the US could not but join with all other Council members in support of Res. 384 (1975), which was adopted unanimously on December 22. The US and the European members could not, as permanent members of the Security Council, have abstained on such a blatant case of armed aggression involving a NATO ally. The Security Council is a more visible body than the General Assembly, and positions taken there carry more significance and weight than in the General Assembly. Hence, the US, French and British votes in the Security Council were different from their votes in the General Assembly.

Security Council Res. 384 (1975) contained a number of important provisions. Operative paragraph one called upon "all states to respect the territorial integrity of East Timor, as well as the inalienable right of its people to self-determination in accordance with General Assembly resolution 1514(XV)." Operative paragraph two called upon "the Government of Indonesia to withdraw without delay all its forces from the Territory." An equally important provision is operative paragraph five, which:

... requests the Secretary-General to send urgently a special representative to East Timor for the purpose of making an on-the-spot assessment of the existing situation and of establishing contact with all parties in the Territory and all States concerned in order to ensure the implementation of the present resolution. [13]

Paragraph six requested the Secretary-General to "follow the implementation of the present resolution and, taking into account the report of his special representative, to submit recommendations to the Security Council as soon as possible." As I shall reveal later in the book, Kurt Waldheim basically ignored this provision, and let the issue be filed in the archives of the Council, where it still remains.

In accordance with operative paragraph five of S.C.Res.384 (1975), Waldheim appointed as his special representative Vittorio Winspeare Guicciardi, Director General of the United Nations office in Geneva, an official with the rank of Under-Secretary-General.

Guicciardi, a tall Italian diplomat, left for the region in the second week of January. Before his departure, I met with him and his staff in New York and briefed them on the situation in East Timor. I strongly urged them to visit FRETILIN-held areas, which I indicated on the map to the UN special envoy. Subsequently, after the departure of the mission for Jakarta, I was in constant touch with the liaison staff in New York. Guicciardi travelled through Lisbon on his way to Jakarta and met there with the then Portuguese Minister for Foreign Affairs, Major Melo Antunes, and the Minister for External Cooperation, Major Vitor Crespo. Lemos Pires, the last Portuguese Governor of East Timor, also briefed the UN team during their transit through Lisbon.

Guicciardi had assembled a small team of very able and dedicated international civil servants: Erik Jensen, a Special Assistant, of Danish and British ancestry but holding Malay citizenship and Gilberto Schlittler-Silva, a Political Officer, a Brazilian national. Both seemed serious and impartial, though I had some misgivings about Erik Jensen when I heard he carried a Malaysian passport. However, I believe he performed with impartiality. I trusted Gilberto because of his previous experience in handling the Portuguese African colonies, his Brazilian background which was an assurance of a better understanding of the aspirations of another Portuguese-speaking people, and his personal charm. A third member of the team was Harald Smaage, a Norwegian who was an Administrative Assistant handling communications and logistics.

Shortly after the adoption of Security Council Res. 384 (1975), the

Indonesians began a series of schemes to render the UN team's mission ineffective. On December 26, through the so-called "Provisional Government" in Dili, a puppet group set up by the Indonesians right after the invasion (the swearing-in of the "Provisional Government" took place on a warship anchored off Dili), a communication was sent to the Secretary-General requesting postponement of the visit. Indonesia had rejected the Security Council resolution, but it could not openly and formally oppose such a UN mission since it was arguing that only Indonesian "volunteers" were helping the "pro-Indonesia parties" in East Timor. The Indonesian authorities resorted then to the cover of a "Provisional Government" to act in their behalf.

From the outset, it was known that the UN mission was meant to fail. A senior UN official involved in the Timor affair in 1975-1976 told me that "Waldheim didn't want Guicciardi to succeed anyway and gave him no support whatsoever." Waldheim, a man preoccupied with reelection to his prestigious and well-paid job, had little time and thought for what he considered a "minor problem." In Waldheim's world, only the US and USSR really mattered, and both countries were on the Indonesian side one way or the other—one more directly involved, the other in a more subtle form. China, the only country of any status that was concerned about East Timor, was not friendly to Waldheim anyway.

Australia was anxious to have the issue buried in the archives of the United Nations bureaucracy. Portugal was not a Britain or France that a Kurt Waldheim had to worry about. Even if the Secretary-General felt strongly about the Timor problem, none of the major powers, with the sole exception of China, wanted his mission to succeed.

Though lacking real power, the Secretary-General has considerable moral authority and a number of devices available to him, provided by the Charter, that may strengthen his role if he has the political will to stick his neck out for an issue. But my impression of Waldheim from the moment I met him in 1975 was that he was a man who knew no principles, and cared little about the UN principles as enshrined in the Charter of which he was supposed to be the guardian.

As Guicciardi's party left for Indonesia early in January 1976, I left New York for Australia in order to be available for direct consultations with him. Darwin, usually a sleepy town, had become a little international diplomatic resort. Thousands of Timorese refugees had fled there during the civil war, and the atmosphere was tense. The scars of the civil war were still fresh and each refugee had his or her own atrocity story to tell. Most were UDT supporters and blamed FRETILIN for the civil war violence, forgetting that it was UDT that started the fight and the murder of FRETILIN supporters. I was quite familiar with the refugee horror stories in Darwin. Between August and November 1975, and particularly during the first few weeks of the civil war, I was completely alone in confronting the barrage of headlines of FRETILIN "atrocities," which proved to be greatly exaggerated; many stories were pure fabrication as I later verified. When I arrived in Darwin in January 1976, the climate had improved, but there was still tension in the air.

In Jakarta, Guicciardi met with President Suharto and Adam Malik. On January 19, he and his team flew to Kupang in West Timor where he met with members of the puppet "Provisional Government" who "happened to be there." As it turned out, these elements were in virtual detention in Kupang and were produced for the UN team as part of an effort to garner some semblance of legitimacy to a "Provisional Government" that existed only in name. The following day, the UN team flew to Oé-cussi, a Portuguese enclave in West Timor where no fighting had taken place, to Ataúro island and to Dili. The first two places were irrelevant for Guicciardi's mission, but were added to his itinerary solely for appearances. Otherwise, the Guicciardi mission would have visited only Dili, the capital, Manatuto and Baucau in a three-day fact-finding mission!

In his Report, Guicciardi said that "at the time the 'Provisional Government' did not deem it possible on technical and/or security grounds for me to visit other centres, roads being largely impassable."[14] What absolute nonsense, to say that it was impossible to travel by road to Remexio and Aileu, 40 and 60 kilometers from Dili, by road! If the UN team could arrange for a helicopter to fly to Manatuto and Baucau, why not use the same means to visit Lospalos, Same, Viqueque, Ossu, Bobonaro, etc.? These places were either under FRETILIN control or were the scenes of violent confrontation involving FRETILIN or Indonesian troops.

From Darwin I phoned Mrs. Tieng, a senior Political Officer in the UN, asking her to convey urgently to the mission a list of places I suggested they should visit. However, the message reached Guicciardi only when he was back in Jakarta. The places I suggested he visit each had an airstrip under FRETILIN control where the UN team could have landed: Suai and Same in the South coast region, Vikeke in the central region, and Con on the Northeastern coast. All four were within one or two hours by air from Darwin and could easily have been reached by light aircraft. But as Mr. Guicciardi stated in his report, neither the Australian nor the Indonesian Governments allowed "for security reasons, the use of, respectively, Australian and Indonesian aircraft and crews, or to clear flights of foreign aircraft from their Territories to East Timor."[15]

As soon as the Guicciardi team arrived in Darwin, I met with them and I was in constant touch with the group during their stay there, in an effort to bring the UN team to visit certain FRETILIN areas. Since the Australian Government was adamant in denying the UN team any logistical support, the Portuguese put at the disposal of the group one of its corvettes stationed in Darwin, which could carry us to the South coast of East Timor. I suggested that the UN team land in Betano, a small port still under

FRETILIN control. The area was free of any military activity at that time. The Indonesians, approached by Guicciardi to cooperate in the venture, responded with the following conditions:

> (1) The Portuguese vessel carrying the mission should fly the United Nations flag;
>
> (2) The sloop used to bring the mission ashore should also display the United Nations flag and be clearly marked "United Nations";
>
> (3) Only the members of the mission would be permitted to disembark;
>
> (4) The crew of the sloop would not be permitted to carry arms;
>
> (5) The Portuguese vessel would not be permitted to come within four nautical miles of the coast;
>
> (6) The Special Representative of the Secretary-General should notify in advance the "Provisional Government of East Timor" of the time and place of landing.[14]

Using the cover of a nonexistent Timorese "Provisional Government" the Indonesian military were dictating the terms under which the UN should discharge its mandate. To my knowledge, neither Waldheim nor Guicciardi protested. The Portuguese also accepted these conditions. I wondered how this "Provisional Government" made up of a few Timorese puppets would have the means to enforce the conditions it put forward had Guicciardi and the Portuguese gone ahead to Betano with the frigate. At that time, I was in constant touch with Alarico Fernandes, a FRETILIN leader in charge of Information and Security, by way of radio. As the Indonesians issued the conditions for the landing in Betano, they also rushed to the area. Alarico informed me of the landing in Betano of hundreds of Indonesian soldiers, and of heavy naval bombardment of the surrounding area. The Indonesians were attempting to create a *cordon sanitaire* before Guicciardi's visit.

FRETILIN leaders and troops had been assembled in Same and were making preparations to descend to Betano. Though I realized the importance of a meeting between FRETILIN and Guicciardi, I was worried about the risks my comrades were facing. They would have to fight their way to Betano to meet Guicciardi, and they would face certain slaughter if they attempted to break through the Indonesian lines. The risks were too high, I told Alarico over the radio.

In the meantime, Indonesian troops had captured the four airstrips I had proposed to Guicciardi for a possible landing by light aircraft. After the capture of the airstrips, the Indonesians, again through the "Provisional Government," issued an invitation to Guicciardi on February 13 to "visit Suai, Same, Vikeke and Lautem" emphasizing now that these places were under "its territorial jurisdiction."[15] A week earlier, all four places had been under FRETILIN control, and had the Australian Government permitted a light aircraft to take off from Darwin, the UN envoy would have accomplished his mission by meeting with FRETILIN leaders face-to-face.

In a hotel room in Darwin, I discussed with Guicciardi the problems that impeded the full implementation of S.C.Res.384 (1975). The UN team had been in Darwin for almost a week now, and Guicciardi was growing impatient. He urged me to issue a statement admitting to FRETILIN's "inability" to arrange a venue for his visit. I had to make recourse to all my self-control not to explode in outrage. Guicciardi knew all along that if anyone should be blamed for his failure to visit FRETILIN-held areas, it was the Indonesian Government, with Australian connivance. Yet, in spite of this, Guicciardi opted to blame the weakest pawn in the game for his failure.

I issued a statement on February 6 putting the blame on the Indonesians, but avoided criticizing Guicciardi or the Australians. Guicciardi, however, was less generous to me. He issued his own statement in which he suggested that this mission was terminated because "Mr. Horta had left Darwin."[16] I left Darwin only because Guicciardi had told me there was nothing else he could do. He had to fly to Sydney on February 7 to meet with Waldheim, who was visiting Australia. I also headed for Sydney and met with Waldheim, and pleaded with him to continue his good offices with a view toward resolving the problem.

Guicciardi's mission was an utter failure for him personally, for Waldheim, and for the UN. The UN team spent a total of three days in East Timor. Guicciardi acknowledged in his report that he "went to certain places only and was unable to travel widely." Yet, he thought it appropriate to write that "there were signs of a functioning administration, and schools as well as health services were working." Guicciardi took at face value what the Indonesians showed him. There was no functioning administration, since the bulk of the civil servants had fled to Australia or Portugal during the civil war, while many others left for the safety of the mountains. Only a handful of educated Timorese stayed behind, and among them many were murdered or imprisoned. The entire school system was paralyzed. At the time of Guicciardi's visit, at least two-thirds of the country and population were living in FRETILIN areas. I am not suggesting that Guicciardi lied; I am suggesting that he was gullible. The fact is that the Indonesians rounded up children and adults to sit in classrooms and offices and shout pro-Indonesian slogans during Guicciardi's visit.

The Indonesians were determined from the outset to sabotage the UN mission. The generals were even considering sinking the sloop carrying the UN team if Guicciardi went ahead with the idea of traveling to Betano on board a Portuguese navy vessel. FRETILIN would be blamed later. This plan was intercepted by CIA monitoring stations in the area and was part of a series of revelations by Dale Van Atta, an associate of columnist Jack Anderson.

Guicciardi's report, contained in Security Council document S/12011 of 12 March 1976, was a classic UN document: bland, cautious, ambiguous. In paragraph 37, Guicciardi wrote: "Any accurate assessment of the situation as a whole remains elusive. Without doubt it continues to evolve. The terrain and conditions in general are such as to rule out front lines and to favour guerrilla warfare."[17] He termed his discussions with the Portuguese and the Indonesians "comprehensive and constructive." Paragraph 39 is very revealing about Indonesian behavior:

> In response to my specific reference to operative paragraph two of the resolution regarding the immediate call for the withdrawal of forces, the Government of Indonesia pointed out that the presence of Indonesian volunteers in East Timor was at the request of APODETI, UDT, KOTA and *Trabalhista* and later of the "Provisional Government of East Timor," in which the four parties were represented, in order to give whatever assistance was necessary to restore peace and order in the Territory, as a prerequisite for the proper exercise of the right of self-determination by the people of East Timor. Consequently, the termination of their presence in, and their withdrawal from the Territory, should be carried out upon the request of the "Provisional Government of East Timor." The Government of Indonesia would be in contact with the "Provisional Government of East Timor" and would co-operate fully in the implementation of such a request.[18]

If there was any doubt about Indonesian intentions, they were soon dissipated by another communication, purportedly issued by the "Provisional Government of East Timor":

> The people and the Provisional government of East Timor have decided for complete integration with the Republic of Indonesia. As far as the people are concerned, they have already exercised their right of self-determination; they consider themselves Indonesian nationals and their territory an integral part of the Republic of Indonesia.[19]

The "Provisional Government" also announced that "the political parties in East Timor have decided on 30 January 1976, to dissolve themselves . . ."
FRETILIN's position, conveyed by me to Guicciardi, was dutifully reflected in his report:

> With a view to achieving a peaceful solution and to establishing the status of the Territory following its decolonization, the representative of the "Government of the Democratic Republic of East Timor" called for:

(1) A cease-fire without delay:

(2) The withdrawal of Indonesian forces and military assistance, and their simultaneous replacement by an international force composed of Portuguese and contingents from Western European countries (preferably Nordic), or composed exclusively of Nordic contingents should it not prove possible for Portugal to participate;

(3) A referendum (one man-one vote) to be held not less than one month, not more than three months, after the Indonesian withdrawal, with a choice between (a) integration with Indonesia, and (b) independence under FRETILIN.[20]

I narrowed the referendum to a choice between Indonesia and independence under FRETILIN for obvious reasons: all other political parties had disbanded themselves. FRETILIN was the only force offering a credible alternative.

The Portuguese agreed with some of the points I put forward to Guicciardi, but did not agree that the referendum should offer only the choice between integration with Indonesia and independence under FRETILIN. The following was the Portuguese response as reflected in Guicciardi's mission report:

The Government of Portugal expressed full support for points (1) and (2) of these proposals, adding that were a Portuguese contingent to be included in an international force, the Portuguese Government would insist on over-all command (on behalf of the United Nations) being held by a Portuguese commanding officer, since Portugal still has legal responsibility as the administering power. However, the Portuguese Government would not oppose an international force being dispatched without inclusion of a Portuguese contingent. Regarding point (3), while in principle favourable to a referendum, the Government of Portugal would wish the people of East Timor to decide on the procedure for themselves, possibly on the lines of the proposal contained in Portuguese Government Law 7/75 of 17 July 1975. But they could not agree to terms of reference for popular consultation offering only a choice between integration with Indonesia and independence under FRETILIN. The Portuguese Government was unable to accept FRETILIN as the only valid political entity in East Timor and would suggest the alternatives be (a) integration with Indonesia, and (b) independence in consultation with all political forces in East Timor. Furthermore, any referendum should be preceded by consultations with all political groups and with the assistance of the United Nations and the Portuguese Government.[21]

In his concluding remarks, Guicciardi stated that "among the divergent views of the governments and parties concerned on the future of East Timor, there is one common element: the need for consultation." There was no such common element between FRETILIN and Indonesia, for Indonesia never intended to allow an adequate process of decolonization to be carried to its conclusion. It knew that in free elections, supervised by the UN, FRETILIN would emerge victorious. Anyway, that was the last time I heard of Mr. Vittorio Winspeare Guicciardi.

The Security Council met again in April to review the Timor situation on the basis of Guicciardi's report. The report had been made available on March 12, but I had asked the Portuguese delegation to request postponement until April, when it would be the turn of Huang Hua of China to preside over the Security Council. I was certain that Huang Hua, as President of the Council, would do everything in his power to turn the debate in our favor.

By April 1976, most of the territory of East Timor was still considered FRETILIN "liberated areas" where the majority of the people could be found living. Heavy clashes were continuing near Baukau, the second largest town; and other smaller towns such as Remexio, only a few miles from Dili, were still under FRETILIN control. However, the human toll had reached horrifying proportions. The first casualty figures came from the Indonesian side. Lopes da Cruz, President of the UDT and deputy "Governor" of East Timor, revealed that as many as 60,000 East Timorese had died.

In a letter dated January 30, 1976, the Portuguese Government complained to the Security Council that Indonesia had been unloading "cars and helicopters" in East Timor, and that the illegal activities of Indonesia were making the implementation of Res.384 (1975) more difficult. In fact, immediately after Guicciardi's visit, Indonesian military presence in East Timor reached new levels.

The Security Council began its second consideration of the Timor problem on April 12, 1976. I addressed the Council three times, making good use of Huang Hua's favorable disposition. My first speech ran about 40 pages. It had been drafted by Mari Alkatiri, my senior in the FRETILIN leadership, and it was my job to translate it into English. Alkatiri always enjoyed inflammatory statements, punctuated by cliches. It never was a pleasant experience to translate his speeches.

For the second Security Council debate, the Indonesians brought along an Australian pensioner, a certain Rex K.M. Syddell, and wife, who had chosen East Timor for retirement and lived on the eastern tip of the island in a secluded farm house. They diligently avoided meeting foreigners, particularly Australian officials. It emerged later that Syddell was sought in Australia on charges of fraud. During FRETILIN's brief interregnum he had offered his services to train young Timorese diplomats, claiming to have been a former diplomat himself. Soon after the invasion, he had switched sides and offered his services to the Indonesians.

Syddell's speech was a disservice to his Indonesian masters. It was full of racist overtones, using words like "primitives" to refer to the Timorese. I requested to speak after Syddell and although I did not want to honor the obscure gentleman by responding to his speech, I could not avoid calling him a "sick white racist." Syddell reportedly moved to Bali in 1976 and settled on a farm donated by the Indonesian Government in gratitude for his passionate defense of Indonesia's position.

Portugal addressed the Council, as did Indonesia and several other countries. Australia, the Philippines, Saudi Arabia and Malaysia spoke in support of Indonesia. Guinea, Guinea-Bissau and Mozambique spoke in support of our stand, as did many other Security Council members. The Malaysian Representative requested to speak at the last minute; and, as in December, showed either utter ignorance of the Timor problem or a blatant disregard for the truth. He argued that the situation in East Timor was "returning to normal" and that the "FRETILIN leadership had left the country."

Galvao Teles of Portugal made a spirited and persuasive speech calling for the "prolongation of the mandate conferred on the Secretary-General by the terms of the Security Council 1975 resolution." He added that Portugal would favor the convening of a conference with the participation of all interested parties, under UN auspices. However, that was the last time the Portuguese made a visible effort on behalf of the people of East Timor. In subsequent months and years, Portugal made only token references to the Timor tragedy in their annual address to the General Assembly.

On April 22, the Security Council adopted resolution 389(1976) which was almost identical to 384(1975). However, this time the unanimity of the December meeting had been lost, thanks to American and Japanese obstruction. The US and Japan abstained. Benin regarded the text as "too weak." In spite of my pleas, the Charge d'Affaires of Benin refused to support the draft; fresh from a coup that brought to power a radical military regime led by the charismatic Mathieu Kerekou, Benin was in no mood for compromises. Addressing the Council, the Benin Representative made a passionate speech on East Timor, the best I had heard.

Japan pursued its efforts to obstruct any meaningful action the Council might take. To this end, the Japanese delegation lobbied hard for certain amendments to the draft introduced by Guyana and Tanzania. The Japanese amendments were tantamount to accepting Indonesian troop presence in East Timor. The Japanese wanted the word "remaining" to be inserted before "troops," so that the amended version would read: "The Security Council calls upon the Government of Indonesia to withdraw its remaining troops from the territory." (Indonesia had claimed that a number of "volunteers" had begun to be repatriated. This was a big lie, of course.) The Japanese amendment was defeated when put to a vote. Eight countries voted for, one against (Benin), and five abstained (Guyana, Rumania, Sweden, USSR, Tanzania). China did not participate. Japan and the US subsequently abstained on Res.389, arguing that because the Council had rejected the Indonesian assertion that "some forces had been and were being withdrawn from the territory," they felt that the resolution was unlikely to serve any useful purpose.

All through both the 1975 and 1976 Security Council debates on Timor, the Japanese delegation was conspicuous in its efforts to soften criticism of Indonesia. There was a crude commercial motive in the Japanese exercise in the Council. In view of this, I question the wisdom of certain proposals that have been floated around the UN to increase the number of permanent members of the Council, one important candidate being Japan. A country so vulnerable to all forms of pressure, and one that has demonstrated on a number of occasions—East Timor not being the only instance—that it can succumb easily to commercial temptations, cannot be expected to play any constructive role as a permanent member of the Security Council.

Security Council Res. 389 (1976) was essentially identical to Res.384 (1975). It called upon

(1) all States to respect the territorial integrity of East Timor, as well as the inalienable right of its people to self-determination;

(2) Indonesia to withdraw without further delay all its forces from the territory;

(3) the Secretary-General to have his special representative continue the assignment entrusted to him under the terms of Res.384 (1975) and pursue consultations with the parties concerned.

This last provision was important; it could have been a pressure on, and an embarrassment for, the Indonesians, had the Secretary-General taken seriously his mandate. No effort was made, however, by Waldheim to have Guicciardi return to East Timor. I was not invited again for any consultations. I crossed paths with Waldheim once in the corridors of the UN; we shook hands, exchanged some brief words, and Waldheim told me how "glad" he was that we had met. To him, that chance encounter was counted as a serious meeting, thus sparing him from wasting time with me in a more formal setting.

On June 22, 1976, Waldheim transmitted the second report by his special representative, which made the point that for "a number of reasons it had not been possible to assess accurately the prevailing situation in East Timor." Again Waldheim was reluctant to offend the Indonesians. As the fighting dragged on with mounting civilian casualties, Waldheim did not even bother to express the traditional, lip-service "deep concern." The Security Council never met again to discuss the Portuguese complaint, even though it remains an item on its agenda of unresolved issues.

It was obvious that neither Waldheim, nor the major powers, were interested in resolving the Timor question, and they all wished the issue would simply fade away. Portugal fell back into an embarrassing silence. It never pushed for another meeting of the Security Council, let alone questioned the inability of the Secretary-General to pursue its mandate. This was not of course the first time that a Security Council resolution remained only on paper, ignored by the countries concerned. In the Timor case there was no major power or regional group pushing the issue. The West continued to supply General Suharto with the military and economic means to continue his savage war against the Timorese people.

NOTES

1. 30 UN SCOR, Supp. (Oct.-Dec.1975) 66, UN Doc. S/11899(1975).
2. "Yearbook of the United Nations," Vo. 29, Chap. V, p. 858, para. 7 (1975).
3. Supra note 1.
4. 30 UN SCOR, UN Doc. S/PV.1864, 15 December 1975, pp. 4-31.
5. Ibid., pp. 31-34.
6. Ibid., pp. 63-71.
7. Supra note 4S/PV.1865, 15 December 1975.
8. Ibid.
9. Ibid.
10. Supra note 2, p. 682, para. 5.
11. Supra note 4, S/PV.1869, 22 December 1975, p. 49-50.
12. Moynihan, Daniel P., *A Dangerous Place*, Little, Brown & Co., Boston (1978), p. 247.
13. Report of the Secretary-General on his Special representative mission to Timor, contained in SCOR.Doc. S//12011, 12 March 1976.
14. Ibid.
15. Ibid.
16. Ibid.
17. Ibid.
18. Ibid.
19. Ibid.
20. Ibid.
21. Ibid.

14

The Games Nations Play

Portugal was an international pariah in the 1960s and early 1970s because of its colonial policies. It shared the world's opprobrium with Israel and South Africa. Portuguese diplomats and officials were on the defensive in every international forum, while the increasingly successful diplomatic war orchestrated by FRELIMO, MPLA and the PAIGC, won over world public opinion.

The 1974 "Carnation Revolution" brought Portugal out of the ranks of international pariahs. The military leaders who masterminded the most bloodless coup in recent history announced their intention to abandon the colonial policies and grant independence to all Portugal's colonies without exception. The new Portugal gained instant recognition as a progressive and democratic country; there was a tremendous reservoir of sympathy for the Portuguese revolution. It was this favorable international political climate that the Portuguese failed to exploit in order to drum up support for East Timor. I am convinced that, had the Portuguese launched an energetic worldwide campaign to internationalize the Timor issue in 1974-1975, President Suharto would not have used force against East Timor. Even after the invasion had taken place, had the Portuguese pursued a determined campaign to dramatize the struggle and suffering of the Timorese, world opinion would have been aroused.

However, after the spirited performance by Galvao Teles in December 1975, and April 1976, during the Security Council debates, Portuguese efforts on the issue became negligible. When the Special Committee on Decolonization and the General Assembly's Fourth Committee again considered the Timor question in August and October of 1976, there was no visible Portuguese participation.

From 1976 until 1982, the Portuguese acted as if they had accepted the *fait accompli*. Portuguese politicians, diplomats and officials simply shrugged when they were approached on the subject of East Timor. The only variance was registered in 1979 when Lourdes Pintassilgo, a chemical engineer, became the first woman Prime Minister in Portugal's history. Speaking before the UN General Assembly, Pintassilgo drew the international community's attention to the suffering of the Timorese. Her speech was such a departure from the wishy-washy language of previous Portuguese leaders that the Indonesians—and many other delegations—were stunned. However, Pintassilgo did not last long in office, and being only a care-taker Prime Minister had very little power to effect any meaningful change in the country's direction.

In contrast, Indonesian embassies around the world have East Timor as a top priority issue. If a trade mission from Europe or Latin America lands in Jakarta, the Timor issue is certain to crop up in the discussions, with the Indonesians leaning on their guests to support Jakarta's position in the next General Assembly session.

In New York, the Indonesian Mission hosts lunches and cocktails for selected diplomats, in groups or individually. The topic is not always East Timor, but the diplomats can get the hint without their hosts having to be too explicit. The Portuguese Mission, in contrast, is amazingly passive. Few of the Portuguese diplomats I have encountered over the years have impressed me as intellectually honest and politically astute. Leonardo Matias, the current Portuguese Ambassador to Brussels (he served previously in the UN and Washington), impressed me the most, although his involvement with the Timor issue was very limited. The late Futsher Pereira, who headed the Portuguese Mission to the United Nations between 1979 and 1981, and later became his country's Minister for Foreign Affairs, was an incorrigible conservative politically, but honest and competent. I maintained a closer working relationship with Antonio Monteiro, one of the new generation of more worldly Portuguese diplomats, at ease in the complexities of diplomacy where charm counts as much as intelligence.

Portugal is a minor player in the NATO club. However, its strategic position on the western edge of the Iberian peninsula, and its control of the Azores and Madeira islands, make it an indispensable element in NATO strategy. The Azores bases proved vital in the 1973 Arab-Israeli war. When all other European countries were reluctant to cooperate in the American airlift effort to rescue the Israeli army, the Portuguese allowed the use of the Azores bases. Had the Portuguese not cooperated in the massive American airlift operation, the outcome of the war would have been different.

The Arab bloc never forgave Portugal for its complicity with the US and Israel in 1973. Relations improved as a result of former President Eanes' and Pintassilgo's embrace of Arafat in 1979. However, the part Portugal played in the 1973 Arab-Israel war contributed to the Arab bloc's decision to side with Indonesia over East Timor—apart of course from the myth of

Moslem and OPEC solidarity. The Portuguese Ministry for Foreign Affairs argues that, because of the Timor problem, Portuguese business interests in the Arab world have been hurt. This is nonsense. East Timor is not even a marginal issue for the Arab countries. For the Arab bloc the single most important issue is Palestine; and if the Arab countries were to use trade as a tool to extract political concessions from Lisbon they would focus on the Palestinian issue rather than on East Timor.

The way countries vote at the UN has little to do with universal principles. There are exceptions but most delegations make use of the centuries-old *quid pro quo* tactic to gain concessions. Diplomats usually understand what the other side expects in return for support on a given issue. During each General Assembly, and often for weeks and months beforehand, delegations begin lobbying to obtain a coveted chairmanship of a particular committee or UN body, a highly paid and visible job, membership in the Security Council, ECOSOC, International Court of Justice, etc. During these rounds, a vote on a totally different item may be secured against the promise of support.

In the Timor case, Indonesia has explored every possible angle, including promises of increased trade, import of arms, export of oil and offers of aid to less endowed countries. Portugal, in contrast, has failed to resort to the same acceptable international practices in order to win votes for East Timor. Lacking political will, successive Portuguese Governments failed, for instance, to persuade the Americans to maintain at least a strict neutrality in the conflict between Portugal and Indonesia.

Mexico, a consistent supporter of East Timor, was a key sponsor in 1981 of a draft resolution being circulated in the Third (Human Rights) Committee on the situation in El Salvador. The El Salvador junta had been supporting Indonesia over East Timor. Common sense suggested that Portugal should side with Mexico. However, the Portuguese were reluctant to vote differently than their European and American allies.

What angered me the most was Portugal's reluctance to side with Greece and Cyprus over Turkey's occupation of Northern Cyprus. Both Greece and Cyprus were consistent supporters of East Timor, while Turkey sided with Indonesia from the very beginning. Lisbon's rationale was that it should not take sides because both Greece and Turkey are NATO members, ignoring the fact that Turkey had committed an act of armed aggression against Cyprus and the majority of the international community supported Cyprus. Only after a lot of phone calls and hectic lobbying did the Portuguese vote for the Cyprus resolution.

There were other resolutions dealing with human rights in Chile and Guatemala. Most Western governments supported the motions critical of the two countries' human rights records. However, it took some effort on my part to convince the Portuguese to send a message to the Chilean and Guatemalan regimes. By coincidence, I travelled from New York to Lisbon

late in 1982, on the same plane as outgoing Prime Minister Balsemao and
Foreign Minister Futsher Pereira. That was a golden opportunity to discuss
with Pereira Portugal's voting record on El Salvador, Guatemala, Chile,
Cyprus, Kampuchea and a host of other issues. I asked him to review
Portugal's position on these issues, bearing in mind the question of East
Timor. I pleaded with him that whenever possible, bearing also in mind
Portugal's own interests, Portugal should exercise *quid pro quo* to gain
votes for East Timor.

Between 1976 and 1982, FRETILIN was virtually alone in the lobbying
effort at the United Nations. Our closest friends were not always there, as
much as their hearts were with us. They too had their concerns, and were
handicapped by limited staff and experience. The painstaking drafting of
the resolutions, the negotiations with key delegations, fell on my shoulders.
I could always count on support from Roque Rodrigues, our Ambassador to
Angola, and Jose Luis Guterres (or Lugo, as he is known to his friends), our
Representative in Mozambique, who joined me during each General
Assembly. Roque was always a tireless worker, fluent in English, French
and Spanish. Lugo is personable with a relaxed attitude—so relaxed that it
is always a struggle to get him to accelerate his pace of work or to get him out
of the bed each morning. If he could abolish the word "work" from the
dictionary, he would have done it long ago.

Each of us had a particular assignment, a number of delegates to contact
each day. I was usually in charge of Western Europe, including the
Scandinavian countries, while Roque was assigned to deal with Asian,
Socialist and Latin American delegates. Lugo's "turf" was Africa.
However, the division of labor was never strict. I often worked on Latin
American delegations as well, and when we wanted to impress a particular
delegation, the three of us would meet them together. Our approach was
always the same: starting with a review of the Timor issue and a briefing on
the current situation, backing up our argument and information with official
FRETILIN documents and press clippings, we would proceed to discuss
the draft resolution (if our interlocutor was on our list of trusted delegations);
ask for its sponsorship (this was always the maximum we aimed for); ask for
its vote and for a statement in the Plenary and in the Fourth Committee.

Our friends from Angola, Cape Verde, Guinea-Bissau, Mozambique,
Sao Tome and Principe, Vanuatu, Zimbabwe and Benin, were asked to
approach other delegations when that was necessary. Obviously, countries
listen more to another government delegation than to a liberation movement.
In the *quid pro quo* game, FRETILIN had nothing to offer.

The most exasperating experience each year was the search for a country
to formally introduce the draft resolution. Though I always drafted the text,
only a Member State could introduce it. The ideal situation is for a country
of the geographical region, with political weight, non-aligned, not classified
as pro-Moscow, to introduce the text. When the issue is popular, like

Namibia, delegations try to outdo one another. On less popular items such as East Timor, the choice is extremely limited. A few times I reached the stage of desperation when one country after another declined to introduce the draft.

The Portuguese were pathetic bystanders to all this. There was no consultation or support, let alone a joint strategy. The Portuguese delegation would limit itself to making a formal statement in the Fourth Committee.

Then, in the Fall of 1982, when public opinion in Portugal demanded action, Portuguese diplomacy began to gear up for some serious initiatives. President Ramalho Eanes forced the executive branch to mobilize the Foreign Affairs Ministry. Under the tenure of Prime Minister Pinto Balsemao, then leader of the Democratic Alliance coalition government, Portuguese embassies were instructed to lobby actively for East Timor, for the first time since 1976. Forty special envoys and ambassadors were sent around the world, carrying volumes of information to back up their case. A paper entitled "The 'Decolonization' of East Timor and the United Nations Norms on Self-Determination and Aggression," by Roger S. Clark, a Law Professor at Rutgers University, was the main document in the Timor dossier. There was an unprecedented flurry of activity in the Portuguese Foreign Ministry, otherwise a sleepy place where it is extremely difficult to reach anyone before 10 a.m., between 1 and 4 p.m., and at one minute past five in the afternoon.

The Portuguese Parliament sent representatives to Australia and Japan. Not everything went smoothly. An envoy sent to Surinam did not manage to see a single official and left the country after delivering a package of material (mostly in Portuguese) to a clerk in the Foreign Ministry. In Monrovia, Chairman "Dr." Samuel Doe gave his word that Liberia would vote in favor of East Timor, but his Mission in New York acted differently.

The sudden Portuguese diplomatic campaign had the immediate salutary impact of injecting new life into the Timor question and giving it a higher profile at the UN and in many capitals. The Indonesians naturally attempted to neutralize this Portuguese offensive with a renewed effort of their own aimed at South America, predominantly Moslem West Africa, and Scandinavia. Their Mission in New York was reinforced. Indonesia also enlisted the personal intervention of then Australian Prime Minister Malcom Frazer and former Prime Minister Gough Whitlam.

A close friend of President Suharto and architect of Australia's subservient posture toward the Indonesian junta, Whitlam had his own personal motives to silence the debate on East Timor. He secured an invitation from Suharto to visit East Timor in March 1982, and spent a total of three days in the territory, accompanied by another apologist for Indonesia, columnist Peter Hastings. Both men were escorted at all times by Indonesian security officers, and were lavishly fed and entertained by their hosts, while hungry Timorese children looked on. Whitlam used this "expertise" when he spoke before the Committee on November 8, 1982, and said: "Most petitioners . . . have never been to East Timor . . . At least I have been there as recently as last March."

Whitlam's decision to petition the Committee had one immediate positive effect: it raised the visibility of the Timor issue in the UN. Carrying his loyalty to General Suharto to new extremes, desperate to rewrite history and erase his shabby part in it, Whitlam said: "It is high time that the question of East Timor was voted off the United Nations agenda . . . " He went on to claim that his visit to East Timor was undertaken "entirely under the auspices" of ICRC: "Both of us [Whitlam and Hastings] had the great advantage of following an itinerary laid down by the delegate of the International Committee of the Red Cross, who had been in the territory for three years and who speaks the Indonesian language."

ICRC formally denied that Whitlam's visit to East Timor was under its auspices.[1] The ICRC delegate he referred to never lived in East Timor for three years; he was based in Jakarta, and his knowledge of the Indonesian language was irrelevant to East Timor, since only a handful of people there speak "Bahasa Indonesia." As on numerous occasions in the past, Gough Whitlam did not hesitate to resort to half-truths, distortions, omissions and outright lies. The first page alone of his speech contained all of these.

After years of struggle against Whitlam's policies, this was the first time I met him face to face. I was determined to publicly expose his record, embarrass and humiliate him on the floor of the Fourth Committee. Whitlam was known to have a big ego and an exaggerated view of himself as a world statesman. He actually believed that his mere appearance in the Fourth Committee would be enough to impress and persuade the delegates. He planned to lecture the delegates into submission, give the Timorese a fatal blow, and walk away with a clean conscience.

At one point in the debate, Whitlam began referring to the "*mestizos*" (mixed-race people) who were behind the independence movement in East Timor, implying that we did not represent the "real" Timorese. This was another lie frequently repeated by Whitlam. Less than five percent of all FRETILIN leaders and cadres had any European background. In any case, I could not recognize in Whitlam—or in any Australian leader—moral authority to dispense judgements on matters of race. In response to Whitlam's remarks, I asked whether he was a black aborigine? Or was he trying to persuade the Committee that he was an albino? Whitlam offered an even worse clarification: all he meant to say was the "the most articulate spokespersons of the Timorese happened to be mestizos"—which implied that only those of us with some European blood were intelligent and articulate!

Whitlam was ridiculed in front of the 200 or so diplomats attending the debate. The Australian delegation was visibly uncomfortable. A New Zealand delegate told me afterward: "My God, I hope Muldoon doesn't show up here one day and go through the same!" Whitlam squirmed under incisive and persistent questioning by Bob Van Lierop, representing Vanuatu; Adriano Cassandra of Sao Tome and Principe; Jose Luis of Cape Verde; and Janis of Zimbabwe. Alfredo Cabral of Guinea-Bissau made an impromptu statement, praising the way the FRETILIN representative was conducting himself in the debate; then he turned to Whitlam and told him that he was mistaken in coming to the Fourth Committee, a committee that is supposed to oversee the dismantling of colonialism, to make an apology for colonialism. "You knocked at the wrong door, Mr. Whitlam," Cabral said.

Whitlam was not the only Australian politician to address the Committee. Gordon McIntosh, a Senator from Western Australia and a member of the Australian Labour Party (ALP), flew to New York armed with a letter signed by 95 percent of ALP Members of Parliament, affirming their support for the Timorese people's right to self-determination. Gordon was certainly much more acquainted with the Timor problem than Gough was. Gordon visited East Timor early in 1975 and has since devoted a lot of time and energy to the issue. He is a man driven by his profound sense of justice. In the Fourth Committee, while Whitlam asked that a wall of silence be erected around the East Timor issue, Gordon made a passionate speech that ended very dramatically. He had brought along a tape of the last words of an Australian journalist, Greg Shackleton, murdered by Indonesian troops in October 1975. The tape, extracted from his last film, was a plea to the United Nations to care. It was played for the entire Committee and the room fell dead silent. Whitlam was even more embarrassed—but not ashamed.

One incident that took place during the 1982 Fourth Committee debate infuriated me. Lance Joseph, a deputy to Dick Woolcot, took the liberty of telling Vanuatu Representative Bob Van Lierop, in the presence of a Caribbean Ambassador, that Australia might cut off aid to Vanuatu because of Prime Minister Lini's support for East Timor. Bob, new to the UN scene, was taken aback and upset by Lance's arrogance.

The incident followed a pattern of pressures and outright blackmail directed by the Fraser Government against Vanuatu. A small island nation of 100,000 inhabitants, Vanuatu became independent in 1981 after about 200 years of joint French and British colonial rule. The first Prime Minister, Walter Lini, a dignified Methodist preacher, invited the displeasure of the Anglo-Saxon overlords of the region because he was not prepared to be another messenger boy of the white man.

I urged Bob to report the incident to Lini because it was a breach of diplomatic etiquette for Lance Joseph to have made such a threat, even if it had been "only a joke," as he tried to excuse it later. Lance Joseph's appearance and manners are not of a refined diplomat; he always struck me as a rough football fan from Liverpool, ready for a fistfight after a few pints.

Dick Woolcot, in contrast, is the quintessential diplomat, refined in his manners, erudite and sensitive. I ignored Dick Woolcot's pleas to forget the whole incident, and Lance himself came to see me shortly after. He tried to explain that it was all a joke. I responded that one doesn't joke with the dignity of a country, and in any case, he owed me no explanation since I was not a Vanuatu Representative. I told him that he could also clarify his remarks to the media, since I intended to bring the incident to their attention.

I watched with a mixture of anger and incomprehension the frenetic activities of the Australian delegation on behalf of Indonesia. Why were the Australians so determined to bury us? Did they have to go to such extremes, to descend so low, to obtain a few more trade deals with the Indonesians? What had my people done to invite such a low blow from our neighbors, the same ones our people shed blood for during the past war?

At times, facing these mean and powerful forces, I felt crushed. Only the thought of men, women and children fighting in the mountains and tropical forests of my beloved island; only the image of those imprisoned, brutalized and murdered, of the thousands uprooted from their ancestral lands and herded into prison camps, or deported to remote islands; only these thoughts and pictures have given me the determination to stand up to these powerful forces.

Even as we, our friends, and the Portuguese were working frantically to win another battle at the UN, we had not agreed on a draft for 1982. I had proposed to the Portuguese, and I had the previous year, that we should try to get the General Assembly to request an Advisory Opinion from the International Court of Justice. I had in fact worked out a draft, inspired in part by the Namibia and Western Sahara cases, which would have asked the Court to give a non-binding opinion on the question of self-determination. Since Indonesia's main argument was that Res.1514(XV) and 1541(XV) had been fully implemented in East Timor and that the people of the territory had decided to join with the Republic of Indonesia, the Court should therefore be asked whether all the provisions of the UN Charter and Res.1414((XV) and 1541(XV) had been observed by Indonesia in regard to East Timor. I was certain that the Court's response would be in our favor. However, the Portuguese rejected the idea on the grounds that Portugal, as the administering power of the territory, was convinced that the Timorese people had not exercised their right to self-determination, and could not therefore put this conviction in question by going to the Court. I and many others could not agree with Portugal's arguments. After all, the Court exists precisely to decide on contentious issues, or to give non-binding opinions on dubious legal issues. But I gave up on the Advisory Opinion draft, since the Portuguese were adamant.

Foreign Minister Pereira crossed paths with me at the United Nations, and told me in his customary pessimistic mood: "I just cannot figure out what kind of a resolution we are going to produce this time." That evening, back in the East 55th Street studio that I shared with a million cockroaches (and eventually with Roque, Lugo and Alakatiri), I read through few cases involving the Secretary-General's "good offices." I was hesitant to trust East Timor to another Secretary-General, since Waldheim's role was still very much in my mind. However, the new Secretary-General appeared to be more decent, and I had a faint hope that he might do more for us than his predecessor.

The authors of a draft resolution usually aim for the broadest possible support, unless the objective is to provoke certain countries into taking a negative stand to cause them embarrassment. Our objective in drafting the text of what ultimately became G.A.Res.37/30 was to gain votes and miminize losses; my comrades Roque and Lugo and I agreed that that seemed to be our only chance to prevent an Indonesian victory. The problem in our case was that no matter how moderate and balanced our draft might be, the US, Australia, Japan and Saudi Arabia, just to mention a few, would always find an excuse to cast a negative vote. No matter what painstaking efforts we had made in the past to draft a "balanced" text, economic interests and political alliances always overrode the merits of the resolution.

I believed that if we were to entrust the problem to the Secretary-General we might achieve two objectives: win the vote; and rekindle some hope, however dim, of a diplomatic solution. I also believed that only the Portuguese were in a position to persuade Javier Perez de Cuellar into accepting such a complex task.

With all this in mind, I prepared the first draft. It read:

The General Assembly,

Recognizing the inalienable right of all peoples to self-determination and independence in accordance with the principles of the Charter of the United Nations and of the Declaration on the Granting of Independence to Colonial Countries and Peoples, contained in its resolution 1514 (XV) of 14 December 1960,

Having examined the chapter of the report of the Special Committee on the Situation with regard to the implementation of the Declaration on the Granting of Independence to Colonial Countries and Peoples relating to East Timor and other relevant documents,

Taking note of resolution 1982/20 of 8 September 1982, of the Sub-Commission on Prevention of Discrimination and Protection of Minorities,

Having heard the statement of the representative of Indonesia,

Having heard the statements of the representative of the Frente Revolucionaria de Timor Leste Independente—the Liberation Movement of East Timor—and various East Timor petitioners, as well as of representatives of non-governmental organizations,

1. *Reaffirms* the inalienable right of the people of East Timor to self-determination, in accordance with General Assembly resolution 1514 (XV);

2. *Requests* the Secretary General to initiate consultations with all parties concerned, namely Portugal, as the administering power, the representatives of East Timor, including the representatives of the Liberation Movement of East Timor—FRETILIN—and Indonesia, with a view to exploring avenues for achieving a comprehensive settlement of the problem, and to report thereafter about the progress and results of these consultations to the 38th session of the General Assembly;

3. *Requests* the Special Committee on the Situation with regard to the Implementation of the Declaration on the Granting of Independence to Colonial Countries and Peoples to keep the situation in the territory under active consideration and to render all assistance to the Secretary General in his endeavours;

4. *Decides* to include in the provisional agenda of its 38th session the item entitled "Question of East Timor."

A long process of consultations was started on this draft. Futsher Pereira brought it up with de Cuellar over lunch. A few days later, the amendments began to pour in. According to Pereira, the Secretary-General insisted on some changes. Operative paragraph one was deleted on the grounds that there was no question that the people of East Timor had the right to self-determination. Then, why delete it? I resisted the deletion of such an important paragraph, but I had to give in in order to gain de Cuellar's acceptance of the mandate. Assured that the right of the people of East Timor to self-determination would not be brushed aside, I went along with the changes. The thrust of the draft was operative paragraph two. Here I took care in specifying that "all parties concerned" included FRETILIN. There was another round of consultations with de Cuellar and his staff, and again I was advised by the Portuguese that the Secretary-General refused to be limited by a resolution telling him who he should or should not contact. He preferred, according to the Portuguese, freedom of movement; and in any case, he knew who the parties to the conflict were. The suggested formula would be:

Requests the Secretary-General to initiate consultations with all parties directly concerned, with a view to exploring the avenues for achieving a comprehensive settlement of the problem and to report thereon to the General Assembly at its 38th session.

There couldn't have been a more vague wording with more risk of different interpretations. I was assured by Futsher Pereira over cappucino in the delegates lounge, that the Secretary-General was conscious of the need to consult the Timorese people themselves. I asked Pereira how we could be certain that the Secretary-General would not try to bypass FRETILIN. He responded that Portugal, as the administering power, would see to it that the people of East Timor were consulted on their future—and that FRETILIN would be included in the consultations. All my discussions with Pereira were faithfully passed on to Roque and Lugo, and to Ambassador Amaro da Luz of Cape Verde in his capacity as Coordinator of the five Portuguese-speaking African countries in 1982.

After a series of consultations we reached a decision: we should go along with the proposed changes in the operative paragraphs, but the preamble should be strengthened. We hoped that our position could be safeguarded in the preambular paragraphs 1, 8, 9 and 10. The latter recalled all previous General Assembly resolutions which reaffirmed the inalienable right of the people of East Timor to self-determination and independence. Though the preamble is not as important as the operative paragraphs, it is nevertheless part of the whole and constitutes the spirit of the resolution. We had another condition to put to Futsher Pereira: that Portugal should cosponsor the draft. He agreed. We regarded this a victory, since this was the first time that Portugal associated itself entirely with a draft resolution on East Timor. We hoped that this would impress Lisbon's European allies who had abstained thus far. We hoped that France and England would side with us. After all, didn't the "Iron Lady" go to war over the right to self-determination of 2,000 settlers in the Malvinas? Wasn't France governed by Mitterrand's Socialist Party, with which FRETILIN enjoyed fraternal relations?

Brazil, the colossus of the South, a fraternal Portuguese-speaking nation, was uppermost in our minds. We believed that if we could only persuade the Brazilians to sponsor the draft along with Portugal and others, a significant victory was assured. To achieve this, we operated at several levels. Angolan Foreign Minister Paulo Jorge, a dedicated friend, was asked to press the matter with his Brazilian counterpart. Chissano of Mozambique and Silvino da Luz of Cape Verde were asked to lean on their Brazilian counterparts. In New York, Amaro da Luz, the Cape Verdeian representative, approached Sergio Correia of Brazil on behalf of the five Lusophone African states. Sergio Correia is one of the most influential Brazilian diplomats, rather sympathetic to our cause. Our friends from Zimbabwe also lobbied on our behalf.

Brazil, though ruled then by conservative military officers, had a progressive foreign policy. Unlike their less sophisticated and less aggressive Portuguese cousins, the Brazilians have a finely-tuned sense of political opportunism. At home, communists and progressives were thrown in jail and mercilessly persecuted; abroad, Brazilian diplomats and officials were seen mingling with Cubans and Russians. Brazil recognized the People's Republic of Angola the day the Marxist MPLA declared the country's independence on November 11, 1975. The Brazilian diplomats I have encountered over the years in the UN have always impressed me as among the most talented in the world. They invariably came from the upper class and aristocracy. They were groomed in the prestigious diplomatic school of Rio Branco, then moved into the highly-paid jobs in Itamaraty. They are archpragmatists who can enjoy a hearty conversation with their fascist Chilean comrades, as well as with the communist Cubans.

After persistent lobbying on our part, we finally secured Brazil's sponsorship. The good news was announced to me and Roque by Bettencourt Bueno. We rushed to inform our friends, who had all failed to show up for a meeting in the Chinese lounge. With Brazil joining the list of countries sponsoring the Timor draft resolution, we were confident of gaining more votes, particularly among Central and South American countries.

I asked later for a meeting of our main supporters—the five African Lusophone states, Portugal, Brazil, Vanuatu, Zimbabwe, Benin and Algeria. Almost everyone showed up for the meeting in the Indonesian Lounge—so baptized because it is decorated with fine carvings donated by the Government of Indonesia. Each country present in this strategy session was asked to help in securing votes for the draft. I raised a remaining question: which of the cosponsors should introduce the resolution? I argued that Brazil was the best choice, because to have maximum impact we had to rely on a country with prestige. Everybody agreed with my suggestion, but not with my choice of words: the implication was that the others were not as important. Adriano Cassandra, the young and opinionated Charge d'Affair of Sao Tome and Principe, a tiny island country of less than 100,000, waited for a private occasion to express his displeasure. He was right, though it was never my intention to minimize the importance of any country. I should have known better, coming from a country often said to be "too small and poor to be viable!"

A country sponsoring a draft and taking the lead in introducing it, shows the importance it attaches to the issue, and invites all its friends to support it. This was the significance of Brazil's stand on East Timor. It is rare for Brazil to sponsor a resolution unless it directly affects its interests or the interests of its region. For this reason, UN delegates were surprised to see Brazil taking such a visible posture on East Timor, with Ambassador Sergio Correia da Costa himself introducing the draft in the Fourth Committee, where he stated:

We are particularly responsive to the situation of the people of East Timor, both because we consider it to be a humanitarian obligation for us to take this position, and because it is in line with the basic guidelines that orient Brazilian foreign policy. And beyond that, there are certain elements that make us identify very closely with the people of Timor, the most significant of which being the fact that we speak the same language and have a cultural background in common. Thus, the suffering of the people of Timor and the difficulties they are going through are a cause of special concern for Brazil.

Though Sergio's statement was cushioned in measured language, it didn't go unnoticed. The Fall of 1982 was to be the most excruciating and fascinating period in my ten years at the United Nations.

The results of the vote in the Fourth Committee were disappointing, but still within our expectations. Some 58 countries voted with us. We could count on a few more when the final vote would be taken in the General Assembly. We could still improve in relation to the 1981 vote or maintain the same level. We mobilized all our meager resources to secure as many votes as possible. Brazil's role was thought to be crucial. I pleaded with Bueno to use his personal influence and charm with his Latin American colleagues, particularly Uruguay, Paraguay and Chile. (He in fact neutralized a particular delegation that had received strict instructions to vote with Indonesia, by inviting the delegate for a coffee just when the voting was going to take place.)

The Portuguese did their best. There was a flurry of cables and telephone calls by President Eanes, Prime Minister Balsemao and Foreign Minister Futsher Pereira to their counterparts in Europe, Latin America and Africa. Eanes talked with Bruno Kreisky of Austria, Senghor of Senegal and Houphouet-Boigny of Ivory Coast, pleading with them to support the Timor draft. He also dispatched former Prime Minister Ms. Lourdes Pintassilgo to a number of European capitals to lobby for East Timor.

I cabled Mario Soares, then still in opposition, and pleaded with him to use his personal contacts and influence as a leader of the Socialist International to win over those fraternal parties in power in Europe and Latin America. I mentioned specifically Sweden, where Palme had just been reelected, Costa Rica and the Dominican Republic. Rui Mateus, Soares' Secretary for International Relations, cabled me back that they were doing their best.

The Indonesians did not relax either. Suharto himself was on the phone with Third World leaders, while a stream of high-ranking military men and special envoys were crisscrossing Africa and Latin America during the crucial weeks before the vote in the General Assembly.

The result was a devastating blow for us: 50 countries voted yes, an equal number abstained, and 46 voted no. A resolution that had been painstakingly drafted so that none could honestly repudiate it as even mildly one-sided, had been adopted by a slim margin of four votes. I began to pick up the bits and pieces and analyze the results to see what went wrong, and reached one firm conclusion: The almost 100 countries voting against us or abstaining did so for no reasons other than sheer hypocrisy, political opportunism and commercial interests. Few succumbed to outright bribery or blackmail. What puzzled me most was that in spite of Brazil's involvement, we made almost no inroads in Latin America. Bolivia changed from a no to an abstention, but this was due more to a change of regime than to Brazilian intervention. Uruguay, Paraguay, Chile, Guatemala—all other Latin American countries with the exception of Colombia, which changed from a no to an abstention—maintained their previous positions. In the Fourth Committee we had gained the votes of Guatemala (thanks to a sympathetic parliamentarian who had followed the Timor question for many years) and of Costa Rica. However, the Indonesians leaned on Guatemala and forced it to reverse the vote in the General Assembly. Guatemala's position was awkward anyway: it covets Belize, which was one of our main supporters and a sponsor of the Timor draft. Though Belize became independent in 1981, Guatemala never renounced its claims, and only the presence of British troops has discouraged the Guatemalan military from imitating their Indonesian comrades and invading. It wasn't difficult, therefore, for the Indonesians to persuade the Guatemalans that they would be shooting themselves in the foot by supporting the Timor draft.

Costa Rica had also voted with us in the Fourth Committee, a departure from its past positions, thanks to Aurora Escalante, a voluptuous Costa Rican delegate who believed in the justness of our cause. Until the very eve of the vote in the General Assembly, Aurora had reassured me that Costa Rica would not deviate from the position taken in the Fourth Committee. However, in the early morning before the vote, a telex arrived with direct instructions from President Monge ordering the mission to vote with Indonesia. As Aurora told me later, she cried—and took a courageous step. She would not disobey the orders of the President, but it could happen naturally that no one would be present in the Costa Rican seat to press the button. And so it happened. Though disappointed by the loss of Costa Rica's vote, I was deeply touched by Aurora's gesture. The abrupt instructions from Monge had been a result of Suharto's personal intervention. Costa Rica, whose relations with the Arab and Moslem groups were tense because of its pro-Israel voting record (it is one of the few countries to have moved its Embassy to Jerusalem), did not want to antagonize the largest Moslem country in the world over so remote an issue as East Timor. There was no counterweight to Indonesia's lobby. Contrary to my expectations, Brazil had not leaned on Costa Rica, thus leaving Monge to choose only between Portugal, which was essentially irrelevant to Costa Rica's interests, and Indonesia.

Indonesian officials had been stunned and extremely worried by Brazil's apparent leading role on East Timor. They reacted angrily and sought to retaliate. A Brazilian trade mission to Indonesia was called off abruptly. Brazilian businessmen, eager to expand their markets in Southeast Asia, were told that their Government's position on East Timor was hampering trade relations between the two countries. Sure enough, the businessmen (who probably had never heard of East Timor, and couldn't have cared less if they had) carried the message to Itamaraty. Arch-pragmatists, the Brazilians tried to play both sides: pleasing the Lusophone community by sponsoring the draft; placating the Indonesians by letting them know that Brazil would not ask other countries to support it. In fact, there were strict instructions from Itamaraty to the mission in New York not to engage in any lobbying whatsoever on behalf of East Timor. Latin American countries eager to discern Brazil's intentions were told to vote as they saw fit. Brazilian diplomats were at pains not to appear to be doing any lobbying in our behalf. The Indonesians had been assured at the highest levels that the Brazilian Mission in New York would not exert any pressure on other countries. The Indonesians had to be content with Brazil's position because they knew that if Brazil were to actively lobby for East Timor, most Latin American countries would be eager to cooperate with the colossus of the South.

The big surprise was reserved for me by Olof Palme of Sweden. The Swedish Social Democratic Party (SDP) had been returned to office in the Fall of 1982. During SDP's brief years in opposition, it had been our best advocate among Western European parties. Its members championed our cause in the Swedish Parliament, never missing an opportunity to castigate the "bourgeois" government for abstaining on East Timor at the United Nations, and for selling "defensive" weapons to Indonesia. When Palme was reelected, I rushed a telex to him, "rejoicing with the great victory of the Social Democrats . . ." And I reminded him that "the people of East Timor, who always had the sympathy and support of the Swedish people, particularly the SDP, count on your continuing support for our just struggle for national self-determination and independence." I pleaded with Palme as the new Prime Minister of Sweden to break with the previous government's "connivance with the criminal dictatorship of Gen. Suharto."

Matts Helstrom, a young SDP parliamentarian who had made a habit of attending all General Assembly sessions each year—during which time he was always eager to help us—happened to be in New York soon after Palme's reelection. I was happy to see him in the delegates lounge. I congratulated him on SDP's victory and asked him to talk to Palme about the Timor draft. Matts' reply was like a bucket of cold water thrown in my face: "They are considering it . . . they don't need my advice." Only a *naif* would have

failed to understand those words as meaning that Palme would not change
the abstention vote on East Timor. I could see in Matts' eyes that he was
embarrassed.

Indonesia had enlisted the powerful lobby of Swedish businessmen,
eager to expand trade relations with Indonesia. Facing an economic crisis
which brought down his opponents, and the prospect of increasing export of
Swedish goods, (chief among them "defensive" weapons and spare parts)
Palme decided to pursue his predecessor's policies and ordered the mission
in New York to abstain, with an explanation of vote expressing pious
concern for the human rights of the Timorese.

Matts Helstrom, who had opposed arms sales to Indonesia, became the
new Minister for International Trade, the man who authorizes arms deals
with foreign countries. I visited Sweden in the Spring of 1983 and was
invited by Matts for breakfast before a speech I was going to deliver at a
seminar on East Timor in Stockholm—financed in part by SDP. We met at
the party headquarters. It was Matts' job to concoct the best possible
explanation for the Swedish abstention. I hoped he knew me well enough to
know that I would not swallow just any lame excuse; yet Matts, or his
colleagues, were less ingenious than I expected. Our conversation went like
this:

"You know I am most disappointed with your abstention," I began. "The
resolution was absolutely mild. It simply called on the Secretary-General to
hold consultations. There was no mention of Indonesia. We did not even
use the word 'negotiations.' How could you have abstained on such a
resolution which simply asked the SG to make use of his good offices?"

"Well," Matts began to respond, "the problem was that we did not want to
give insoluble problems to the Secretary-General. It is our view that the
Secretary-General's role should be strengthened, and not weakened with
insoluble problems."

"But how do you weaken his role when you support a resolution that asks
him to use his good offices? Besides, Matts, the SG had given his agreement
to the Portuguese beforehand. Otherwise we would have considered
another approach."

"We know he is not happy with it."

"I find it hard to believe what you are saying. The SG did not say such a
thing to the Portuguese Foreign Minister when both first discussed the idea.
Well, someone is lying . . ."

The truth was that regardless of the nature and thrust of the resolution, the
Palme Government—like almost all Western governments—would have
abstained anyway. Commercial interests, not moral principles, determined
their vote.

Though disappointed and hurt, I did not lose respect and faith in Palme. I believe that under Palme and SDP Sweden has had an outstanding record worldwide. In fact, Sweden's position on a wide range of issues—ranging from disarmament to sanctions against South Africa, support for liberation struggles in Southern Africa, human rights in Latin America, development aid and humanitarian assistance to the poorest of the world—should be a model for the rest of the industrial countries of the North. Palme was for me what John F. Kennedy was for millions of Americans, and myself, in the early 1960s. He was a humble and accessible man whom I met casually several times during his frequent visits to the UN in New York. I learned of his sudden violent death one evening in Geneva. I was stunned when the news of his assassination flashed over the TV screen. I could only murmur helplessly, "It is not possible. I cannot believe it . . ."

Of the Scandinavian countries, only Iceland has been a consistent defender of the rights of the Timorese people. A small country, proud and fiercely independent, Iceland resents the arrogance and cajoling tactics of the larger powers, including its Nordic brothers. One would not think that Indonesia would find any angle through which to blackmail distant Iceland. There is no trade link between the two countries, and the Reykjavik government does not aspire to be a major trading partner with Indonesia. However, the devilish generals and colonels found a way to blackmail the Icelandic government. The Indonesian authorities discovered that Icelandic families had applied for adoption of abandoned Indonesian children. It passed the word to the families that their case would be resolved only when their government stopped voting against Indonesia at the UN. The interested families brought up the subject with the Ministry for Foreign Affairs; however, this crude tactic did not sway the Icelanders onto Indonesia's side.

Norway has abstained on East Timor from the very beginning in 1975, for very selfish commercial reasons. Late in 1975, Norway was awarded a lucrative ship-building contract by the Indonesian government. The contract had been awarded originally to the Netherlands, but it was abruptly cancelled by the Indonesians in a show of displeasure over the Dutch Government's handling of an incident in which South Mollucan separatists took over the Indonesian Consulate in Amsterdam and murdered at least one diplomat.

> Let us speak of the forgotten man, abandoned, lost, delivered over to the powers that crush him. People in most places are dying of hunger, of misery and solitude, a whole people was killed in Cambodia, and another is being killed in Timor. (Francois Mitterrand, 1981)

These poetic, moving words were spoken when Mitterrand was still only dreaming of sitting on the peacock throne of the French Republic. They were forgotten the moment he took office. In a formal note addressed to the Portuguese in 1983, Quai d'Orsey informed them that France would oppose any resolution on East Timor if the issue came to a vote in the General Assembly in the Fall of 1983. In 1982, France, along with all the other European countries—with the notable exceptions of Albania, Cyprus, Greece, Ireland and Iceland—had abstained. However, there was to be no occasion for the French to cast their vote with Indonesia in 1983, since the question of East Timor was deferred to the following General Assembly session, and deferred again in 1984 and 1985.

The French defend their position with the argument that the situation in East Timor has improved, pointing to the fact that the provincial "governor" is an indigenous person. When I met with a French diplomat in New York, shortly after Quai d'Orsey announced its position to the Portuguese, I told him that his government's position reminded me of Marshal Petain's betrayal of the French Republic. It seemed as if the French still believed that as long as an indigenous puppet is figurehead, foreign military occupation is tolerable.

If any European country should be elected to preside over the international arms traffic, France would be the choice. Its arms sales to Indonesia have increased dramatically and continue to expand. Indonesia's arsenal include French tanks and "Puma" and "Allouette" attack helicopters, all frequently used in East Timor. The "Allouette" is FRETILIN's major fear. Its versatility and speed allows it to operate effectively in jungle and mountain areas to chase retreating guerrilla forces or flush them out of their bases.

Regis Debray, the one-time revolutionary who posed for photographs with Che Guevara in the jungles of Bolivia, is among the most enthusiastic proponents of increased French-Indonesian relations. He was honored guest and keynote speaker in a seminar on French-Indonesia relations sponsored by the Jakarta-based Center for Strategic and International Studies (CSIS). Modeled after the Georgetown think-tank institution, CSIS produces pseudo-academic papers in defense of the military regime. A brainchild of the late General Ali Moertopo, CSIS was instrumental in the propaganda war and diplomatic campaign designed to prepare world public opinion for the bloody 1975 invasion of East Timor. It was this Mafia-type setup that was honored by Debray.

Few people still have illusions about France's commitment to human rights. When the Socialists were elected in France for the first time in many decades, hopes were high that French trade relations with some of the despotic regimes on earth could come to an end. Africans expected a decrease in trade relations with South Africa. However, in the first two years after Mitterrand took office, trade between the two countries increased dramatically.

Some would argue in the defense of the Socialists that all has not been negative in the Mitterrand government's relations with the Third World;

look at France's relations with Nicaragua, for instance. However, it has to be noted that French interests in Central America are negligible. The famous French-Mexican joint communique of 1982 on Central America reflect, if anything, Mitterrand's eagerness to court favor with the Mexicans as an alternative source of energy to the Middle East. A policy toward Nicaragua that might be perceived in the region and within France as an affirmation of France's "independence" *vis-a-vis* the ugly Americans, and yet does not carry with it any political or economic costs to France, can only be to French advantage.

Canadian official attitudes toward East Timor and other issues such as Cambodia and Afghanistan are a study in contrasts. Canada joined with the US, Japan and others in voting against any and every resolution on East Timor. It explained its stand in the 1981 "Annual Review" of the Canadian Department of External Affairs:

> On East Timor, the General Assembly again called for *self-deter-mination and humanitarian assistance* for the former Portuguese colony *annexed* by Indonesia in 1976. *Canada* and over 40 other countries *voted against the resolution* on the basis that the *integration* of East Timor, while not entirely consistent with the principle of self-determination, is now *an accomplished and irreversible fact.* No resolution on the subject could change the principle of self-determination and the international community should now focus on the humanitarian and developmental problems faced by the inhabitants. (emphases in the original)

The Canadian Foreign Office has another explanation for its position on Afghanistan:

> Canada lent strong support to a [UN] resolution . . . *which con-demned the invasion* of Afghanistan, called for the *immediate withdrawal of foreign troops* and reaffirmed the right of the Afghan people to *self-determination*, free from outside interference. (emphases in the original)

Such double standards are explained by the growing Canadian economic and military relations with Indonesia. Canada ranks fifth among member countries of the Intergovernmental Group on Indonesia (IGGI), a consortium of Western countries that fund Indonesia's economy. In 1975, within weeks of Indonesia's invasion of East Timor, Canada signed a $200 million aid and loan agreement with Indonesia. By 1981, Canada ranked third, after the US and Japan, in foreign investment in Indonesia. The Canadian government has authorized General Motors of Canada to sell light tanks to the Indonesian government, violating its own laws barring weapons exports to conflict areas. Pratt & Whitney of Canada, one of the biggest aircraft engine manufacturers in the world, has built engines for the Indonesian air force, including 16 T-34C Beechcraft "Mentor" and six Bell 212 helicopters. DeHavilland of Canada has supplied the Indonesian air force with seven DHC-3 "Otter" transports. These weapons play an important role in the war in East Timor. But how does the Canadian government explain the weapons exports to Indonesia if Canadian law states that export permits should be issued only for "non-conflict" areas? Simply by asserting that there is no armed conflict in East Timor—knowing that to be a lie.

The Malvinas conflict provided another example of how selective Western "principles" can be. In 1982, Great Britain went to war with Argentina over a group of barren islands inhabited by sheep and penguins— and a mere 2,000 settlers, most of them employees of British absentee landlords. Thatcher discovered, though belatedly, that those settlers, few though they might be, had a right to self-determination—something her government did not recognize for the 700,000 Timorese! Any student of history and international law would have little difficulty in ascertaining that Argentina's claims over the islands are rather solid. Thatcher didn't think so, and when Galtieri ordered the liberation of the Malvinas—as a diversion from Argentina's mounting economic and social problems—the "Iron Lady" proved that she could send a *macho* Latin American general running. I followed the entire Malvinas debate at the United Nations, and was impressed—if not always amused—by the British Ambassador's emotional defense of the "inalienable right to self-determination" of the Falklanders. Wasn't Galtieri's arsenal supplied by England? Where was British commitment to democracy when thousands of Argentinian families were being tormented? The Western democracies that financed the fascist junta in Argentina were stunned when their hands were bitten by the mouth they fed.

The Malvinas debate at the United Nations provided a colorful view of the games governments play. Both countries used their ablest diplomats and political clout to appeal for Third World votes. Portugal, which maintains with Great Britain a 600-year-old alliance, gave full support to its ancient ally, allowing British planes to refuel in the strategic Azores bases en route to the South Atlantic. Argentina, which styles itself as a European enclave and actually takes offense when referred to as a Third World country, woke up to a bitter truth: The West, of which it considered itself a part, sided with the Anglo-Saxons and not with some Italian emigrés. The Argentinian fascists—who had abducted and murdered thousands of leftists, alleged leftists, their families and friends—began to season their vocabulary with revolutionary rhetoric, appealing for Third World solidarity. The Soviet Union, which had always maintained fraternal relations with the fascist junta because of its supposedly nationalist credentials, stepped up its moral support for the Argentinian claims. Castro, never wanting to miss an opportunity to make life miserable for the Brits and *gringos*, rallied behind the fascist Galtieri.

I watched it all with incredulity and amusement. Fascist Argentina had been a consistent supporter of Indonesia, because Jakarta had persuaded the Argentinians that the Malvinas and East Timor were one and the same issue—both representing anachronistic legacies of European colonization. (Had the Argentinians cared to study the Timor dossier they would have found out that in fact the two issues have rather different historical and legal backgrounds.) The progressive Third World group believed that no matter what kind of regime reigned in Buenos Aires, there was an issue of principle involved—and that was Argentina's rightful claims over the Malvinas. With our friends I argued for an abstention on the Malvinas issue, as a mild reminder to the Argentinians of their negative stand on East Timor.

Our friends disagreed and preferred a principled stand. One of them said: "We can win them [the Argentinians] over with our moral stand." I doubted that principles alone would impress the Argentinian fascists. However, the consensus was that we should request a meeting with the Argentinians to inform them that our group would support them in the General Assembly. The meeting took place in the Indonesian lounge, and the Argentinians promised to "review" their position on East Timor. To the advantage of the Argentinians, the Malvinas vote came up in the General Assembly before the vote on East Timor—as always, Argentina voted with Indonesia.

In the Fall of 1983, I drafted a memo to our friends in the UN, urging them again to establish a linkage between their stand on the Malvinas issue and Argentina's stand on East Timor. I could sympathize with the dilemma our friends were facing. On a historical and legal plane, I fully agreed with Argentina's claims. I believe that Argentina's claims over the Malvinas are indisputable in history and law. On the other hand, the use of force in international relations (like the use of institutionalized terror against human beings) must be thoroughly condemned.

As it turned out, the Indonesians were the winners. They got Argentina's vote on East Timor, and a British abstention—as well as British weapons. Not surprisingly, British rhetoric on self-determination and non-use of force in international relations did not apply to East Timor—or to South Africa, where Britain ranks first in direct foreign investment. Since 1978, there has been a strong drive by the British to increase defense contracts with the Indonesian military. In 1978, British Aerospace won a contract to supply Indonesia's air force with advanced trainer/combat "Hawk" ground-attack aircraft. A total of 17 have been supplied since, a number of which have been used in East Timor. The Baukau International Airport, closed to civilian traffic and off-limits even to friendly foreign visitors, is the base for British "Hawk" aircraft as well as American OV-10 "Broncos" and French "Allouettes" and "Pumas." Frigates were ordered from Vosper-

Thorneycroft in 1984, and a $200 million deal was struck between Indonesia and British Aerospace, also in 1984.

Prime Minister Thatcher visited Indonesia in April 1984, as part of a 10-day tour of Asia, a trip designed to consolidate British economic relations with the Indonesian military, particularly in the field of weapons supply. Thatcher, pressured by the British Parliamentary Group on Human Rights, reportedly raised the issue of East Timor during talks with Suharto. Yet, her government continues to supply the Indonesians with the very weapons they use to pursue their brutal war.

Certainly no particular country or regional group holds a monopoly on double standards and hypocrisy in international relations. These are the trademark of the United Nations, even if all members subscribe to the lofty principles and purposes of the Charter. If one listens to an Arab delegate launching a tirade against Israel's "aggression," one might believe that all the problems in the Middle East are of Israeli making. If one listens to the likes of Mobutu (fortunately Dr. Idi Amin Dada and His Majesty Emperor Jean Bedel Bokassa I are gone from the scene) we might believe that the white South Africans are the only oppressors and exploiters in Africa. Unfortunately, we can find in Asia, Africa and the Middle East some of the worst barbarians in the world.

While the industrialized countries vote on issues on the basis of their objective and perceived interests, regardless of the merits of each resolution, the voting pattern of the Third World group is equally illustrative of the inconsistencies that plague the UN.

The Palestinian issue has been the lifeblood of the "Arab cause." Each fall in New York, the General Assembly debates the Palestinian question and denounces Israel's annexation of the Golan Heights, incursions into Lebanon, and human rights violations in the occupied territories. Often an emergency session of the General Assembly is convened by the powerful Arab group. Sadly enough for the Palestinians, who are still languishing in refugee camps after 40 years, these exercises are little more than a convenient way for the Arab states to exhibit their lip-service support for the Palestinian cause. The General Assembly and the Security Council floors are the only battleground where many Arab megalomaniacs have the courage to fight for their Palestinian "brothers," in sterile speeches against Israel. On the real battlefield, as in the summer of 1982, the Palestinians are left to fend off the Israeli army by themselves—when they do not have to fight off assaults and massacres by other Arabs. When Yasser Arafat was under siege in West Beirut in 1982, the Arab League Foreign Ministers could not even agree on a venue for a meeting. Weeks later, when the Israeli army finally relented on the siege—under pressure from hundreds of thousands of Israelis who took to the streets in Tel Aviv to protest the war— the Arab League decided to call for an emergency session of the General Assembly. An African Ambassador told me in anger and frustration: "This is outrageous. They didn't lift a finger to help the Palestinians when they were in desperate need. Now that the worst is over, they call for an emergency session!"

It is certainly not the purpose of this book to analyze the Palestinian and Arab issues. My intention is only to illustrate the hypocrisy that has characterized the offical Arab attitude toward the Palestinian question— and, not surprisigly, toward East Timor. I must emphasize the word "official" because there are millions of Arabs who do not endorse the perverted behavior of the ruling elites. I would also commit a grave injustice if I did not single out Algeria and, particularly, Democratic Yemen as exceptions to the rule. Both nations have resisted strong pressure by Indonesia and continue so far to support our struggle. South Yemen is particularly vulnerable to pressures by Indonesia, because there are over half a million people of Yemenite ancestry living in Indonesia, whose remittances to their country are not negligible. Algeria and Democratic Yemen, and to a certain extent Kuwait, are Arab countries whose attitudes toward the Palestinian problem, and relations with African countries south of the Sahara, are commendable.

I'm often asked where Syria, Iraq and Libya stand on the Timor conflict. Since the three are allegedly the most staunchly anti-imperialist of the Arab group, my questioners react in disbelief when I explain that both Syria and Iraq actively support Indonesia. Among progressive people in the US and Europe there is a false assumption that Syria and Iraq are progressive, when in fact both countries are ruled by megalomaniacs. Assad has probably more Arab blood, both Palestinian and Syrian, on his hands than Ariel Sharon. Libya has opted for a neutral position between us and the Indonesians.

"Islamic solidarity" and "Afro-Arab brotherhood" are invoked when it suits the interests of the Arabs. The Africans south of the Sahara are often called upon to lend their support for Arab-sponsored resolutions at the United Nations. However, in these times of horrendous crises in Africa, Arab generosity toward their black "brothers" is almost nil. Arab petrodollars are invested elsewhere—in the US, Switzerland, Germany, Britain, France, etc. Only miserable crumbs go to black Africa. Indonesia invokes "Islamic solidarity" to win Arab and Moslem votes on East Timor. Although Indonesia is nominally the largest Moslem country in the world, with its 170 million people of whom 90 percent are at least nominal Moslems, it is ruled by a military oligarchy in which the most influential elements are Protestants and Catholics. Armed Forces Chief Benny Murdani, the second most powerful man in the country, is a devout Catholic—as good a Catholic, presumably, as Stroessner of Paraguay, Pinochet of Chile and Roberto d'Aubuisson of El Salvador. Murdani is also a confessed admirer of Israel. Under his control, the Indonesian state security and intelligence agency, BAKIN, has working relations with

Israel's MOSSAD as well as America's CIA and South Korea's KCIA. Israeli weapons are a familiar sight in the Indonesian army and police. An item in *The New York Times* of December 14, 1984, makes interesting reading:

> A crowd of 1,500 people described by the Government as Moslem extremists ran through Jakarta's port area Wednesday night... Today, scores of troops with armored cars stood guard in the port area... About 60 youths on motorcycles escorted an ambulance carrying the body of one of the dead rioters... They gave the clenched-fist salutes and shouted 'God is great!' while soldiers with Israeli-made Uzi submachine guns looked on.

Israel itself has maintained a studied distance from the Timor issue. In the General Assembly it has abstained on every resolution—a stand slightly better than that of most Arab countries. However, it has become evident that Israel's relations with Indonesia, particularly through Benny Murdani, have moved to active levels. Not only Uzi submachine guns have been purchased by Indonesia. Directly or via the US, more advanced weaponry, including US aircraft no longer in use by the Israeli air force, have been transferred to Indonesia. The Israeli Council for Israeli-Palestinian Peace (ICIPP) took up the issue of Israeli weapons supply to Indonesia in a letter, dated June 26, 1985, signed by the group's secretary, Adam Keller, addressed to Abba Eban, Chairperson of the Knesset Defense and Foreign Affairs Committee. The basis for ICIPP concern was an article published in the Israeli newspaper *Hadashot* of April 14, 1985, which stated: "Diplomatic sources in Washington believe that Jakarta's new approach (the lifting of the prohibition of travel to Israel by Indonesian nationals) stems from its desire to import military equipment from Israel, in conjunction with the security connections between the two countries' secret services." Keller appealed to Eban "to act in time, before we find Israel to be involved in the oppression of the inhabitants of East Timor."

The Israeli-Indonesian cooperation does not constitute surprising news for those familiar with Israeli involvement with some of the worse regimes on earth. One must concede that the Indonesians have perfected hypocrisy into a high art. They manage to portray themselves as champions of Islam, while actively collaborating with the "satanic Zionist entity."

Stories of bribes among UN delegates have circulated for some time. Prices for a vote are said to range from a wristwatch to several thousand dollars. More elegant, official forms of coercion on the state-to-state level co-exist with outright threats and blackmail. The US is a long-time practitioner of state bribery and blackmail, but Jeanne Kirkpatrick perfected it. This obscure political scientist-turned-ambassador instituted a loyalty test aimed at rewarding friends and punishing enemies of the US. What is it if not bribery and blackmail when a country offers rewards and promises retaliation for votes? Of course, there are countries that cannot afford the methods of blackmail perfected by Kirkpatrick and have to settle for the simpler old ways under the table.

In 1977, still a novice at the UN, I had my first encounter with this ancient institution. I approached a certain delegate (I omit his name and nationality out of respect for his country) and pleaded with him to reverse an abstention his subordinate in the Fourth Committee had cast on the draft resolution on East Timor. He was taking a well-deserved nap during a speech while I explained to him my problem.

Still half-asleep he asked: "Is your Minister still in town?"

I immediately realized that he thought East Timor was another Member State. I answered "no," thinking of Alkatiri, our External Relations Minister, who had in fact left New York.

"Well . . . if he was here maybe we could make some financial arrangement," he said, looking at me in a very conspiratorial manner.

I still didn't understand and thought that by "financial arrangement" he meant a donation to our struggle. I immediately liked him. However, knowing how long a donation would take to materialize, and anxious to get his vote, I gave the worst possible answer:

"I thank you a lot, but money is not our problem. My problem is the vote. All I want is your vote when the resolution on East Timor comes to the plenary."

"I'm glad you said this. So you have money? Well, I want to tell you something. You know, my colleague lost money in the hotel . . . if you could help him, I would appreciate it very much."

Dumb, dumb! I thought to myself, only now realizing what he meant by "financial arrangements." And I had fueled his greed! More hesitantly now I asked:

"How much did your colleague lose?"

"About $1,000 . . . "

My heartbeat increased. Where would I find that much money? Were I to pay a few more delegates that much for their votes, FRETILIN would file bankruptcy pretty soon. I tried another tactic:

"I'm prepared to contribute some for your colleague. How much?"

"A couple of hundred bucks would be okay," he said nonchalantly.

What a relief! I hastened to respond that I would be happy to help with $200.

He looked more serious and whispered: "Put it in a manila envelope. Be discreet."

I excused myself and left after promising him the money "within a few days." I began to play for time. I concocted a story that I needed clearance from my superiors. When a few days had passed I had to add details to the original story: the money had been sent but my name was not properly spelled, and the bank was withholding payment until they got clearance. "You know how strict the American banks are," I said.

I did plan to make the payment, but our friends to whom I told the story advised me against it. Guinea-Bissau's Counsellor Arnaldo Araujo was most adamant. Disciplined by years of hardship in the jungles during the bitter war against the Portuguese, Araujo became one of his country's first senior diplomats and served with competence, always careful in taking positions at the UN, never compromising his country's non-aligned posture. His opposition to giving in to bribes was a reflection of his personal integrity. I followed his advice, but continued to stall. One morning, as I was on the escalator leading up to the General Assembly hall, I heard someone calling me by my first name. It was my "friend." He took me by the elbow and led me to a far corner. In a low voice he asked:

"Where's the thing? You know, Hassan also promised to help."

Hassan was an Indonesian delegate in charge of East Timor. That was bad news, since I could not compete with the Indonesians when it came to giving bribes. "Don't trust this Hassan. The Indonesians are big liars!" I told him in desperation.

"Jose, don't worry. We'll vote with you. It's a matter of principle—but hurry up with the money."

I almost cracked up when I heard that it was a "matter of principle—but hurry up with the money." What a line!

On the morning of November 28, 1977, the General Assembly voted on the Fourth Committee report and on the item entitled "Question of East Timor." Moments before the vote, I went to see my "friend" and sat behind him. Leaning forward, I whispered: "I have the money now." He reassured me of his support and suggested that we meet in the delegates lounge for a drink to celebrate. As the lights flashed on the electronic voting board, he pressed the green button and joined with 66 other countries that cast a yes vote on G.A.Res.32/34. Twenty-six voted no, 47 had abstained. It was a significant victory, though as with the previous resolutions—and as in the following years—it would remain a resolution without binding effect.

The following year, my "friend" did not show up for the 33rd session of the General Assembly. I met a new delegate from his country who informed me that the person in question had been ordered into early retirement by his President. The new delegate explained that apparently the Indonesians had paid him money and complained when the vote wasn't cast as had been promised to them.

If in 1977 I had my first personal experience with a corrupt diplomat, I also met one of the most decent and intelligent men in the UN that year. In fact, I had met him a few months earlier: Donald Blackman was a political science professor at a predominantly black college in New York State where I had been invited to give a talk. A native of Barbados, Prof.

Blackman was invited by the tiny Caribbean nation to head its Permanent Mission to the United Nations. An outstanding scholar in his 40s, Don was unpretentious, humble, and yet very firm in his convictions. He was disappointed and angry at what he saw as indifference on the part of Member States to the plight of the Timorese and other oppressed peoples. What a contrast between Don and his predecessor, who was credited with one of the most amusing and shameful incidents in UN history. Donald's predecessor had actually tried to claim "diplomatic immunity" for his vicious dog that was accused of attacking neighbors and passers-by!

Don Blackman restored respectability to his country. When he decided in 1977 to sponsor and introduce the Timor draft in the Fourth Committee, there was surprise among some delegates. A Rumanian delegate asked if the US was behind Don's move, explaining that often the Americans use a third country to push something that they themselves cannot for one reason or another. I answered no, and explained that it was Ambassador Blackman's independent judgement on the merits of the issue that compelled him to take a stand on behalf of a people remote from his country. Later, he drafted a superb speech for one of his senior aides to read it before the Committee. Two years later Don was appointed to a senior cabinet post in Barbados.

Saint Lucia, a newly-independent Caribbean island state, is many times smaller in size and population than East Timor. Like most other microstates it sympathized with the fate of a fellow Lilliputian nation trampled upon by its giant neighbor. Its Permanent Representative was August Barry, a man who took special care of his physique and attire. The second in charge of the Mission was Dr. Charles Flemming, a bright young diplomat with a doctorate in Indian Ocean studies from New York University. Under these two men, Saint Lucia consistently supported all UN resolutions on East Timor. Then there was a change of government back home. Indonesia lost no time in sending a delegation to congratulate the new government, to discuss East Timor—and to offer economic assistance. When the Portuguese wanted to send a delegation to Saint Lucia, also to discuss East Timor, they were turned down. The Indonesian Ambassador struck up a friendship with the new PM of Saint Lucia. Both men were seen enjoying lunch in a Chinese restaurant a block from the UN. There is nothing wrong with two men enjoying some Hunan specialty. What is unusual is for a visiting Head of Government to sneak away to lunch with an Ambassador; and what is unusual becomes a topic of speculation when the PM is not accompanied by anyone from the Mission's staff.

When I heard of this incident, I lost all hope that Saint Lucia would stick with us. I figured that it would change from sponsor of East Timor resolutions to an abstention. The change was more brutal. Under the new PM, Saint Lucia made a 180 degree change. I could only speculate that the Indonesian Ambassador must have made a rather attractive donation to a charitable cause.

Another surprise came during the crucial 1982 General Assembly vote. Liberia had voted with us in the Fourth Committee. It did not abstain; it voted yes. It is unusual for a country to switch votes from a Committee to the General Assembly. Changes do occur when a country decides to move from an abstention to an affirmative vote, or from non-participation to an abstention; but diametrical change, from yes to no, is rare. Chairman "Dr." Doe had assured a Portuguese envoy that Liberia would vote for the Timor draft. In fact, instructions to this effect had been sent to the Head of the Mission in New York, Ms. Jane Adeoudu.

The day of the vote, Roque, Lugo and I began our frantic efforts to make sure that our friends and all those we were reasonably sure would vote with us were present in the General Assembly halls. This was always the most anxious moment of our work. We would rush to the phones to call the Missions and plead with them to send somebody. Often, a lazy secretary would answer: "But no one is here. They all went to the UN." We would survey the delegates' lounge, the Indonesian and Chinese lounges, the numerous conference rooms and the hidden corridors where indolent types would be dozing off behind dark glasses or newspapers. The most difficult to get were the ones hanging out at the bar; they often pretended to be engaged in serious consultations and did not appreciate being disturbed.

I noticed that the Liberian Permanent Representative was present. My heart almost stopped when I saw the devilish Indonesian Ambassador Kamil greeting Madame Ambassador effusively, as if congratulating her for having won a beauty contest. That scene did not augur well for us. Roque whispered to me: "We lost that one." And so we did. To the surprise of many observers, and of her own staff, Ms. Adeoudu changed Liberia's vote from a yes in the Fourth Committee to a no in the General Assembly.

Apparently it was not the first time Madame Ambassador had pushed the wrong button.

The Soviet Union and China were looked upon in the post-war period as the natural allies of the Third World peoples struggling for national emancipation. Both countries, along with Cuba and Yugoslavia, and to a much lesser extent the Eastern European members of the Warsaw Pact, made a significant contribution to the cause of liberation of the colonized peoples of Africa and Asia. Though not entirely philanthropic, China and Cuba have been by far the most genuine friends of the Third World. China's economic assistance and military aid to liberation movements and newly-independent countries has been, in most cases, free from political pressures on the recipients. Chinese economic assistance was and is still offered on the best possible terms.

The Sino-Soviet split of the late 1960s had a serious adverse impact on the progressive Third World movement. It divided and weakened the anti-imperialist struggle. Third World revolutionaries were forced to choose between one camp or the other. FRELIMO of Mozambique and PAIGC of

Guinea-Bissau and Cape Verde were among the few organizations that managed (and only to a certain extent) to maintain a balance in their relations with Moscow and Beijing. In Angola, the MPLA leadership found it harder to establish the equilibrium. This was not because the Angolan leaders deliberately chose the Moscow and Havana camp, but because of Mao's intransigence. Angola thus fell victim to the communist schism, with China supporting the reactionary and corrupt factions of the FNLA of Holden Roberto and UNITA of Jonas Savimbi, while the Soviet Union gave token support to the MPLA. Only when victory was at hand, when the MPLA had consolidated its power base in the capital, Luanda, with Cuban and Yugoslavian help, did the Russians throw their military weight behind Agostinho Neto's faction.

In Asia, both Moscow and Beijing played with the struggles of the peoples of Vietnam, Cambodia, Thailand, the Philippines, Malaysia and Indonesia. Those movements that were foolish enough to have entered the Sino-Soviet schism in the 1960s paid dearly. The Thai Communist Party, for example, was closely aligned with China. Its relations with the Vietnamese, if not the best, were correct. However, when the Vietnam-Cambodia conflict blew up, there was a sudden realignment of forces in the region, with the Chinese aligning with the reactionary ASEAN bloc, thus effectively supporting the Thai military regime against Vietnam and dumping the Thai Communist Party. The history of shifting alliances and outright treasons committed by the two communist powers is a long one. Their support, in the best of circumstances, was never automatic and usually less generous than claimed by Western intelligence and myopic journalists and scholars. In the case of Moscow the level of support was always in direct proportion to the strategic value of the country seeking aid. Moscow's support was always weighed against its regional and global interests.

In Mozambique, China was FRELIMO's primary backer throughout the 1960s. The Soviet Union came in late, around 1972, "when victory was just around the corner," according to a veteran of the Mozambiquan liberation struggle. However, neither the Chinese nor the Russians were the first to offer military assistance to FRELIMO and other African liberation movements. In fact, Israel was the first country to give FRELIMO's soldiers military training and medical help. This relationship, however, was terminated in 1967 with the Arab-Israeli war. Sweden was the first country to offer humanitarian assistance to the liberation movements fighting the Portuguese in Africa, back in 1964.

It is not in the scope of this book to analyze in detail the policies of the two communist giants in regard to the Third World, their support or betrayal of the liberation movements. In any case, such an analysis would have to take into consideration the different historical periods in China and the Soviet Union.

In the history of the anti-colonial struggle, two countries deserve a place of honor: Algeria and Cuba. Their support for the liberation movements has always been there, unconditional, never contingent on alignment with one particular bloc. I feel I'm unbiased on this particular issue, since FRETILIN owes no special favors to either Algeria or Cuba, their support having been limited to the votes in the United Nations. Algeria, having fought for its independence in one of the most celebrated epics in human history, became the Mecca for revolutionaries from all over the world. Cuba, though close to Moscow, never made its support for a liberation movement dependent on ideological alliance with Moscow. Only the utter ignorance or ideological blindness of Western journalists, scholars and government officials, allows them to maintain that every Cuban step in foreign policy is inspired by the Kremlin; in fact, Cuba's involvement in African liberation struggles has had more to do with Cuba's own African heritage.

The Indonesian Communist Party (PKI) was the third largest in the world until its virtual destruction in 1965-1966. A coup initiated by an obscure army officer against the CIA-backed Council of Generals backfired when General Suharto astutely neutralized other army divisions and isolated the putschists. Suharto's counter-coup resulted in the worst bloodbath since the Holocaust. An estimated 500,000 to one million Indonesians were massacred in a six-month period. The West applauded the destruction of the PKI and praised the "moderation" of the new regime.

When the pro-Beijing PKI was destroyed, Moscow did not rejoice at the news, but did not make a big fuss either—as it did when Allende was overthrown. The Indonesian generals, accusing the Chinese of aiding PKI's drive for power, broke off relations with Beijing. This pleased the Russians, who have since been eager to cultivate relations with the Indonesians. The Suharto regime, though decidedly pro-Western, has maintained a certain independence from Washington, particularly in regard to American military presence. Unlike Thailand and the Philippines, Indonesia does not allow foreign military bases on its soil.

In Indonesian strategic thinking, the threat to ASEAN in the immediate or foreseeable future does not emanate from the Soviet Union or Vietnam. China, because of its economically powerful minorities in the region, and particularly in Indonesia; and because of its enormous population and potential wealth, is seen by the Indonesians as the real threat to ASEAN. A logical development of this fear is the growing relationship between Jakarta, Moscow and other Warsaw countries. Though savagely anti-communist at home, Suharto and his army colleagues welcome the Russians as a counterbalance to the Chinese. Indonesia's warm relations with Moscow and Hanoi can be detected in Jakarta's low-key approach to Vietnam's intervention in Cambodia and the Soviet Union's intervention in Afghanistan.

The Soviet Union has grown into a superpower with global reach. While the CPUSSR proclaims rhetorical commitment to all oppressed peoples around the world, the Soviet State operates on a more cautious and pragmatic level. For this reason, Soviet relations with Third World liberation movements and states are often compromised by Moscow's and Washington's own agendas.

Moscow's relations with the Indonesian military regime were a carbon copy of its relations with the Argentinian juntas up until the abrupt return to civilian rule following the Malvinas war. Trade and strategic considerations counseled Moscow to seek normal, if not friendly, relations with both Buenos Aires and Jakarta. Certainly, the oppressed people of Argentina, the thousands of *desaparecidos*, their widows and relatives, those tortured in jail for crimes never committed, could not understand Moscow's embrace of the fascist junta. The same goes for the peoples of Indonesia and East Timor, particularly those languishing in prison camps.

The Soviet Union has voted yes on all resolutions on East Timor since 1975, including the Security Council resolutions 384 (1975) and 389 (1976). Between 1975 and 1978, all Eastern European Warsaw Pact members voted the same way. Rumania dropped out of the group in 1978, moving from a yes vote to non-participation; since then, Rumania has abstained. In 1979, in spite of our strenuous lobby, the Eastern European group switched sides: Bulgaria chose to be absent; Czechoslovakia, the German Democratic Republic and Hungary abstained. Poland chose also to be absent in 1978 and 1979, but has abstained since. Byelorussia and Ukrania, the two Soviet Republics with voting rights in the UN, obviously voted with Moscow.

UN observers were surprised by the "split" in the Soviet camp, the first such event ever. Eastern European delegates could not offer a sensible explanation for their "defection" from the anti-colonial bloc.

The fact is that the "split" was planned at the annual meeting of the Warsaw Pact Foreign Ministers, at which common strategies are defined for each General Assembly. Every single item in the UN is scrutinized during the meeting, usually held in September. The Soviet bloc's decision to split their vote on East Timor was a conscious one, meant to reward Indonesia for its accommodating position on Cambodia and Afghanistan and its long-standing anti-Chinese posture. There was another factor that influenced the bloc's change of heart on East Timor: negotiations were underway between the Eastern European countries and Indonesia for the repayment of some $2 billion owed by Jakarta, a debt Suharto inherited from the deposed Sukarno regime. Indonesian negotiators blackmailed their Socialist counterparts by promising to honor the debt if the bloc dropped its support for East Timor. Other elements were taken into consideration. Ever cautious and pragmatic, the bloc members were skeptical about chances for a FRETILIN victory. Hence, in their view, there was no point in antagonizing the Indonesians any longer. A Lusophone scholar told me in 1979: "Our President discussed the Timor problem with Brezhnev twice. It seemed to us that the Russians were afraid of a confrontation with the Americans since that region was within an American zone of influence."

Lest I'm misunderstood, I must say that this and other instances of Soviet failures and weaknesses in no way diminish the USSR's enormous contribution to the changes that took place in colonial-dominated Africa and Asia in the 1950s and 1960s. Russian support was not automatic—and when it came, it carried with it implication for the future of the recipient country. However, much is owed to Russian advisers and hardware.

Soviet support for East Timor has been limited to its vote at the UN. No Soviet or Eastern European delegate ever bothered to make even a perfunctory reference to East Timor in any of their countless speeches in the Decolonization Committees of the UN. In 1975 and 1976, Soviet representatives did speak on East Timor, but as Permanent Members of the Security Council they had to anyway. Yacob Malik dozed off most of the time during the debates. His deputy Ovnikov, speaking on behalf of the Soviet delegation during the Security Council debates in April 1976, didn't even bother preparing a written statement, and never mentioned Indonesia by name.

No FRETILIN representative has ever visited Moscow or any Eastern European country, even though we spared no efforts in courting the Russians, just as we court the US and the Western European countries. However, while we are basically free to travel to all Western countries (except Australia and New Zealand between 1977 and 1983), our repeated requests to visit Moscow were invariably turned down. Soon after the invasion, a FRETILIN delegation was instructed by our Central Committee to visit Moscow. Visa applications were filed at the Russian Embassy in Maputo. There my comrades were told that they should apply for the visa in Lisbon because the Embassy in Maputo didn't have a visa stamp! Alkatiri, who was supposed to lead the delegation to Moscow, swallowed his pride (something that always demanded a major effort on his part) and flew to Lisbon, where he waited for several days before being told that a visit to Moscow wouldn't be appropriate "at this time." In the summer of 1985, an East Timorese cultural delegation was invited to join the International Youth and Students Festival in Moscow. That seemed to be a major step forward and was achieved thanks to the lobbying of the Portuguese Communist Party and the Angolan and Mozambiquan national preparatory committees. However, once in Moscow, the Timorese delegation was barred from taking part in the opening parade. The Russians were rather frank about it. They had good relations with the Indonesians and did not want to upset them.

While Moscow kept FRETILIN at arm's length, Beijing extended lavish hospitality and active diplomatic support. I personally visited the People's Republic of China early in 1976, as did other FRETILIN representatives. China provided us with strong words of support at the United Nations, as well as financial contributions. However, FRETILIN never took sides in the Sino-Soviet split. We spared no efforts in balancing our relations with China with visits to Cuba and Vietnam, while Moscow refused us even a discreet visit. Some of my comrades visited North Korea and Democratic Kampuchea, but never obtained any financial, let alone military, support from these countries.

1978 was a disastrous year for FRETILIN. In East Timor, Nicolau Lobato, FRETILIN's immensely popular leader, died of bullet wounds after a ten-hour battle against a far superior enemy force. Indonesian intelligence had tracked down Nicolau's whereabouts and for weeks elite troops were ferried by helicopters to vantage points for the assault. The Indonesians had been aided by Alarico Fernandes, a former FRETILIN Minister of Security, who had defected after some bloody clashes with Nicolau's loyal faction. The encirclement operation involved some 2,000 troops. On December 31, 1978, the clash took place. Outnumbered and encircled, Nicolau and his men fought to the bitter end. Armed with a captured M-16, Nicolau kept firing, his wife at his side, also firing with a captured American-made machine gun. Hit in the leg and stomach, Nicolau began to bleed profusely. When the fighting died out, most of the FRETILIN fighters had been killed or gravely wounded. Some managed to escape. Others surrendered. Nicolau was rushed away in an Indonesian army helicopter. The Indonesians wanted to keep him alive so that he could be persuaded to call on his comrades to lay down arms. However, Nicolau died before reaching the hospital.

Nicolau's death was a crushing blow to FRETILIN and to the tens of thousands of Timorese who, though not affiliated with the movement, admired and respected his courage and saw in him the hope for a liberated East Timor. Nicolau's death had been caused as much by FRETILIN's internal divisions as by Indonesia's firepower. The handful of FRETILIN senior cadres overseas did not escape the infantile spasms of sectarianism, and we found ourselves bitterly divided. Accused of "treason," "capitulation" and "connivance with the CIA," I was abruptly pulled out of the UN on the eve of the Fourth Committee's discussions on East Timor. That year, 1978, we suffered a double setback—in East Timor and at the UN where we lost 10 votes in relation to 1977. When the mess was cleared and I was absolved of any intentional political wrong doing (at least for a while), I returned to the UN in time for the 1979 General Assembly session. With the tireless Roque assisting me, we plunged into a desperate battle to reverse the trend. In spite of the defection of the Eastern European bloc, we managed not only to stop the downward trend, but gained three votes in relation to 1978. The figures for the three years show the trend:

1977: 67 yes; 26 no; 47 abstentions
1978: 59 yes; 31 no; 44 abstentions
1979: 62 yes; 31 no; 45 abstentions

Democratic Kampuchea was one of our earliest and most vocal supporters. Influenced in part by the Chinese, the Pol Pot government extended formal recognition to FRETILIN and the government established after the 1975 UDI. Between 1975 and 1977, little was known of what was happening inside Cambodia. However, there were persistent reports of human rights violations on a large scale. As important as our relations with Democratic Kampuchea were to us, I was troubled by the reports. We in FRETILIN were in fact among the few people in the world who had access to Democratic Kampuchea. As a result, I learned a great deal about Pol Pot's "dark age" policies and his provocations of the Vietnamese. Eyewitnesses told me in 1977 of the shelling of Vietnamese territory by Khmer Rouge troops. During a meeting that year with Ien Sari, Pol Pot's right hand man and Foreign Minister, in the Chinese lounge of the UN in New York, I cautiously raised the troubling questions of human rights violations in Cambodia. I told Ien Sari that I could not believe the reports to be true, and suggested that to dispel any doubts, his government should allow foreign correspondents to visit Democratic Kampuchea. Ien Sari looked at me with surprise and politely turned the conversation to another topic, as if to say, "Worry about your struggle and let us take care of our problems." I did not persist.

Soon after the Vietnamese intervention in Cambodia, Pol Pot reversed his stand on East Timor. Though this was not entirely unexpected, it came as a rude shock. During the Fourth Committee proceedings in 1981, the Pol Pot delegation was absent most of the time. However, when the Committee gathered for the vote on the Timor draft, the Kampuchean delegate walked in; he had come to cast the vote for Indonesia. All of us—Abilio Araujo, Mari Alkatiri, Roque Rodrigues and myself—were furious. I met later with a senior Chinese delegate and expressed to him my anger at the Kampuchean about-face. He volunteered to talk to the Cambodians about it, but I said: "Don't worry. We don't need their vote. They are in good company with the Indonesians."

NOTES

1. In a letter dated 26 July 1982, addressed to the author, ICRC Director of Operational Activities Jean-Pierre Hocke wrote on Gough Whitlam's claims that his visit to East Timor had been arranged by ICRC:

    > Mr. Whitlam, former Prime Minister of Australia, did not visit East Timor "entirely under the auspices of the International Red Cross," but, as he himself stated during a Press conference in Jakarta, without having made any prior contact with our institution. It was solely with the agreement of the Indonesian authorities that Mr. Whitlam visited East Timor. Hence, it was not the ICRC that asked the latter to visit (East Timor) to "observe its activities."

15

The Non-Aligned Movement and Our Struggle

1985 was a year of historical anniversaries: the 40th of the end of World War II and the founding of the United Nations; the 25th of the Declaration on the Granting of Independence to Colonial Countries and Peoples (as contained in UN General Assembly resolution 1514 (XV) of 14 December, 1960). Equally important—or more so for hundreds of millions in the Third World—1985 marked the 30th anniversary of the Bandung Afro-Asia Conference, precursor of the Non-Aligned Movement (NAM). Hosted by the late Indonesian President Sukarno, founding father of modern Indonesia, the Bandung Conference attracted leaders from 29 countries of Africa and Asia, among them some of the most inspiring leaders of the Third World— Nasser of Egypt, Nehru of India, Nkrumah of Ghana, Chou En Lai of China. Held after the Korean war of 1951 and the Geneva Conference of 1954, the Bandung Conference was called to discuss the problems of Korea and Indochina. A declaration was issued after the conference affirming the principle of peaceful co-existence and calling upon the newly emerging nations to strengthen their anti-colonialist and anti-imperialist solidarity.

Thirty years later, the days of anti-colonial and anti-imperialist fervor are gone, and more than ever the Third World is plagued by political instability and oppression, economic disarray, poverty, mass famine—and utter dependency on the West. The dominating agenda is no longer Third World solidarity, but rather fratricidal conflicts such as the Iran-Iraq war; the Cambodia-Vietnam quagmire in which some fellow members of the Third World join with the US in bitter denunciation of Vietnamese "expansion-ism"; and Western Sahara, in which a leading member of the Movement is the new colonialist aggressor. Indonesia, host to the first Afro-Asia Conference which proclaimed as its sacred goal the total elimination of colonialism, continues to occupy East Timor.

In those early years, the enemy was easily identifiable—the white man, the obvious source of all the ills affecting the developing nations. England, France, Belgium, Portugal, Spain—these were the enemies. Today, only Namibia and South Africa remain as white bastions. Ian Smith's dream of white rule in Rhodesia for "One Thousand Years" lasted only a few years. British and French anthropologists who predicted that the whites could count on ruling Africa well into the 21st century proved to be ignorant. In the South Pacific region, a few remnants of *pied noirs* are trying desperately to retain a white enclave in New Caledonia, an island country that is like a Club Med for the whites but where the indigenous Kanaki inhabitants are denied both land and dignity.

By and large, the era of European colonialism is gone. However, new colonial forces have emerged. With the demise of Spanish colonial domination of Western Sahara, King Hassan of Morocco descended on the Saharawi nomads and since 1974 has been waging a savage war against the POLISARIO Front. The colonialist in this case is a fellow member of the "brotherly" Arab bloc. The sad irony is that Morocco was among the early supporters of African liberation movements, and its contribution to the victories celebrated in the 1970s is undeniable. In 1975, it was the turn of Indonesia—another vocal member of the anti-colonial alliance—to trample upon the Bandung principles with its invasion of East Timor. The colonial power is no longer European. The oppressor, a million times more brutal than the Portuguese, is none other than the country that hosted the first gathering of Third World leaders. In April 1985, while Suharto played host to a lavish gathering in Bandung of some 90 Third World delegations to mark the NAM's 30th anniversay, Indonesian troops were slaughtering Timorese freedom fighters and defenseless civilians.

The Heads of State and Government of the Non-Aligned Movement met in Colombo, Sri Lanka, a few months after Indonesia's 1975 invasion of East Timor. Much to Indonesia's surprise, the Colombo summit did not ignore the issue. The Final Declaration endorsed UN Security Council resolutions 384 (1975) and 389 (1976) which called upon Indonesia to withdraw all its forces from East Timor. Indonesia had counted on its prestige to silence any debate on East Timor. However, three factors worked against this: One, the progressive camp remembered that the regime of General Suharto had come to power in a bloody coup against Sukarno, one of the founders of the NAM; second, the African members of the Movement had grown in numbers and were extremely sensitive to attempts at changing colonial boundaries; third was the presence at the Colombo summit of five new member states that had achieved independence one year earlier from Portugal after protracted liberation struggles that captured the imagination and sympathy of most of the world. The five took a leadership role in championing the independence of East Timor. They had gained considerable prestige for having defeated the Portuguese and brought about the fall of the 50-year-old fascist regime.

Three years later, at the Havana meeting of NAM Heads of State and Government, Indonesia was again isolated. The Final Declaration included reaffirmation of the Movement's endorsement of all United Nations General Assembly and Security Council resolutions on East Timor. The mood that had prevailed in 1976 at the Colombo meeting had not dissipated. However, Indonesia did not relent on its campaign to see that the thorn that the East Timor issue had become for its position in the Movement be removed once and for all. In 1981, during a NAM Ministerial meeting in Havana, East Timor was heatedly debated in the Political Commission chaired by Zambia's Ambassador Paul Lusaka. The debate showed how divided the Movement was on the issue of East Timor—only because the culprit was not a Western colonial power, but a leading member of the Third World. In the absence of a consensus, Lusaka ruled that the paragraphs on East Timor that had appeared in the original draft declaration should be deleted. The Zambian diplomat, who was eyeing the Presidency of the United Nations' General Assembly (to which he was elected in 1984) had decided to use a procedural trick to please the Indonesians and gain their support for that glamorous job. In 1983, when NAM met again at the level of Heads of State and Government, the host country was India which was committed to Indonesia. Not surprisingly, East Timor did not figure in the draft declaration; this made our effort to have a paragraph or two in the Final Declaration an impossible one. The Indian hosts were so blatant in their support for Indonesia that they literally censored the televised speeches. References to East Timor by Samora Machel of Mozambique and Jose Eduardo dos Santos of Angola were cut from the TV broadcast.

In 1985, with Malaysia's backing, Indonesia's Foreign Minister Mochtar Kusumaatmadja began to prepare the terrain within NAM for Suharto's coronation as the next Chairman of the Movement after India. The lavish Bandung gathering was designed to present Suharto as the elder statesman and leader of a country that had paid its dues and now deserved such an honor. The fact that contenders to the post were countries such as North Korea and Libya, unlikely to win consensus, encouraged Suharto's candidacy. We were worried; Suharto's election would have meant NAM's endorsement of Indonesia's occupation and annexation of East Timor.

The decision to hold a Ministerial meeting in Luanda had been made in New Delhi, three years earlier. For the MPLA, such a meeting—if successful—would mean an enormous diplomatic victory against its domestic and external enemies. From the outset, powerful forces worked to undermine the Luanda meeting. The Pretoria regime and its ally Savimbi of UNITA tried to discourage other governments from attending the meeting. Morocco, Saudi Arabia, Egypt, Indonesia, Malaysia and Singapore were among those that wanted to see the Luanda meeting fail. Indonesia would have boycotted the conference, and would have encouraged Malaysia, Singapore and others to do likewise, had Angola made clear its intentions to invite FRETILIN. We deliberately kept a low profile so as not to give the Indonesians any excuse to boycott the meeting.

However, once they had secured the confirmation of participation from every NAM member, the Angolans revealed their commitment to our struggle. Working always in consultation with us, they included three paragraphs on East Timor in the draft declaration, and invited a FRETILIN delegation to the meeting—the first time ever we were invited by a host country of the Movement. An Indonesian delegation of 40 senior diplomats, led by Foreign Minister Mochtar Kusumaatmadja, arrived in Luanda in a special plane, confident that East Timor would not be a major nuisance and their President would be the compromise candidate for the presidency of the Movement. This optimism was reflected in Jakarta newspaper editorials on the eve of the Luanda meeting. In spite of our own worst fears and Indonesia's high expectations, the 1985 Luanda Ministerial meeting turned out to be a victory for us and a humiliation for Indonesia. The debate on East Timor in the Political Commission lasted five hours, longer than on any other issue except the Iran-Iraq war. True, Indonesia had mustered more voices in her support than we had. However, one immediate casualty of the debate was Suharto's candidacy. Another positive side of the debate was that it proved that the ghost of East Timor will not cease to haunt Indonesian diplomats. Indonesia was the big loser. Having aspired to lead the Movement for the next three years, it had campaigned lavishly and feverishly to that end, only to suffer in the end a humiliating defeat.

To our further satisfaction, the Luanda meeting was enormously successful for the MPLA government. UNITA did not fulfill its threats to render Luanda insecure; on the contrary, it was on the run in the Angolan deep south, barely surviving a fierce onslaught by government troops. Organizationally, the Angolans surprised the skeptics and managed to run the entire operation smoothly.

On the negative side, the Luanda Ministerial meeting brought again to the surface the double standards that have become the hallmark of the United Nations. The Arab bloc, always eager to launch verbal assaults on Israel, almost unanimously sided with Indonesia over East Timor. Only Democratic Yemen remained firm in its principled support for our struggle. Algeria, though not joining the rest of the Arab bloc, kept a studied silence. Malaysia and Singapore, always hysterical in their condemnation of Vietnamese presence in Cambodia, supported Indonesia. Singaporean delegates, with their customary arrogance and self-rightousness did not mince words in private and in public to justify Indonesia's brutal occupation of East Timor. To our dismay and the displeasure of our Angolan hosts, the Yugoslavian delegation launched a verbal assault against FRETILIN. A delegate in the

Political Commission made a statement in which he referred to East Timor as a "corpse" that should not be "resurrected." Because of its historical relation to Indonesia, Yugoslavia stood by Indonesia from the day East Timor was invaded.

Robert Mugabe of Zimbabwe was elected NAM President. Under Mugabe's leadership there are hopes that the Movement will be instilled with renewed optimism and courage to tackle the problems facing the Third World.

16

The Good Offices of the Secretary-General

> The parties to any dispute . . . shall . . . seek . . . a solution by negotiation, enquiry, mediation, conciliation, arbitration, judicial settlement . . . (Chap. 3, Art. 33, para. 1 of the UN Charter)

The Secretary-General is the "chief administrative officer" of the United Nations. Article 100, para. 1, of the Charter, states that "in the performance of their duties the Secretary-General and the staff shall not seek or receive instructions from any government. . . " Paragraph 2 seeks to reinforce the independence of the office by calling on Member States to refrain from trying to influence the man occupying the executive suite on the 38th floor of the Secretariat building overlooking the East River.

Having reviewed the history of the most prestigious office in the world, I could say that the UN has been fortunate in having had outstanding individuals governing it since its inception. Most tried and did their best to live by Art. 100 of the Charter. If at times they seemed to have taken sides, this was often more the result of public perception than of deliberate action by the Secretary-General and his staff.

As much as I believe that senior UN officials can be credited with integrity, this does not mean that they do not bring to the 38th floor their own prejudices. They all have their own sympathies and loyalties. For instance, Kurt Waldheim, an Austrian diplomat, believed that only two powers really mattered: the US and the USSR. His predecessor, the Burmese U Thant, was more sensitive to Third World problems and demands. When Javier Perez de Cuellar, a career diplomat from Peru, was elected, a UN official from a Third World country remarked: "After Waldheim, the Europeans got another European as Secretary-General," referring to Cuellar's reputation as culturally and emotionally more European than South American.

While Cuellar won praise for his acknowledgement of the weakness of the UN, and has spoken out at times on such controversial issues as the American-inspired "linkage" concept for the independence of Namibia—under him the system remained over-bureaucratized, overstaffed, overpaid and, by and large, incompetent. The "Austrian Mafia" on the 38th floor was replaced by a "South American Mafia," in the words of a UN official.

Member States often disregard the sanctity of the Secretariat's independence. The worst culprits are the two superpowers. The recent "election" of a Swiss national, Jean-Pierre Hocke, to the well-paid and glamorous job of UN High Commissioner for Refugees is an example of superpower manipulation. Hocke was backed by the Americans against at least three other candidates, each with better qualifications. However, only Hocke was politically acceptable to the Americans—and the Secretary-General dutifully picked him for the job.

In my ten years of active involvement with the UN as FRETILIN Permanent Representative, or following other issues of interest to me personally, I witnessed countless instances of Member States seeking to influence the Secretary-General, and other violations of the rules by staff members. For instance, there was an American working in the Department of Political Affairs, Trusteeship and Decolonization (PATD), who was seen visiting the American Mission quite frequently and passing on to them information about his Department's working papers on Micronesia.

There are of course many UN employees with outstanding qualifications, both academically and professionally, whose loyalty to the Charter is unquestionable. This latter group is often subjected to administrative harassment precisely because they try to perform their duties with moral and intellectual honesty.

The question of East Timor provides good evidence of how Member States try to influence the Secretariat. Every year, PATD prepares working papers for the use of the Special Committee on Decolonization, covering every item on the list of "Non-self-governing Territories." These working papers are supposed to reflect the information supplied by the colonial power administering the territory, as required by Art. 73(e) of the Charter, in regard to the social and economic conditions of the people under its jurisdiction, and the steps it is taking to bring about the independence of the territory. In the case of East Timor, Portugal has not been able since 1975 to comply with the provisions of the Charter in regard to transmission of information to the United Nations Secretariat.[1] In case of the inability or unwillingness of the administering power to comply with Art. 73 e., the practice of the Secretariat has been to gather information from other sources: international news media, NGOs, local church officials and the indigenous peoples themselves. However, in the case of East Timor, the authors of the working paper, in 1984 and 1985, gave little space to the information available on the true conditions in the territory, and relied instead on official claims by Indonesia. The working paper on East Timor prepared by the Secretariat for consideration by the Special Committee on Decolonization in August 1984 read like a propaganda handout issued by the Permanent Mission of Indonesia.[2]

It was this blatant bias that reinforced my (and many others') distrust of the team of advisers the Secretary-General had chosen to deal with the issue of East Timor. The following year, the working paper was slightly more balanced, but the space given to Indonesia's fantastic claims about "progress and development" in East Timor took precedence over the central question of the right of the people of the territory to self-determination.

In pursuance of General Assembly resolution 37/30 (1982), the Secretary-General assembled a taskforce on East Timor. He picked Under Secretary-General Rafeeuddin Ahmed, a Pakistani, as his Special Representative. Ahmed is also de Cuellar's representative for Humanitarian Affairs in Southeast Asia. "Humanitarian" is in fact a neutral word used to cover Ahmed's important role in trying to arrange a peaceful resolution of the Cambodian conflict. Ahmed is assisted by Hedi Annabi from Tunisia, whose main job in the UN is Secretary of the Ad Hoc Committee on Kampuchea. Their involvement in the Kampuchean conflict put the two men in constant contact with ASEAN governments and particularly with the Indonesians. It became quite obvious to me and to many others (except the Portuguese) that Ahmed and Annabi did not appear to be the best choices to handle the Timor issue. I never questioned their professional competence or integrity; however, the choice of mediators from countries with strong ties to one of the parties to the conflict does create suspicion and distrust, and may in fact condemn them to failure.

In a meeting in October 1982, in New York, I conveyed to Portuguese Foreign Affairs Minister Futsher Pereira my serious reservations about the possible choice of Ahmed as the Secretary-General's Special Representative for the Timor problem. My reservations were expressed even before the adoption of Res. 37/30 in November 1982; but in fact Ahmed had already been appointed by the SG to head a taskforce on East Timor much earlier in the year.[3]

I made my point so strongly to Pereira that he was startled and responded that I was "interfering in Portuguese affairs." I urged Pereira to propose another name to the Secretary-General, as Portugal was entitled to do as one of the parties directly concerned. I suggested Tom Vraalsen, the Permanent Representative of Norway, since he is a diplomat with impeccable credentials, very familiar with the Timor dossier. He had been president of the Fourth Committee and was widely respected among Third World delegates. Indonesia would certainly not reject Vraalsen's name, since Oslo and Jakarta entertained excellent diplomatic and trade relations (which explained Norway's abstention on East Timor in every General Assembly resolution since 1975).

Though the preamble of a resolution is not as important as the operative, it is an integral part of the whole and should not be disassociated from the operative. FRETILIN is referred to in paragraph 6 of the preamble of G.A. Res. 37/30—as it had been mentioned in previous General Assembly resolutions, some of which had in fact included FRETILIN in the operative part. All this adds up to a recognition of FRETILIN as a valid entity representing the people of East Timor, even if it does not carry the more formal recognition bestowed upon the PLO, SWAPO or the ANC. On the other hand, there was never any need for the General Assembly to formally recognize a liberation movement or insurgency group before accepting its *de facto* existence and indispensability in a process of conflict resolution. FRETILIN is so widely acknowledged, both inside and outside East Timor—and by the Indonesian authorities themselves—that it would be an exercise in absurdity to try to resolve the problem without the involvement of the movement's representatives.

During the drafting stages of G.A. Res. 37/30, I was assured by Portuguese Foreign Affairs Minister Futsher Pereira that the Secretary-General was conscious of the need to consult the people of the territory as to their own future. There was no question, according to Futsher Pereira, of Portugal accepting an arrangement that did not satisfy the legitimate aspirations of the people of East Timor. I was also assured by the Mission's Counsellor, Antonio Monteiro, that FRETILIN's position was safeguarded in the preambular part of the draft. These assurances were given to me to allay my fears that the amendments the Secretary-General (or Mr. Ahmed) was suggesting would short-circuit FRETILIN and the people of East Timor. I agreed to the amendments, and the final text referred only to "all parties directly concerned." It didn't take long before I was told that the office of the Secretary-General interpreted G.A. Res. 37/30 much more narrowedly than I had been led to believe. For Javier Perez de Cuellar and Rafeeuddin Ahmed there are only two parties to the conflict: Portugal and Indonesia. According to this interpretation, only these countries should be consulted—and this is what has taken place—while the people of East Timor, whose very fate is the subject of the negotiations, are ignored. To this day, the Secretary-General's office maintains that only Portugal and Indonesia are parties to the negotiations. This interpretation is faulty at best, for the people of East Timor continue to have a right to self-determination as recognized in the Charter. Until this fundamental issue of self-determination is resolved, East Timor will remain a subject of international responsibility, and not just between Portugal and Indonesia.

Former President Eanes and Foreign Affairs Minister Gama told Mr. Ahmed, during a series of separate meetings held in Lisbon in the fall of 1984, that Portugal remained commited to the East Timorese people's right to self-determination and that FRETILIN should be involved in the consultation process. This Portuguese stand has not been altered, and I am certain it will not be altered in the foreseeable future, since the political costs for any government in Lisbon that might be tempted to sell out East Timor would be too high. No Portuguese political personality will want to be remembered as the one who betrayed the East Timorese—and Portugal's own history and national dignity.

In his exchanges with Eanes and Gama, Ahmed argued that FRETILIN was not recognized by the UN; and that, furthermore, Res. 37/30 makes reference only to Portugal and Indonesia. Res. 37/30 mentions "all parties directly concerned" without reference to *any* specific party to the conflict. Ahmed's position was in conflict with the spirit and letter of Res. 37/30, as well as the two fundamental General Assembly resolutions on self-determination. Ahmed's position was also a denial of the assurance I had been given by Foreign Affairs Minister Futsher Pereira that the Secretary-General was conscious of the need to consult the Timorese. Had I not been given such an assurance at the highest level, I would have stuck to my original draft which made specific reference to FRETILIN in operative paragraph 1.

Shortly before the inauguration of the 38th session of the General Assembly, the Secretary-General issued a brief note stating:

> In view of recent developments regarding the question of East Timor, I do not consider it opportune to submit a substantive report on my efforts to contribute to a comprehensive settlement of the problem to the General Assembly.[4]

The "recent developments" were the first direct contacts established between FRETILIN leaders in East Timor and senior Indonesian army commanders. Face to face talks between FRETILIN President Xanana Gusmao and Lt. Colonel Purwanto, commander of Indonesian forces in East Timor, were held in a region under FRETILIN control in March 1983. This dramatic development raised cautious hopes that peace might be in sight after eight years of a brutal war, and encouraged the Secretary-General to propose that debate on the Timor question be deferred to the following session. Direct contacts had been established between Portuguese and Indonesian representatives in New York, with Ahmed sitting in between. Needless to say, I was not consulted by the Portuguese about the decision to postpone the debate on East Timor.

There were reasons that counseled a postponement, among them the fear that we simply lacked the numbers in the General Committee if Indonesia, through one or two of its friends, raised objections to the inclusion of the Timor question in the agenda of the plenary. In 1983, Portuguese diplomacy was completely paralyzed on East Timor. There was no effort whatsoever on the part of the Portuguese to build support for our position.

In the summer of 1984, the Secretary-General issued a four page "Progress Report" which was, in fact, a bland chronological narration of his efforts to discharge his mandate.[5] He cited a series of discussions he and Mr. Ahmed had held with both the Portuguese and the Indonesians. de Cuellar's report referred at length to the humanitarian situation in East Timor, but did not say a word about the widespread violations of human rights. On the humanitarian side, it is true that both the Secretary-General and Under Secretary-General Ahmed did their best to pressure the Indonesians to allow free access to East Timor by UNICEF and ICRC. However, even in this regard, the Indonesians made only token gestures designed to neutralize negative criticism in the West.

It would be unfair and incorrect to suggest that the Secretary-General's efforts have been fruitless. If he has not achieved more, this is attributable to the hypocrisy of the Western countries—and to Indonesia's other friends, particularly within the Arab League, who opposed G.A. Res. 37/30. Whatever limited access to East Timor ICRC now has must be credited to de Cuellar and Ahmed—certainly not to the US State Department or the Australian Foreign Affairs Department. The role of American Congressman Tony Hall (D-Ohio) and Senator David Durenberger (R-Illinois) has been effective in drawing international attention to the problem, thus strengthening de Cuellar's hand.

Above all, the Secretary-General and his special representative Ahmed can be credited with a major breakthrough in getting Indonesia to negotiate with Portugal. The Indonesian side had rejected G.A. Res. 37/30 on the grounds that East Timor was Indonesia's "27th province," and therefore an "internal affair" of the Republic, outside the competence of the UN. The Secretary-General managed to persuade Indonesia's Foreign Affairs Minister, Mochtar Kusumaatmadja, to direct his representatives to meet with their Portuguese counterparts in New York. The argument used by de Cuellar (which was acceptable to the Indonesians) was that they were not negotiating "within" the framework of 37/30, but rather in "parallel" to it. Mochtar had his own calculations, that he might gain international acceptance of Indonesia's occupation of East Timor through protracted negotiations.

The negotiations have dragged on for almost four years, and the root of the problem has still not been addressed.

I personally believe that both the Secretary-General and his special representative, Rafeeuddin Ahmed, share the feeling that a great injustice is being committed against the East Timorese. In spite of my earlier reservations about Ahmed, I do not believe their reluctance to involve FRETILIN in the consultations can be attributed to some evil scheme to sell out the Timorese. The Secretary-General knows that Indonesia would gladly walk away from the negotiations the moment the Secretary-General invited FRETILIN or UDT. I have met with Ahmed a number of times in a setting which he skillfully describes as "informal" and *not* in the framework of Res. 37/30. These meetings have helped to diminish my earlier suspicions of him. However, Ahmed is such a diplomatic fox that one can never pin him down.

In September 1985, the Secretary-General issued his second "Progress Report" on Timor.[6] A modest step forward was the first meeting ever between the Portuguese and the Indonesian Foreign Ministers with the Secretary-General himself sitting in between. Previous meetings had been at ambassadorial and senior official level, with Ahmed representing the Secretary-General. However, the two parties again discussed only side issues of humanitarian nature, such as the repatriation of Portuguese nationals and Timorese civil servants who refuse to abandon Portuguese nationality. The fact that there is even talk about "repatriation of Portuguese nationals" implies Portugal's recognition that East Timor is no longer a Portuguese territory. A government does not repatriate its nationals from its own territory!

In his latest report on East Timor, the Secretary-General emphasized the need for a solution to the conflict "acceptable to the international community." No reference was made to self-determination. What could be an "acceptable" solution? A bilateral arrangement between Portugal and Indonesia, bypassing the Timorese people and any genuine act of self-determination, could constitute an "acceptable" solution, since it is conceivable that such an arrangement could get majority support in the General Assembly. I believe, however, that any Portuguese Parliament, President or Government would have to reject such a scheme—if not for love of the Timorese, then for the realization that the political costs, both domestically and with the five Portuguese-speaking African countries, would be too high.

The Indonesian side has been preparing for a long time the inclusion of East Timor in Indonesian parliamentary "elections" scheduled for 1987. I was asked by both Ahmed and Gama about this, and I made it quite clear that FRETILIN as well as all other sectors of the Timorese society reject such a farce. "Elections" in Indonesia, manipulated and controlled by the military regime, are an Indonesian domestic political charade, absolutely irrelevant to the problem of East Timor, which can be resolved only through an act of self-determination organized and supervised by the UN.

By avoiding any specific reference to self-determination, the Secretary-General's intent was to continue the process he had begun with some modest success. I can only assume that his intentions are good. Conscious of the Secretary-General's difficult task—and our own weakness—FRETILIN has bent over backward to allow room and time for the negotiations to produce results. FRETILIN will not, however, accept any bilateral arrangement that bypasses the people of East Timor. No arrangement that does not involve the Timorese in a free, UN-supervised referendum or general elections will be acceptable to the people of East Timor, the FRETILIN leadership inside and outside the country, the UDT or the Catholic Church of East Timor.

Both Foreign Minister Gama and President Eanes reiterated Portugal's official stand on the question of East Timor during the 40th session of the United Nations General Assembly. Speaking during the 15 minutes allocated to each Head of State and Government during the 40th anniversary celebrations, Eanes devoted a considerable portion of his statement to the Timor problem. He thus reminded the international community—and the Indonesians—of Portugal's commitment to the East Timorese people's right to self-determination.

Speaking to the General Assembly, Jaime Gama also expressed his country's firm belief in the "fundamental principle of self-determination of the peoples, and this is the core of the question of East Timor."

Newly elected President Soares did not deviate from Eanes' position in his inaugural speech. He reaffirmed Portugal's committment to self-determination and independence for the Timorese. There is not one single voice in the Portuguese Parliament that disagrees with Portugal's moral and constitutional commitment to East Timor.

NOTES

1. See "Information from Non-Self-Governing Territories transmitted under Article 73 e. of the Charter of the United Nations," Report of the Secretary-General, Annex, p. 3, note c, UN Doc.A/AC.109/837, 30 July 1985.
2. "East Timor, Working paper prepared by the Secretariat," contained in UN Doc.A/AC.109/783, 3 August 1984.
3. "Question of East Timor, Progress Report of the Secretary-General," UN Doc.A/39/361, 25July 1984, para. 1, 2, 3.
4. "Question of East Timor, Note by the Secretary-General," UN Doc.A/38/352, 19 August 1983.
5. Supra note 4.
6. "Question of East Timor, Progress Report by the Secretary-General," UN Doc.A/40/622, 11 September 1985.

17

The UN and Human Rights

The United Nations' concern for human rights may be "traced to humanitarian traditions, to the unceasing struggle for freedom and equality in all parts of the world and, as far as more recent developments are concerned, to the historic pronouncements of English, American, French and Russian leaders" from the 17th century onward, according to UN official documents.[1] At the end of World War I, Member States of the League of Nations accepted the Mandate System, established by the Covenant of the League, and commited themselves to the well-being and advancement of the peoples placed under their mandate.[2] Then came the International Labor Organization (ILO) based on the conviction that universal peace could be achieved only if it were based on social justice.

The United Nations Charter refers to human rights in its preamble and in six articles. In the preamble, signatory Member States pledge to uphold "fundamental human rights" and express their faith "in the dignity and worth of the human person, in the equal rights of men and women, of nations, large and small." Yet the fact is that the world situation cannot be said to have improved much since the adoption of the Charter. Millions around the world are denied the most basic human rights. Unelected beasts trample on the rights of their subjects with impunity. In spite of its fancy rhetoric, the UN has been, in most cases, a silent observer. The inability of the United Nations and its organs to deal effectively with cases of human rights violations—even those so flagrant and of such genocidal proportions as in Uganda under Amin or Cambodia under Pol Pot—stems from the principles of state sovereignty and domestic jurisdiction. The general conviction is that any attempt by the United Nations to enforce the relevant clauses of the Charter would be at odds with Article 2(7):

Nothing contained in the present Charter shall authorize the United Nations to intervene in matters which are essentially within the domestic jurisdiction of any state ...

For a perspective in assessing the UN's inability to enforce the Charter clauses on human rights, I would distinguish between: (a) human rights of colonized peoples and (b) human rights in sovereign states. In terms of self-determination of colonized peoples, the adoption of G.A.Res.1514 (XV) and 1541 (XV) constituted historical landmarks. Millions in Africa and Asia benefitted from an activist role by the UN. However, even in this area, there is a tendency to exaggerate the UN's contribution. In the British and French colonies, the UN had little or no role in the decolonization process. In other cases, notably Portuguese Africa, it was the bloody guerrilla campaign waged by indigenous movements that forced the metropolitan power to finally acknowledge its inability to hold on to the colonies. The UN simply provided an international forum for these movements, which helped to isolate Portugal.

When one moves from decolonization to the question of individual human rights in sovereign states, there is little the UN can claim to have achieved. The difficulties in monitoring human rights violations and enforcing the Charter guidelines are insurmountable. In most cases, governments reject attempts by United Nations agencies to investigate reports of human rights violations. More often than not, the UN does not even make the attempt!

Indonesia's actions in East Timor since the occupation in 1975 are in violation of virtually every human rights provision in the United Nations Charter, the Universal Declaration of Human Rights and the Racial Discrimination Convention; as well as the provisions of the two Covenants that make up the International Bill of Rights, namely the International Covenant on Economic, Social and Cultural Rights, and the International Covenant on Civil and Political Rights.

Both Covenants make specific reference to the right to self-determination of all peoples. As has been amply demonstrated in this book, the people of East Timor have been prevented from freely determining their political status, let alone "their economic, social and cultural development." A foreign language, religion and culture, are being imposed upon the indigenous peoples of the territory. "Bahasa Indonesia," a language as alien to the indigenous inhabitants of the island as Chinese or Arabic is to the Swedes, is now a compulsory subject in the school curriculum. All civil servants are required to devote several hours a week to the study of the language.

The provisions of the two Covenants covering freedom of expression and political association, the right to form trade unions, freedom of movement within the territory and the right to leave it, have all been trampled upon in a systematic manner. No political activities in any form (except those in support of the regime) are tolerated. Timorese are subjected to arbitrary arrest without due legal process or trial.

All available evidence points to one conclusion: Indonesia's actions in East Timor amount to a crime of genocide as defined in the 1951 United Nations Convention on the Prevention and Punishment of the Crime of Genocide. Art. 2 provides a thorough coverage of all the elements that constitute a crime of genocide. Some scholars and jurists argue that for a crime to be classified as "genocide," it has to be established that there was "intent" on the part of the defendant to "destroy, in whole or in part, a national, ethnical, racial or religious group as such."

Nazi Germany's persecution and killing of Jews constituted a crime of genocide inasmuch as the "final solution"—the physical liquidation of the Jews as a people—was an official policy of the Third Reich. Idi Amin of Uganda and Pol Pot of Kampuchea never proclaimed their "intent" to exterminate their own people or a particular tribe. However, under the principles of International Law recognized in the Charter of the Nuremberg Tribunal and in the Judgement of the Tribunal, Idi Amin and Pol Pot would have been declared guilty—as would President Suharto and General Benny Murdani of Indonesia, as well as the commanding officers responsible for the conduct of the war in East Timor.

The deaths of 100,000 to 200,000 East Timorese, representing 10 to 20 percent of the territory's population, cannot be attributed to negligence or recklessness. When there is a pattern in the killing and destruction, covering a period of several years, there is definitely an intent to decimate the indigenous population of the territory as the "solution" to a political and military problem. The following pattern of violence and oppression shows that the Indonesian generals have a well-thought-out *policy* to resolve the problem of East Timor—as well as the problem of West Papua—through mass extermination:

—Deportation of Timorese to remote Indonesian islands.

—Forced removal of people from their ancestral lands and their concentration in so-called "resettlement camps" without medical care, sanitation or land for cultivation. (Starvation and disease have killed thousands in these camps);

—Forced sterilization of women and men.* (East Timor does not have a problem of overpopulation; quite the contrary, at least one-third of its population has perished in less than a decade);

---

*Indonesia has imposed on the Timorese a family planning program which is nothing but an attempt to further reduce the indigenous population. How can one justify family planning through forced sterilization in a country that has lost at least

—Arbitrary arrests, "disappearances" and mass killings of non-combatants; use of chemical weapons such as napalm against "suspected" areas.

In the UN system, there are two bodies that are supposed to work towards the protection of individual human rights around the world: the Commission on Human Rights, and the Sub-Commission for the Prevention of Racial Discrimination and Protection of Minorities. The latter is made up of 26 "experts" who are supposed to be "independent" of their home governments and act according to their consciences. Fine enough on paper, but anyone who believes that the Rumanian "expert" acts on the basis of his conscience and not according to Ceacescu's curious views of human rights, should be given a medal for good faith. Of course, the Eastern European "experts" are not alone in toeing the line of their respective governments. Certainly the American "expert" took the advice from the Indonesia desk of the State Department on how to behave on the issue of East Timor in the Sub-Commission in 1984.

The Commission on Human Rights is made up of 43 countries, the representatives being government officials. It is a highly politicized body, subject to the same conflicting national interests that paralyze the General

one third of its population in less than ten years? On top of this, Indonesian authorities have declared East Timor a transmigration zone for model Javanese and Balinese farmers, in the same manner as it has done in West New Guinea for the past two decades. Several hundred Indonesian families have been resettled in the Maliana valley area, taking away the best land from the local population. The World Bank funds this Indonesian scheme though it knows it to be in violation of the Bank's own regulations. In a letter addressed to Carmel Budiarjo of the British *Tapol* (a London-based human rights organization), World Bank officer for Indonesia Ann O. Hamilton argues that "as long as there are large parts of the country which are lightly populated, it is the Government's purpose, understandably, to assist in the redistribution of the existing population." If East Timor is "lightly populated", then why does the World Bank support a family planning program there? On the other hand, World Bank involvement in family planning activities in East Timor is in violation of UN General Assembly resolutions since the Bank seems to have recognized East Timor as part and parcel of the Republic of Indonesia. While the General Assembly called upon UNICEF, UNHCR and the World Food Program to render assistance to the people of East Timor within their respective fields of competence, the World Bank was *not* asked to fund Indonesia's forcible sterilization of the Timorese people, aimed at rendering the indigenous people a minority in their own land! It is clear from the World Bank's correspondence on this subject that it knows of the implications of its involvement with Indonesian authorities in East Timor, both on a legal and moral plane, and yet it chooses to participate in this immoral strategy of physical and cultural genocide of the Timorese people.

Assembly and the Security Council. Poland, where no more than a dozen people were killed in a whole year, became the darling "human rights" issue of the Commission. If Polish workers refuse to go to work and demand an extended weekend, this becomes an issue for the West; if Lech Walesa is bothered on his way to work, this becomes a major "human rights violation." However, this same Western group opposed discussion of the killing of thousands of non-whites in East Timor, Indonesia, the Philippines and South Korea because the beasts running these countries are "benevolent authoritarian regimes," not totalitarians. The Socialist group has no love for the Commission because it sees it as a tool of the West. The Commission is therefore rendered useless.

In March 1985, the 41st session of the Commission, held in Geneva, voted to remove the question of East Timor from its agenda. The vote was close: 11 for, 9 against, 20 abstentions. Japan and the US were among the 11 voting for the elimination of the issue. The Japanese government, ever subservient to the Indonesian generals, did not care to hear the information and documentation on East Timor.

NOTES

1. *"United Nations Action in the Field of Human Rights,"* (New York: 1980), Chap. I, para. 1, p. 5.
2. Ibid. para. 3.

18

Self-Determination as a Principle and A Right

...Free, open-minded, and absolute adjustment of all colonial claims, based upon a strict observance of the principle that in determining all such questions of sovereignty the interests of the population concerned must have equal weight with equitable claims of the Government whose title is to be determined.

Though Woodrow Wilson's 1918 proclamation did not refer specifically to self-determination, he is honored by many writers as the progenitor of the concept. Other writers point to far older origins such as the Greek city-state, the Peace of Westphalia and the French Rights of Man.

There are authors who enjoy endless debates over whether self-determination is a right or merely a *principle*. They point to the fact that the United Nations Charter does not refer to it as a *right*. Article One, Paragraph Two of the Charter calls for "... friendly relations among nations based on respect for the *principle* of equal rights and self-determination of peoples ... " The omission of the word *right* led many governments, among them the Portuguese, to argue that there was no binding legal obligation on the part of Member States to relinquish their colonies. This debate went on through the 1950s and 1960s, while the movement toward colonial emancipation gained impetus with the independence of India, Indonesia, Algeria, Ghana, and other African territories.

As the Afro-Asian group grew in numbers and in strength, with the support of the Soviet bloc, self-determination became an issue that pitted this group against the colonial powers. The post-World War II anti-colonial movement was simply unstoppable, and was in sharp contrast to the defunct League of Nations of the post-World War I period, when the victorious powers extended their dominions to include the colonies of the defeated countries.

Inis Claude wrote in *Swords into Plowshares*:

> The critical difference between the political context of 1945 and that
> of the early League era lies in the fact that a widespread attack upon
> the very existence of the colonial system had gathered momentum by
> the end of World War II.[1]

As the author pointed out, "colonialism had become a global question,"
and it was no longer possible for the colonial powers to hide behind the
sacrosant "internal affair" umbrella. In 1960, the General Assembly
adopted by overwhelming majority the "Declaration on the Granting of
Independence to Colonial Countries and Peoples (hereafter, the Declaration,
or Resolution 1514). A second resolution, 1541 (XV) was adopted the
following day, December 15, 1960. Both resolutions established concrete
formulas for the decolonization process. Critics retorted that, since the
General Assembly has no law-making capacity, the Declaration could not
constitute an international legal instrument. Supporters in the anti-colonial
camp contended that since it was adopted without a negative vote (there
were nine registered abstentions), the Declaration reflected a consensus
among States that the Charter principles are legally binding.

While certain Western scholars maintain that juridically the notion of a
legal "right" of self-determination is nonsense, the International Court of
Justice (ICJ), the highest legal authority in the United Nations system,
concluded in its opinion on the Western Sahara case that "the right of self-
determination for non-self-governing territories has become a norm of
international law."

A far-reaching step in the development of the *principle* of self-determina-
tion into a *right* was when Resolution 1541 (XV) was inserted into the
"Declaration on the Principles of International Law Concerning Friendly
Relations Among States in Accordance with the Charter of the United
Nations." (A/8082):

> By virtue of the principle of equal rights and self-determination of
> peoples enshrined in the Charter of the United Nations, all peoples
> have the right freely to determine, without external interference, their
> political status and to pursue their economic, social, and cultural
> development, and every State has the duty to respect this right in
> accordance with the provisions of the Charter.
>
> The establishment of a sovereign and independent State, the free
> association or integration with an independent State or the emergence
> into any other political status freely determined by a people constitute
> modes of implementing the right of self-determination by that people.
>
> Every State has the duty to refrain from any forcible action which
> deprives peoples referred to above in the elaboration of the present

principle of their right to self-determination and freedom and independence. In their actions against, and resistance to, such forcible action in pursuit of the exercise of their right to self-determination, such peoples are entitled to seek and to receive support in accordance with the purposes and principles of the Charter.

It would be an exercise in futility to continue the argument that self-determination is only a *principle*, when some 100 new nations have joined the United Nations since the early 1960s, having exercised their *right* to self-determination.

Resolutions 1514 (XV) and 1541 (XV) called for speedy decolonization of the non-self-governing territories, a list of which had been adopted, covering some 74 such territories. According to Art. 73 (e) of the Charter, administering powers were required to transmit periodic information on conditions in the territories and on the steps being taken to move them towards self-government and independence. Portugal refused to comply with Art. 73 (e), arguing that it did not possess "colonies" but only "overseas provinces." In response to this, Principle IV of Resolution 1541 (XV) stipulates that a "prima facie" obligation to comply with Art. 73 (e), exists when a "territory is geographically separate and ethnically and/or culturally distinct from the country responsible for its administration."

The General Assembly proceded to list the territories it considered "non-self-governing" under Portuguese administration. This list, contained in Resolution 1542 (XV), included Angola, Cape Verde, Guinea, Mozambique, and Sao Tome e Principe (Africa); Goa, Daman, and Diu* (Indian sub-continent); Macao (China); and Timor.

Thus East Timor benefitted from the activism that characterized the United Nations in the 1960s and early 1970s, when its right to self-determination was officially recognized by the General Assembly. Indonesia did not raise any objections to the inclusion of East Timor in such a list, nor did she advance any territorial claim.

The General Assembly took a step toward enforcing the provisions of Resolution 1514 (XV) and 1541 (XV) with the adoption of Resolution 1654 (XVI) which established the Special Committee of Seventeen. Its membership was later increased and became known as the Committee of

---

*The Portuguese conquered Goa around 1510 and maintained there an effective administration for almost five centuries. While the British succumbed to India's cry for independence, led by Gandhi, the Portuguese stubbornly resisted India's calls for negotiations toward restoring Goa and its enclaves, Daman and Diu, to India's sovereignty. In December 1961, Indian armed forces invaded the three enclaves. The Security Council failed to take action because the Soviet Union vetoed a draft resolution introduced by the United States and co-sponsored by France, Turkey and the United Kingdom. A second draft, favoring India's position, co-sponsored by Liberia, Ceylon (Sri Lanka) and Egypt got only four votes and thus failed to pass.

24. Its task was to follow the implementation of Resolution 1514 (XV) and 1541 (XV) and to report to the General Assembly on the progress (or the lack of it) toward self-determination of colonized territories and peoples.

Later resolutions, such as Resolution 3070 (XXVIII) called upon all states ". . . to offer moral, material, and any other assistance to all peoples struggling for . . . their inalienable right to self-determination and independence." Resolution 33/24 supported the legitimacy of the anti-colonial struggles for independence "by all available means." The General Assembly, through Resolution 3070 (XXVIII) and 33/24 endorsed the use of violence as a legitimate form of struggle for independence.

The General Assembly established certain explicit ground rules to be observed by the Administering Powers in implementing self-determination. A United Nations involvement in all stages of the process leading up to the act of self-determination, was considered an imperative. As early as 1954, for instance, General Assembly Resolution 850 (IX) stated that:

> . . . a mission, if the General Assembly deems it desirable, should, in agreement with the Administering Member, visit the non-self-governing territory before or during the time when the population is called upon to decide on its future status.

When the Committee of 24 was created in 1960, one of its functions was to supervise:

> . . . the self-determination process in non-self-governing territories, particularly in those situations where the people are being asked to decide on a constitutional formula falling short of independence or where concern has been voiced regarding the full respect for democratic processes during the electoral consultation.

While General Assembly Resolution 1541 (XV) provided for a choice between independence, integration with another independent state, and free association with an independent state, independence has been the general outcome of a process of decolonization. The General Assembly refused, for instance, in the case of French Somaliland, to accept changes in the status of non-self-governing territories not involving independence and in which the Administering Power did not invite a United Nations involvement.

Following the 1975 invasion of East Timor by the armed forces of the Republic of Indonesia, the United Nations Security Council, in a rare show of unity, adopted a resolution "deploring" the invasion and calling upon the aggressor to "withdraw all its forces without delay from the Territory." Needless to say, Indonesia did not comply and stepped up its military operations in the territory in flagrant violation of the Charter and General Assembly Resolution 1415 (XV) and 1541 (XV).

Five months later, with fierce fighting still raging in many parts of the country (including the vicinity of the capital) the Indonesian authorities announced the formation of a "People's Assembly." On May 31, 1976 this "Assembly" met in a movie house in Dili to vote on the single item of its agenda: the integration of East Timor into the Republic of Indonesia. As expected, the "People's Assembly" voted "unanimously" for integration.

On the basis of this action by an obscure "People's Assembly" which was never elected, Indonesia announced that the people of East Timor had exercised their right to self-determination in accordance with Resolution 1514 (XV) and 1541 (XV).

The "People's Assembly" consisted of 28 delegates, of whom 25 were selected in accordance with traditional practices, according to the Indonesians. One of the East Timorese delegates later explained to me how he was "selected":

> I was walking along the street leading to the city center, desperately trying to arrange a passport for myself and my family to leave the country as soon as possible. I was scared to death when a military jeep full of Indonesian soldiers stopped right next to me. Shouting in Bahasa, "Come with us!" they shoved me into their car. I was too terrified to ask questions or to protest. The officer told me that I was going to be a delegate, and I was going to join the others to vote for integration. When I got to the "Sporting Club," I saw many other familiar faces, and they all looked so miserable! We were all powerless, completely at their mercy, and we were going to sign away our country! I felt like crying. I knew what everybody else felt. With the exception of two or three, we all wanted independence for our country.

This experience was confirmed by other participants in the May 31, 1976 "People's Assembly," who have since left East Timor and taken up residence in Portugal or Australia.

The United Nations was not involved in any way, shape or form in the procedings leading up to May 31. Indonesia's efforts to have the United Nations lend some credibility to the farce were rebuked. Invitations were sent to the Secretary-General, the President of the Security Council and the Chairman of the Committee of 24 to witness the Assembly proceedings. Their refusal to attend was correct, and was an unequivocal statement of the illegality of Indonesia's actions, as well as of the illegitimacy of the "People's Assembly."

Only a few junior diplomats based in Jakarta, and a handful of journalists, attended the May 31 proceedings—and were not allowed to talk to the "delegates"! Roger Clark, Professor of Law at Rutgers University, wrote of the "People's Assembly" in his comprehensive analysis of the "decoloniza-tion" of East Timor:

The role of the United Nations or other observer group in an act of self-determination is to ensure impartiality and fairness. The failure of the seven diplomats at the Popular Assembly to make public reports contrasts sharply with the practice of United Nations observers. . . and with the observers at the 1980 Zimbabwe elections who published their reports. . .

The author endeavored to obtain copies of the reports from each of the seven governments. The Thai Mission to the United Nations kindly transmitted a four page report(in Thai). The report is. . . critical of the haste with which the Assembly was convened and of the absence of its consideration of any alternative other than integration with Indonesia. Neither the New Zealand nor the Indian governments wished to release their reports.[2]

Adding one more comic note to the farce, President Suharto of Indonesia, though touched by the decision of the "Assembly" to solicit integration with the Republic, decided to send a "fact-finding" mission, led by his Interior Minister, to ascertain the wishes of the people. At the end of this three-day "investigation," the Minister pronounced himself satisfied.

Acting on the "Assembly's" decision and the "fact-finding" mission's report, the Indonesian Parliament, which is a rubber stamp for the military regime, approved a bill for the integration of East Timor into Indonesia. Under tight security—with hundreds of Indonesian security men dressed in Timorese civilian clothing, mingling with the crowds and encouraging them to display enthusiasm—President Suharto visited Dili on July 17, 1976. It was a symbolic gesture to underline Indonesia's sovereignty over the Portuguese colony of East Timor.

Paragraph 6 of Resolution 1514 (XV) provides: " . . . any attempt aimed at the partial disruption of the national unity and the territory integrity of a country is incompatible with the purpose and principles of the Charter. . . " The authors of the Declaration had in mind arbitrary actions by the colonial powers in dismembering units that pre-dated the colonial era. In the cases of Goa and Macao, both territories were part of the Indian and Chinese territories, respectively. East Timor is also different from the Malvinas. Here, Argentina can justly claim that the islands formed part of the same territory under Spanish Administration.

In the case of Western Sahara, Morocco resorted to arguments based on "historical ties" as the basis for her claims over that Spanish colony. When the issue was brought before International Court of Justicé, the court found that no ties existed between Western Sahara and Morrocco or the "Mauritania entity" which "might affect the application of resolution 1514 (XV)." The Court ruled also that vague assertions of historical claims were insufficient to support territorial claims.

Indonesia has even poorer claims to historical ties. Throughout the 1960s and early 1970s, neither Sukarno nor Suharto made any claim to East Timor when the territory was under colonial occupation. After the invasion, Indonesia tried to concoct some "historical ties" between the people of East Timor and Indonesia. When he received the petition for integration from the "People's Assembly," President Suharto made this claim:

> This archipelago was once united, with an area approximately the size of the present territory of the unitary State of the Republic of Indonesia. History noted the famous Srivijaya Kingdom, as well as the well known Majapahit Kingdom.

Noted historians such as G. Goedes never made any explicit reference to Timor as part of the two ancient kingdoms. However, if Suharto's reasoning were to be carried to its logical conclusion, then part of Malaysia and of the Philippines as well as the island of Madagascar across the Indian Ocean should be included in "Greater Indonesia".

The UN Charter and modern and customary international law forbids the use of force in international relations. The exception to this is strictly defined in Article 51:

> Nothing in the present Charter shall impair the inherent right of individual or collective self-defense if an armed attack occurs against a Member of the United Nations . . . Measures taken by Members in the exercise of this right of self-defense shall be immediately reported to the Security Council. . .

Not one inch of Indonesian territory was violated or occupied by FRETILIN forces at any stage of the border conflict between September and December 1975. As we have seen in previous chapters, it was Indonesia that systematically intervened in East Timor during that period. If there were any "armed attacks" by FRETILIN against Indonesia, evidence of them was never produced before the United Nations Security Council. Even if such FRETILIN incursions had taken place, Indonesia's subsequent actions were grossly disproportionate to any such incursion.

Indonesia's most insistent argument was that it was invited to intervene by "four political parties representing the majority of the people of the territory" to assist them against "Portuguese colonialism" and "FRETILIN's reign of terror." Even if this were true (and it wasn't) the four parties never constituted the internationally recognized government of an independent East Timor. Portugal, the internationally recognized "Administering Power" of the territory, never solicited Indonesia's military assistance

Quite the contrary, it protested Indonesia's earlier military intervention in a note to the Security Council; and on December 7, 1975, the day of the invasion, the Portuguese Council of Ministers broke off diplomatic relations with Indonesia in protest. Portugal also lodged a complaint in the Security Council against the invasion and called for an urgent meeting of the Council.

Between mid-September and December 1975, FRETILIN was the *de facto* authority in the entire territory, the only party with any degree of international recognition. On November 28, 1974, as Indonesian military pressures mounted and the Portuguese failed to uphold their obligations, the FRETILIN leadership made a Unilateral Declaration of Independence (UDI). This UDI was as valid as the 1973 declaration of independence by Guinea-Bissau which was promptly recognized by a majority of the international community. It was no less valid than Indonesia's own 1945 UDI or the American Declaration of Independence. FRETILIN was the only entity with any measure of legal right to call for assistance from third countries.[3]

Evidence abounds that the "invitation" issued by the "four political parties" was obtained under duress. The leaders of UDT, the only party besides FRETILIN with significant political influence in East Timor, were virtual prisoners in West Timor. It is significant that the UDT leaders who stayed behind in Dili denounced their comrades' action. UDT's platform called for the independence of East Timor, and whatever support UDT enjoyed among the people of East Timor was based on the party's original platform, which was never altered, calling for independence with close association with Portugal. Had UDT espoused the goal of integration, as did APODETI, its following in East Timor would have been as minuscule as APODETI's.

Two other fringe parties claimed to exist in East Timor—KOTA, a monarchist group; and *Trabalhista*, a vaguely defined group that claimed to represent the workers. Neither of the two merited Portuguese official recognition. They were never able to produce a written platform. However, it was handy for Indonesia to talk about "four political parties." To give legal authority to any of these four groups to call for armed intervention is like recognizing the Ku Klux Klan's right to call on a foreign power to intervene in the continental United States and annex it.

One of the most outspoken and visible pro-Indonesian leaders was Jose Martins, head of KOTA. During the Security Council consideration of the Timor issue in December 1975, he was Indonesia's star witness. In April he managed to escape while on a tour of Europe and addressed this letter to the Secretary-General of the United Nations in April 1976:

> I am writing to your Excellency as President of KOTA Party and as an East Timorese who has witnessed and experienced Indonesian

bloody intervention in East Timor which has already cost many thousands of lives.

My views reflect the feelings and sufferings of my countrymen and women who are now struggling for self-determination and the independence of East Timor. Those who like me were forced to cross the border into Indonesian territory are prisoners and realize now the evil nature of the Indonesian military. The very moment we entered Indonesian territory in the first week of September 1975, fleeing from advancing FRETILIN forces, we became instruments of the Indonesian government. The dismembered leadership of APODETI, UDT, KOTA, and *Trabalhista* soon realized that while looking for "freedom" we fell into the hands of the Indonesian military.

With the leaders about ten thousand people also entered into Indonesian territory. I wish to stress the fact that while the Indonesian authorities claimed that over forty thousand East Timorese sought refuge in West Timor, the real figure was no more than twenty thousand. It is also necessary to stress that these people did not flee to Indonesian territory because they wanted to join Indonesia. They were just looking for a safe place until they could return to their homes. But they also fell into the hands of the Indonesian authorities; they soon realized that while seeking peace, they found only maltreatment and misery. The refugees were either forced to take military training and fight against FRETILIN or to work without pay for the Indonesians. Their belongings were confiscated, such as money, jewelry, and so on. As early as October, the refugees wanted to return to East Timor, but the Indonesian authorities did not allow them to do so. Obviously the Indonesian government was using the "forty thousand refugees" as a political weapon against FRETILIN. This was also a trick to get funds and aid from the International Red Cross and foreign governments![4]

While Indonesia did not formally invoke the so-called "humanitarian intervention" doctrine, some of her pronouncements were obviously an effort to portray the intervention in that light.* Though the "humanitarian intervention" doctrine has been largely discredited and is unacceptable to most of the international community, some authors contend that it can be invoked if the following elements exist: 1) widespread and immediate threat to human rights with loss of lives of nationals of the country considering such an intervention; 2) proportional use of force; 3) minimal effect on the local authority structures; 4) a quick, speedy withdrawal once the objectives of the intervention have been achieved; 5) immediate full reporting to the Security Council and appropriate regional organizations.[5]

In East Timor, none of these elements existed. The civil war had ended in

September and in no way affected the safety and lives of Indonesian nationals. There was no Indonesian minority community in East Timor at any time. Human rights in the territory were being monitored by ICRC and other agencies. Indonesia's subsequent actions exposed its real intentions of annexing the territory, regardless of the wishes of the people, trampling upon their fundamental rights to self-determination and liberty.

Indonesia's invasion of East Timor was an act of naked armed aggression in its classic definition. Article 3(3) and (4) of the Charter state:

> All members shall refrain in their international relations from the threat or use of force.

> All members shall settle their international disputes by peaceful means. . .

Actions that are in violation of Article 2 of the Charter are defined as aggression. The "Definition of Aggression," contained in General Assembly Resolution 3314 (1974) states:

> Article III:
> Any of the following acts, regardless of a declaration of war, shall, subject to and in accordance with Article 2, qualify as an act of aggression:
> 1) the invasion or attack by the armed forces of a State on the territory of another State, or any military occupation, however temporary, resulting from such invasion or attack, or any annexation by the use of force of the territory of another State or part thereof. . .

Though the "Definition of Aggression" refers only to States, it cannot be argued that because East Timor was not a State at the time of the invasion, Indonesia's actions could not constitute "aggression." The Indonesians cannot have it both ways. East Timor was either an independent nation (DRET) under the UDI of 1975; or it was and remains today a territory under Portuguese jurisdiction in accordance with international law and various General Assembly resolutions. Either way, Indonesia is guilty of aggression under the UN Charter.

---

*In the last few years, two cases of armed intervention could be seen as coming within the scope of "humanitarian intervention": 1) the Tanzanian intervention in Uganda which, though officially termed as self-defense and retaliation against an attack on Tanzanian territory by Idi Amin's troops, served also to put an end to a brutal regime that was universally condemned; 2) the multinational force sent into Lebanon in the aftermath of the massacre of Palestinians in refugee camps by

Christian phalangist troops. The United States intervention in Grenada was portrayed by the Reagan Administration as a "humanitarian intervention" to rescue 1,000 American students whose lives, the Administration claimed, were in immediate danger. The real reason for the intervention was political and strategic, and it was under consideration long before the assassination of Prime Minister Bishop and the subsequent crisis.

NOTES

1. Claude, Inis, "Swords into Plowshares: The Problems and Progress of International Organization," (1964).
2. Clark, Roger. "The 'Decolonization' of East Timor and the UN. Norms on Self-Determination and Aggression," *The Yale Journal of World Public Order* (1980).
3. See Decision on Timor of the Permanent People's Tribunal, session on Timor, held in Lisbon, June 19-21, 1981. Reprinted in *note verbale* dated August 11, 1981, from the Permanent Representative of Cape Verde to the United Nations, addressed to the Secretary General, U.N. Doc. A/36/448. Also Robert, Michel, statement before the Special Commitee on Decolonization, 8 August 1985, on behalf of the *Ligue Internationale pour les Droits et la Liberation des Peuples*.
4. A copy of Jose Martins' letter is in file with the author. Also on file with the author is a detailed report entitled *"Cem Termos Acusatorios Contra o Estado Indonesio: a Invasao de Timor Leste"*, prepared by Jose Martins, leader of the KOTA party, dated April 1976.
5. Supra, note 2.

19

The Quality of Mercy

The title of this chapter is borrowed from William Shawcross' superb book on the Cambodian tragedy and the world's response. As I read Shawcross's book in the basement of my New York apartment, as a Timorese I could not help but envy the Cambodians. In spite of their immeasurable suffering, the world woke up to the Cambodian tragedy. ICRC, UNICEF, US Catholic Relief Services (CRS) and OXFAM tried as hard as competitors at a trade fair to outperform one another. Donor countries poured millions into UNICEF, UNHCR and ICRC coffers and used their political muscle to make sure the agencies discharged their humanitarian missions.

During the Vietnam war, Cambodia was a place of no great importance. The bombing of that neutral country was only a "sideshow" in a larger theater of operations. When Vietnam invaded Cambodia, forcing tens of thousands to flee and starve in the process, the US was more interested in punishing Vietnam than in saving Cambodian lives. If sending surplus food to starving Cambodian children and welcoming with great fanfare the "boat people" would embarrass the Vietnamese communists, so much the better. Crocodile tears flooded the Thai-Cambodia border. The Kissinger legacy was forgotten, as was Pol Pot's dark age. The refugees were starving pawns in a well orchestrated campaign to embarrass Vietnam and its allies.

But Indonesia is not Vietnam. It has been a prize of the West since General Suharto massacred over half a million and imprisoned 750,000 Indonesians in 1965-1966. We Timorese only wished Indonesia were a Vietnam run by the communists; then, our tortured land would be flooded with crocodile tears, our tragedy would be sung by international stars, Western governments would condemn the violation of our human rights, Christian agencies of mercy would race with each other to help us. But because Indonesia is not Vietnam, the West doesn't give a damn about the

Timorese. And to cover up for their ignominious silence, they resort to distortion, deceit, half-truths and outright lies.

A document circulated by the US State Department is typical of this disinformation campaign. It labels FRETILIN "an avowedly Marxist faction" regarded by the Indonesian government as a "threatening movement." Indonesia's strategy of "search and destroy," designed to starve the population into submission, is not seen by the State Department as the reason for the famine; instead, the Department argues that it is "the dislocation and damage caused by the insurgency [that] have undermined agricultural production. . . " As to the "allegations made that food situation in East Timor is deteriorating and that famine threatens some areas. . . [these allegations] proved to be unfounded." This report was written at a time (1983-84) when a major Indonesian offensive was being undertaken against FRETILIN forces, a military campaign which the report acknowledges, has had "a negative impact. . . [on] the food situation in parts of the province. . . " Yet, it decides to contradict reliable and often agonizing appeals for food from church officials in East Timor.

Of foreign governments, the Australian is best placed to gather reliable information on conditions in East Timor through its Embassy in Jakarta; and if it wanted, it has thousands of refugees in Portugal and Australia readily available to be interviewed. However, the Australian official attitude has always been to dismiss the tales of horror that poured out of East Timor. In an effort to establish the facts on the situation in East Timor, Labor Sen. Gordon McIntosh of Western Australia, Chairman of the Senate Standing Committee on Defense and Foreign Affairs, undertook a year-long inquiry and received some 200 oral and written testimonies in 1981. Of the East Timorese who testified, often in closed session for fear of reprisals against their relatives back home, not one was a FRETILIN member. I had written to the Committee indicating my desire to appear before it. However, the government of Malcolm Frazer, true to its commitment to free speech, denied me a visa to enter Australia. In fact, between 1977 and 1982, no FRETILIN Representative was able to visit Australia, even in a private capacity. Of those who testified before the Committee, most were either supporters of the conservative UDT or were not related to any of the political parties. All the testimonies agreed on the catastrophic consequences of Indonesia's brutal occupation in terms of human lives and property destruction. However, the Foreign Affairs Department referred to these reports as "unfounded allegations" and was "not able to prove or disprove them."

While the Western media takes at face value the stories of Cambodian refugees, the personal accounts of countless Timorese in the refugee camps in Portugal or resettled in Australia are ignored altogether. The same newspapers that refuse to publish the stories of the refugees, never hesitate to print official Indonesian propaganda, which they temper with remarks from "credible" Western diplomatic sources in Jakarta. The most reckless and unethical reporting on East Timor in a long time has been by Barbara Crossette of *The New York Times*. She visited East Timor for a mere four days in July 1985, in a visit completely controlled by the Indonesian security forces. Crossette treated the East Timorese with a condescending attitude verging on crude racism, while the Indonesians were presented as "do-gooders." Crossette described East Timor as an "Indonesian province" and those fighting the foreign occupation of their land as "separatists."

Not a single journalist has ever visited East Timor without the stamp of approval by the military. One who managed to see beyond the security curtain was Australian Peter Rodgers, a former diplomat stationed in Jakarta, whose dramatic pictures of emaciated children hit the front pages of major newspapers around the world in 1979. Another was Pulitzer Prize winner Rod Nordland, then the Bangkok-based correspondent for the *Philadelphia Inquirer*. Nordland sneaked out to see local church leaders, nurses, nuns and common people. His findings were a devastating exposure of Indonesia's record in East Timor, and a true masterpiece of investigative journalism.

ICRC rushed to East Timor as soon as the civil war broke out in the summer of 1975. Its mandate covers protection of civilian population in armed conflicts, prison visitations and protection of prisoners of war and political prisoners, and tracing of missing persons. In 1975, ICRC operated both in Indonesian West Timor, providing assistance to some 20,000 refugees who had fled with the UDT forces; and in East Timor, then under FRETILIN control. In East Timor, ICRC delegates were able to discharge their responsibilities without hindrance. They were able to visit every single prison without giving us prior notice, survey the food situation without any restriction as to their movements, and interview anyone they wished. FRETILIN's cooperation was acknowledged in the 1975 ICRC Annual Report:

> The ICRC conventional activities developed rapidly, with visits to prisoners, exchanges of Red Cross messages, listing of missing persons, searches, relief, etc. (p. 17).

> The ICRC obtained the approval of the FRETILIN to visit freely all the places of detention under its control. Within two days after its arrival in East Timor, the head of the delegation made three visits to some 100 UDT prisoners in the hands of the FRETILIN. (p. 18)

In the first few days of the civil war in August, both UDT and FRETILIN detained Portuguese soldiers and officers. UDT was holding 23 in West Timor, where they became hostages of the Indonesians and were unable to leave for almost a year in spite of ICRC's persistent efforts to obtain their release. FRETILIN had taken prisoner 28 Portuguese soldiers. I personally discussed their release with Portuguese Minister for External Cooperation Almeida Santos, in Darwin. In its "International Review" of October 1975, the ICRC reported that on September 10, 1975, only a few days after FRETILIN gained control of the capital, "Twenty-eight Portuguese soldiers, liberated by the FRETILIN, were transported from Dili to Darwin . . . [and] returned to Portugal."

ICRC's performance in East Timor during the months of September and November 1975—until December 6, the eve of Indonesia's invasion—was flawless. This was because we strictly observed the Geneva Conventions. The ICRC couldn't have functioned effectively in the territory had FRETILIN refused to cooperate. Certainly our good will toward the ICRC was not entirely altruistic. We desperately needed all the help we could get. All Portuguese medical personnel had abandoned the country and we were left with one Goanese doctor who was drunk most of the time.

In its "Annual Report" of 1975, the ICRC reported on its last visit to East Timor: "The final visits took place on 5 and 6 December at Dili, where about 680 persons, mainly UDT and APODETI soldiers, were still held by the FRETILIN. During these visits, the delegates distributed relief consisting for the most part of blankets, clothing and underclothing, toilet articles and cigarettes." The irony was that our opponents who had been detained were better fed and clothed than our own soldiers!

ICRC was not the only outside agency operating in East Timor during our administration. A shadowy Australian agency, "Australia Intercountry Aid-Timor" (ASIAT) made an unexpected appearance in Dili as the fighting still raged in the outskirts of the capital. In other places of the world, a group of foreigners daring enough to show their faces in the midst of civil turmoil could expect less gentle treatment than Dr. John Whitehall and his group received. The ASIAT medical team was able to work in Dili and visit other places without any hindrance on the part of FRETILIN. There was some suspicion that the group's coordinator, Bill Bancroft, was a CIA agent. These rumors were never confirmed—and didn't disturb us in the least. ASIAT appeared to be a group of well-meaning, conservative missionaries rather than a gun-toting gang of mercenaries. I remember one of their Australian nurses crawling under the bed whenever there was an outburst of gunfire in the middle of the night in Dili.

The Australian Council for Overseas Aid (ACFOA) took an early interest in East Timor. An umbrella organization of some 60 NGOs, ACFOA is one of the best run and most dedicated organizations of its kind I have encountered anywhere in the world. As early as 1974, I approached ACFOA in Canberra to brief its leaders on the situation in East Timor and to interest them in our development projects. During our brief administration, we opened up the territory to all NGOs wishing to work with us. ACFOA responded promptly in spite of the Australian government's efforts to discourage such cooperation. We were rather optimistic, maybe naively so, about the prospects of an economically self-reliant East Timor. With a territory endowed with fertile land and a relatively small population, we believed that modest assistance would be enough to help us realize our strategy of self-reliance in the agricultural sector. However, Indonesia's invasion nipped our dream in the bud.

Efforts by the ICRC to return to East Timor after the invasion were fruitless. As the organization itself reported, "from 7 December onward, the ICRC intervened repeatedly with interlocutors in Jakarta, Geneva and the United Nations in New York, seeking permission . . . to return to East Timor . . .". Between 1975 and 1979, ICRC was kept out of East Timor while tens of thousands of Timorese were massacred, starved and denied medical care. Thousands were thrown into prison camps where they died from degrading and horrifying torture methods. Men were decapitated by the hundreds. Women were gang-raped by the soldiers and killed. Children were murdered. Prisoners were thrown from helicopters. Entire villages were razed to the ground. By 1979, the more than 80 percent of the territory's population who lived in villages in the interior had become displaced persons, refugees in their own land—but not recognized technically as refugees because they were inside their own country!

Was there Western outrage over this? There was only silence. The Americans, British, Australians and Dutch, with elaborate monitoring facilities in the region, continued to minimize the extent of Indonesia's brutal war against the Timorese people, and lied about the unfolding tragedy in the island.

ICRC was allowed to reenter East Timor in mid-1979—almost four years after the invasion—with a limited emergency operation in East Timor affecting only some 60,000 persons. There was no prison visitation program, no protection of the prisoners still alive let alone tracing the tens of thousands of "disappeared" persons. By then the Indonesian army had achieved important military victories, and FRETILIN had been seriously beaten in the pacification onslaught of 1977-1979. I talked with survivors of Indonesia's siege of FRETILIN's last stronghold in the Matebian mountain range, who gave a vivid description of the effects of napalm on women and children. They told of hundreds of dead in the three-week siege and of the cries of women pleading for help to alleviate their children's pain. Matebian was like a scene from Dante's *Inferno*. During all that period, ICRC remained silent. When it was finally allowed to return, the West praised the Indonesian military for their moderation!

After two years of relative quiet (because FRETILIN had withdrawn into the mountains to regroup) another major offensive was launched by the Indonesian military in the summer of 1981. This was the so-called "fence of the legs" campaign in which tens of thousands of East Timorese between the ages of nine and 60 were forced to march in front of the soldiers as a shield. Again, on the eve of the offensive, ICRC pulled out of East Timor.

The "fence of the legs" resulted in hundreds of deaths. Elderly people conscripted into the operation died of exhaustion and starvation. Children were left abandoned in the bush and died. In spite of the appeals by then Apostolic Administrator of East Timor, Msgr. Martinho da Costa Lopes, to Generals Yussuf and Murdani to stop the campaign, it went on for weeks. It did not achieve its military objectives, but the human toll on innocent women and children was catastrophic. When they finally were allowed to return home, the land had not been cultivated and an acute food shortage decimated hundreds more in the following months. Had ICRC resisted Indonesia's "suggestion" that it leave the territory, had it appealed for international action, maybe the "fence of the legs" would not have been put in motion.

The small island of Atauro off Dili had become a prison for those suspected of being related to FRETILIN. Children did not escape imprisonment in the island and were not given medical care or food. Famine and disease became rampant in Atauro, whose original population of about 5,000 had swelled to 9,000 with the influx of prisoners. Only in 1982 was ICRC allowed to undertake relief action and medical assistance in Atauro.

Soon after the "fence of the legs" campaign, ICRC was again allowed to reenter East Timor for a limited program in cooperation with PMI, the Indonesian Red Cross. However, ICRC's role was limited to material assistance. PMI is anything but an impartial humanitarian institution. Its operations in East Timor are authorized by the military and it is required to report all its movements, as well as its findings, to military intelligence. In fact, willingly or unwillingly, PMI is an intelligence-gathering service of the military. However, knowing the nature of PMI and the extreme corruption that plagues this militarized agency, ICRC and UNICEF, as well as Western governments, do not hesitate to channel most of their assistance to East Timor through it.

In July 1983, the ICRC announced that it had "suspended its activities on the main island of East Timor following the refusal of the Indonesian authorities to grant ICRC delegates access to all villages requiring assistance." The truth was that Indonesia was gearing up for yet another major offensive, following the breakdown of the four-month-old ceasefire both sides had agreed upon in March, 1983. As on previous occasions, the Indonesian authorities decided to clear the territory of ICRC's "neutral" presence, following the simple logic that a crime without witnesses is no crime.

ICRC decided to pull out because it was "unable to apply usual International Red Cross criteria for the provision of aid" (ICRC Situation Report No. 10, September 1983). However, ICRC's previous agreements with the Indonesian authorities, between 1979 and 1981 and between 1982 and 1983, had the same restrictions, and yet it went along with them. I believe that ICRC was fully aware of the pending offensive, code named "Operation Clean Up," as it had been forwarned of the 1975 invasion. Had the ICRC insisted on staying, it could have saved thousands of lives. It is this inconsistency on the part of ICRC that has raised serious questions about the integrity of the institution's handling of the Timor tragedy.

In 1985, the Indonesians allowed more freedom of movement to the ICRC delegates for the purposes of surveying the food and medical needs of the population. However, only 40,000 people were reached by the delegates. A total of three visits were made in 1985 to prisons in Dili and Jakarta. Hundreds of prisoners in inhuman detention centers in Baukau, Laga, Lospalos, Ainaro, Ermera, Aileu and Same were beyond the reach of the ICRC. Puppet "Governor" Carrascalao told me once how his Indonesian colleagues fooled the ICRC delegates. Whenever a prison visit was scheduled, Indonesian security personnel would order the prisoners to clean the cells and don clean uniforms, then distribute blankets and cooking pots, all of which would be taken away after the visit. Since the visits were infrequent, the delegates could not tell when somebody had been subjected to torture a month or two before. Prisoners who were murdered or died under torture were reported as having been freed.

ICRC retains as a consultant none other than Liem Biau-Kie, director of the Jakarta-based Center for Strategic and International Studies (CSIS). Liem is a notorious Chinese Catholic, instrumental in the regime's propaganda machinery. With his late boss General Ali Moertopo, he masterminded the destabilization campaign against East Timor in 1974-75, and has been deeply involved ever since in the regime's efforts to silence its foreign critics. That ICRC knew the background of the CSIS director, and yet hired him as its consultant on East Timor and Indonesia, might explain its periodic statements putting Indonesia's record in East Timor in a favorable light. On more than one occasion, ICRC has produced misleading reports on the situation in East Timor, giving the impression that the food situation and humanitarian problems there had improved. When it is criticized for not denouncing Indonesian obstructions of its work or lack of compliance with Geneva Conventions, ICRC defends itself by arguing that it does not make public its findings. However, it does make public the findings that put Indonesia in a favorable light!

General Assembly resolutions 34/30 and 35/27 requested UNICEF as well as the World Food Program (WFP) and the High Commissioner for Refugees (UNHCR) to "render, within their respective fields of competence, all possible assistance to the people of East Timor." The tragic situation in East Timor certainly required UNICEF's intervention. Yet the agency remained inactive for several years. Even after the adoption of G.A.Res.34/30 and 35/27, its bureaucratic machinery did not move. Finally, UNICEF decided to take action—and teach "Bahasa Indonesia" to the mothers of

East Timor! The explanation was that this would enable them to understand the nutrition instructions. In fact, what UNICEF did was to help in the "Indonesianization" efforts of the illegal occupying power. Almost all UNICEF funds for East Timor were channeled through PMI. When I confronted UNICEF officials in New York about the UNICEF/PMI relationship, I was told that the agency always tried to rely on the local people to carry out its programs. However, PMI is not a local agency, and "Bahasa Indonesia" is a language alien to the local people. I wonder when UNICEF will begin classes in Hebrew for the Palestinians, and Afrikaans for the Namibians!

The US Catholic Relief Services (CRS) is the only NGO allowed by the Idonesians to operate in East Timor since 1979. It is widely perceived as a foreign policy arm of the US State Department, concerned not only with saving lives and feeding the hungry, but also with perpetuating the status quo in places such as Indonesia, Chile and Paraguay, to mention only a few of the dictatorships that are haven for the conservative Catholics who run the organization. Officially, CRS is not supposed to take political stands; however, in private discussions its members show themselves to be finely attuned to political considerations.

"Let's face it, it's a fact—Indonesia now owns East Timor," Jewel Slingerland, former CRS assistant regional director for the Asia-Pacific region, told two visitors during a conversation in 1982. In a separate interview, another CRS official, John Donnelly, said that he and two of his colleagues had visited East Timor "and saw no instances of violations of human rights." (Apparently the Indonesians had not organized a torture show for the benefit of their American visitors!) Donnelly, who was only briefly in the territory, dismissed persistent reports from local church officials of gross human rights abuses with the usual State Department language: "Charges of human rights violations have not been substantiated." When asked how CRS could monitor the situation if it did not have a permanent presence in the territory, Donnelly said: "The area is too desolate for CRS staff to live there . . .Dili is so backward, we would not inflict it on any American full time." Asked to comment on the human rights situation, Miss Slingerland responded: "We concentrate on feeding and cannot engage in human rights activities. That is political. The word human rights makes us uncomfortable. It is a word that is not welcome here."

Not surprisingly, the CRS record on East Timor is clouded with questions—as has been its handling of the $100 million collected for the Ethiopian relief program. In the field, Timorese find it difficult to distinguish between the Catholic agency and the Indonesian military, in view of their close collaboration. Frank Carlin, who served in Jakarta and East Timor, confessed to two visitors that "no more than 20 percent of CRS aid is distributed through the local Church. The rest goes through the

Indonesian government infrastructure" (which is to say, the military). However, Donnelly, who visited East Timor in March 1980, declared himself "satisfied" that "there was no evidence of diversion of aid."

According to Slingerland, "CRS is going where the Government of Indonesia wants it to go and doing what the Government of Indonesia wants it to do . . . CRS is restricted in East Timor." When asked the reasons for CRS's hostility toward the concept of self-determination for the Timorese, it was Miss Slingerland who displayed the agency's ignorance and anti-communism: "East Timor relies on the Russians; it's been said around here and it's enough to influence judgements around here."

The Geneva-based World Council of Churches (WCC) encompassing Protestant denominations world-wide, figures prominently in the struggle for human rights in South Africa, South Korea, the Philippines and other parts of the world. To its supporters WCC deserves a Nobel Peace Prize; to its detractors on the right, WCC supports "terrorist" organizations through its financial contributions to liberation movements. The Indonesian Council of Churches (DGI) is an influential member of the parent institution. While WCC denounces injustice, poverty, and human rights violations in many parts of the world, its stand on East Timor has been one of embarrassing silence. To understand WCC's position, one has to understand DGI's relationship with the ruling military oligarchy in Indonesia. DGI is led by retired army general Simatupang, a man intimately associated with the military elite. Though a minority in Indonesia, Christians hold far greater power and privilege than the majority Moslems and see their interests as intimately linked with the regime. Perpetuation of the status quo is their goal. DGI is the largest Asian representation in WCC and therefore commands enormous power.

DGI delegates to meetings of WCC or other regional bodies oppose any discussion whatsoever—let alone adoption of any constructive resolution—on the question of East Timor.

During a meeting in Seoul in July 1985, of the Christian Conference of Asia (CCA), the Indonesian delegation demonstrated its loyalty to the military regime with an emotional outburst against efforts by some CCA members to have a discussion of the Timor situation. Some 110 churches and Christian organizations in Asia, Australia and the Pacific had signed a petition drawing CCA members' attention to the plight of the Timorese. The petition was presented to the Seoul meeting by Father Fernandes, a Timorese Catholic refugee in Australia who had been invited for informal meetings with CCA delegates. A certain Reverend Thobias from Indonesia questioned the "integrity of the organizing committee" that invited "a person from East Timor to be present." A Dr. Supit of Sulawessi then read a prepared statement in which he refuted the reports of brutalities perpetrated by Indonesian army troops, and said: "It is not true to speak about genocide in East Timor. The purpose of the Indonesian army is not to kill but to assist families to be reunited!" A Mr. Tumiwa, also from the Indonesian delegation, objected to the distribution of leaflets on East Timor. A member of the Philippines National Council of Churches, Mr. Sabug, intervened with a question to the Indonesian delegation: "Why are the Indonesian churches so afraid of this issue?" Why, indeed. The Indonesian church is afraid of the truth about East Timor because it is too intimately associated with a murderous military regime, and because it knows the extent of the regime's crimes against the people of East Timor. How could it acknowledge these bare facts and at the same time explain its relationship with the regime?

The American Quakers, like Quakers around the world, have been in the forefront of nonviolent peace and liberation struggles. However, they have kept their distance from the Timor problem. In September 1982, an appeal signed by Carol M. Bragg, Noam Chomsky and Jerry Elmer was addressed to the Philadelphia headquarters of the American Friends Service Committee (AFSC). The introductory letter to a five-page report and proposal for action read:

> A human catastrophe of immense proportions is occurring today in East Timor. The Indonesian war against the East Timorese people has cost at least 100,000 lives. Two additional matters make this situation specially alarming. First, the Indonesian war has been literally genocidal for some of the 28 indigenous tribes, several of which may have already been entirely exterminated. Second, the war—carried out with extensive United States assistance—has been almost completely ignored by the American press and public; the only response to this crime of genocide has been a deafening silence.
>
> This silence must be broken. It would be impossible to overestimate our personal anguish as we contemplate the tragedy of East Timor. We appeal to the AFSC to respond to this crisis by initiating a program of relief for the people of East Timor.

The New England regional office endorsed the appeal in a note dated December 11, 1979. However, when the AFSC met early in 1980, the Asia Panel had before it a memorandum from a Dave Elder stating that "need alone has not justified a new program." After arguing against an AFSC project in East Timor because of "a probable loss of agency identity," and other legitimate concerns such as being subject to "the control of Indonesian Military Intelligence," Elder discouraged any "further exploration at this time."

It is understandable that, in the absence of freedom of action in East

Timor, the AFSC and other like-minded organizations should see no point in lending themselves to manipulation by the Indonesian military. What is less understandable is the Quakers' general attitude of indifference toward the Timor tragedy. Apart from some token gestures, the Quakers have refused to petition the various United Nations bodies that deal with issues of self-determination and human rights. In Geneva, the Quakers kept silent during discussions on East Timor in the Sub-Commission and in the Human Rights Commission. One or two individuals in the Quakers' UN office did initiate an educational project about the Timor problem with UN delegates and Quaker membership. What is interesting to note, however, is that the one or two people who have expressed concern have been young non-Quaker interns, and not the professional Quaker human rights activists!

NGOs have a general function of raising sensitive issues that UN diplomats are reluctant to deal with. While some NGOs, particularly the European ones, are genuinely concerned with peace and justice, bread and development, many others exist only for themselves. In ten years of working with NGOs, I have come across a number whose disappearance would not cause a tear in anyone's eye. American NGOs are notorious in this respect. They pick issues that hit the front pages and are endorsed by well known personalities or institutions. The poor and forgotten of the world are ignored by many of the hundreds of NGOs in the US. They seek issues that can generate easy money to keep them going.

Amnesty International (AI) is easily the most effective and respected NGO. It has a narrow and strict mandate: release of political detainees and abolition of the death penalty. It does not engage in the promotion of any political cause. Though its mandate seems narrow to some, it is the only hope for many of those languishing in prisons in Latin America, Africa and Asia.

The role of the Church in East Timor is similar to the role of churches in Brazil, the Philippines, Nicaragua during Somoza's dictatorship, South Korea, etc. It has become a refuge for those living in Indonesian-controlled areas. The Church has become the moral fortress of the oppressed. The enemy has tried to break down its thick walls through campaigns of intimidation and persecution. But what the Indonesians have achieved with this brutal occupation has been a dramatic increase in conversions. Before the invasion, the Timor Catholic population was about 150,000 to 200,000. Today, it is well over 400,000. Within a few years, there will be an almost exclusively Catholic population in East Timor. Indonesia's efforts through bribes and intimidation to win conversions to Islam has failed because Islam is seen as a religion of the enemy; and the same has happened with DGI's attempts to win conversions to Protestantism.

While priests are harassed and Church properties have been ransacked, I would not agree with the charges that the Catholic Church in East Timor is persecuted as an institution. Those few priests, like the Goanese Monteiro and Brito, who collaborate with the military are loaded with favors. Those who do not cooperate, and speak their conscience, are blacklisted and harassed. This cannot be interpreted as persecution of the Church as an institution. In Indonesia, and particularly in the power centers in Jakarta, Catholics hold enormous power and wealth, far beyond their minuscule numbers.

In 1983, Monsignor Martinho da Costa Lopes, Apostolic Administrator of the Dili Diocese, resigned from his post and departed for Portugal. The resignation was a culmination of years of struggle against human rights abuses. He had succeeded Dom Ribeiro, who until 1977 was Bishop of Timor. When Dom Ribeiro retired and returned to his native Portugal, tortured by the Timor tragedy, Msgr. Lopes, a native of East Timor, was consecrated Apostolic Administrator. The moment he took office, he sought dialogue with the Indonesian military as a way to resolve the problems of human rights abuses. He chose diplomacy instead of confrontation. Waves of arrests, torture, rape, massacre and "disappearances" swept the country from the moment the Indonesians landed in East Timor. Lopes talked to the Indonesian officers and pleaded with them to put an end to the reign of terror. In vain. The Vatican was kept fully informed about what was going on in East Timor. Both the pro-Nuncio in Jakarta as well as Cardinal Cazarolli, the *"eminence grise"* of the Vatican, received detailed reports about the horrors being done to the Timorese people.

After five years of fruitless "quiet diplomacy," during which the Church remained silent, Msgr. Lopes reached the painful conclusion that for the sake of his own conscience and the credibility of the Church of Christ he would have to speak out. He chose May 13, 1981, the day of the festivities of Our Lady of Fatima, to deliver his first public denunciation of the system of terror that had been installed in East Timor. The open air mass held at the seashore square of Our Lady of Fatima was attended by thousands of believers—and by Indonesian security thugs. Shortly after the mass, Msgr. Lopes was invited to army intelligence headquarters for questioning. He was faced by six officers who did not refute his charges and pleaded with him not to say "these things in public" and report to them instead. Lopes reminded them that that was exactly what he had been doing for five years to no avail.

The head of the Catholic Church of East Timor became Indonesia's "public enemy number one." Three Timorese were hired by the Indonesians to assassinate the prelate. However, when they came to the Monsignor's residence to carry out their mission, they burst into tears and confessed to him instead.

What was the Vatican's reaction? About the time when Lopes was consecrated Apostolic Administrator of East Timor, the Vatican appointed the Spaniard Pablo Puente as its pro-Nuncio—the Vatican's Ambassador—to

Jakarta. Puente began his mission by courting the men of money and power, two attributes that have been intimately linked to the Holy See since the Middle Ages. Puente struck up friendship with a Catholic army officer, Benny Murdani, one of the most powerful men in Indonesia, the man who masterminded the invasion of East Timor and holds exclusive power over the territory. Thus the churchman "goes to bed" with the most feared and hated man in Indonesia. Puente is the quintessential diplomat, mingling with ease in the social circuit, enjoying all the worldly pleasures of expensive French wine, gin and tonic, scotch on the rocks and sex. Power, money and pleasure are the three interests that unite the two men.

The Vatican was informed (or misinformed) about the situation in East Timor *via* Murdani and Puente. The Church of East Timor, a Church of the poor and persecuted, was kept in the dark and felt abandoned and betrayed. Msgr. Lopes remembers that during all those years he received only one message of solidarity, from a French priest. I remember the many approaches I made to Churches in the US, pleading with them to send messages of solidarity and support to Lopes, who I knew was in physical danger. There was no response! The Pope prayed for Poland, but not for East Timor. Msgr. Lopes wrote to Cardinal Cazarolli requesting a meeting with the Pope. Such meetings are in fact standard procedure every five years. However, Msgr. Lopes was denied a meeting with the Holy Father.

The culprit was not so much John Paul II, who I believe wouldn't have minded taking a half hour from his anti-communist crusades to meet with the prelate from East Timor. The culprit was the Spaniard, Pablo Puente. Not content in denying Monsignor Lopes a hearing in Rome, Puente began a campaign to discredit him. This campaign began in Jakarta and was picked up by the Vatican's embassies in key European capitals. Monsignor Lopes' credibility was questioned whenever information from him appeared in the press. Though an indigenous Timorese, he was portrayed by his detractors as a Portuguese missionary who resented his loss of privileges. Gough Whitlam, the unrepentant former Australian PM who has made his life a crusade against East Timor, was among the Timorese churchman's most vocal critics.

Monsignor Lopes finally resigned in 1983. With humility and reverence toward his superiors in Rome, he did not think for a moment to question the Vatican's "invitation" to resign. In June 1985, I accompanied him in a tour of Federal Republic of Germany, during which we both met with a German bishop. The issue of the resignation came up and he explained without rancor the painful circumstances of his departure from his native land. "Please don't think badly of the Vatican and the Holy Father," he said. "My resignation was God's design. It was God that wanted me to leave Timor so that I can speak for my people to the rest of the world." I could not help but be touched by his generosity and faith.

When we talked one evening over a meal in Bonn, I learned more about da Costa Lopes, the human being. He explained that he could have refused to resign, but his profound sense of discipline and loyalty to the Vatican prevailed. "After working so hard, after doing so much, for the Church, for the people, I was advised to resign . . . Yes, there were political pressures." His eyes revealed the depth of his pain and anguish. The more we talked, the more I learned about the greatness of his heart, his strong personality and courage. He never expressed any anger against the Vatican that had betrayed him and the Church of East Timor. For Pablo Puente he had only kind words. For the Pope, a loving respect, adulation and faith. Does he believe in the Pope's infallibility? "In matters of religion, the Pope is infallible. In matters of politics, he is as fallible as any human being."

* * *

These past twelve years have been years of pain, anguish, frustration, hopelessness, but also of faith and satisfaction. During these years, I met countless individuals in the US, Europe, Australia, New Zealand, Japan, men, women and even children, whose concern, love and dedication, towards our people have touched me profoundly. I cannot forget the loving gesture of two American children who wrote to Jimmy Carter on Christmas 1979: "Dear Mr. President: We are friends of José (they assumed that Carter should know me by name . . .). He told us about the poor children in East Timor. We are sending you all our savings from our piggy bank so that you buy some food and send to the children in East Timor". An Australian child, 6 year-old Christopher, wrote to me a few years back, and told me of his plans for the future: "When I grow up, I want to become a secret agent and go fight for Timor". With them, I learned the dimension of people's solidarity that breaks political frontiers, race and creed; My humanist upbringing has been reinforced by their example; my belief in individual human rights has been strengthened by their dedication to people's freedom. It would take too many pages if I were to list our many friends around the world—and I would not certainly make justice to anyone if I were to mention only some. And the struggle is not over. Most of them, I believe, will be with us in the years to come until the Liberation Day parade.

20

The Long March To Peace and Freedom

Ten years and 200,000 dead later, the dream of independence is as alive and strong as ever in occupied East Timor. Indonesia's brutal occupation has only strengthened our collective will and resolve to continue our struggle, or *funu*, which is Tétun for liberation war. Independence is now the desire of everyone, including those who had illusions about Indonesia 10 years ago. Independence is seen as the only alternative for peace. Indonesia's efforts to "pacify" us have failed, as have the attempts to destroy Timorese cultural identity. Throughout the country, in the occupied towns and resettlement camps, in the liberated areas, there is a tremendous cultural movement in the form of Tétun music, songs, plays, and other indigenous forms of expression. The Tétun language, which was spoken by slightly over 50 percent of the population, is now used by everyone and has gained tremendous strength and vitality. As yet another form of resistance to foreign domination, the Catholic Church has seen its membership increased 100 percent since 1975.

But the people have paid a terrible price. Entire tribes have been liquidated. Hundreds of villages have disappeared. People continue to die— and to fight. The Indonesian people have paid as well for their leaders' aggression, with over 10,000 dead and many thousands wounded and mutilated. There are hundreds of new graves of Indonesian soldiers in Dili, Baukau, Lospalos, Same; in Atambua, Kupang, Denpassar and Jakarta. The authorities cannot hide the ugliness of the war forever from the Indonesian people, particularly from those who have lost their relatives in a strange war in a strange land.

Can Indonesia defeat FRETILIN militarily? It has not been able to do so for more than 10 years now. On the other hand, the prospects of a FRETILIN military victory are also remote. Indonesia has almost unlimited manpower reserves; however, its economic and military resources are limited. It does not have an arms industry of any relevance, depending entirely on the West for even light weapons such as machine guns. Indonesia's external debt is now $30 billion, with $5 billion going to service this debt annually. The war in East Timor cost Indonesia more than $1 million a day. The oil boom that sustained Suharto's regime for the past 20 years is over. The crunch has already arrived.

Most wars of national liberation end in negotiations. There is almost no precedent of a guerrilla movement defeating an established government by military means alone. Vietnam and Nicaragua are the two most recent examples of how a combination of factors—armed struggle, political mobilization of the peasants, mobilization of world public opinion, demoralization of the opponent's army and population by a war of attrition combined with political propaganda—determine the outcome of the war. In both Vietnam and Nicaragua, public opinion in the US and to a lesser extent in Europe, contributed significantly to the end of the conflict.

However, unlike Vietnam and Nicaragua, East Timor is not part of the East-West strategic rivalry, where the victory of one is the loss of the other. Neither the Soviet Union, nor the US, would have much to lose or to gain, if Indonesia were forced to pull out. East Timor is in fact one case in which the West could play an effective and constructive role. The Indonesian generals, in spite of their loud talk and arrogance, fear any move by the West to bring an end to the Timor problem. They know too well that they could not continue the war in East Timor for long if the West were to suspend weapons shipments to Indonesia. A combined effort by the US and Great Britain, with which Australia could be associated, would certainly persuade the Indonesian generals to seriously negotiate an end to the war.

Such a diplomatic effort could be undertaken directly by the US or through the Secretary-General, who has been attempting to resolve the problem for the past three years without any support whatsoever from the major Western countries. A combination of the Secretary-General's moral weight and diplomatic ability, with the constant prodding of the Indonesians by Washington and other industrialized countries, would be certain to bring about a breakthrough. The leaders of FRETILIN and UDT have taken significant steps to reconcile themselves and work together. FRETILIN has stated its solemn commitment to a multiparty, parliamentary system in a free East Timor. This is a firm guarantee that an independent East Timor would not fall under the influence of any power hostile to Western interests in the region. FRETILIN and UDT leaders have also stated support for and interest in joining ASEAN and the South Pacific Forum, the regional organization of the countries of the South Pacific. Indonesia should have no reason for fearing an independent East Timor whose relationship with its larger and sensitive neighbor could certainly be inspired by the Finnish-Russian *entente*.

The alternative is the continuation of the war with all its human toll. The West will bear direct responsibility for the fate of the Timorese if it continues not only to ignore the problem, but to actually connive with the military regime in its war of aggression.